The aim of the Biblical Theological Classics Library
is to make available at the lowest prices new editions
of classic titles by well-known scholars. There is a
particular emphasis on making these books affordable
to Eastern Europe and the Two-Thirds World.

For current listing see overleaf

GOD'S PEOPLE
IN GOD'S LAND

CU00952202

MAKING THEOLOGICAL BOOKS AFFORDABLE

Authors in the Biblical and Theological Classics Library:

G.R. Beasley-Murray
Baptism in the New Testament (10)
D.A. Carson
Showing the Spirit (1)
William J. Dumbrell
Covenant and Creation (12)
Jacques Ellul
The Meaning of the City (15)
John Goldingay
Theological Diversity and the Authority of the Old
Testament (2)
Bob Goudzwaard
Capitalism and Progress (11)
Walter L. Liefeld
New Testament Exposition (3)
Richard N. Longenecker
Biblical Exegesis in the Apostolic Period (5)
I. Howard Marshall
Biblical Inspiration (6)
Kept by the Power of God (7)
New Testament Interpretation (16)
Leon Morris
The Cross in the New Testament (4)
Waldron Scott
Bring Forth Justice (13)
Willem VanGemeren
The Progress of Redemption (8)
William A. Heth & Gordon J. Wenham
Jesus and Divorce (9)
Christopher Wright
God's People in God's Land (14)

GOD'S PEOPLE
IN GOD'S LAND

Family, Land and Property in the Old Testament

CHRISTOPHER J.H. WRIGHT

paternoster
press

Copyright © 1990 Wm. B. Eerdmans Publishing Co.

First published in the UK 1990 jointly by Paternoster Press and Eerdmans
255 Jefferson Ave. S.E., Grand Rapids, Michigan 49503, USA

This edition published 1997 by
Paternoster Press in the Biblical and Theological Classics Library

03 02 01 00 99 98 97   7 6 5 4 3 2 1

Paternoster Press is an imprint of Paternoster Publishing,
P.O. Box 300, Carlisle, Cumbria CA3 0QS

The right of Christopher J.H. Wright to be identified as the Author of this
Work has been asserted by him in accordance with the Copyright, Designs
and Patents Act 1988.

*All Rights Reserved. No part of this publication may be reproduced, stored in
a retrieval system, or transmitted, in any form or by any means, electronic,
mechanical, photocopying, recording or otherwise, without the prior
permission of the publisher or a licence permitting restricted copying. In the
U.K. such licences are issued by the Copyright Licensing Agency, 90
Tottenham Court Road, London W1P 9HE.*

Unless otherwise noted, the Scripture quotations in this publication are from
the Revised Standard Version of the Bible, copyrighted 1946, 1952 © 1971,
1973 by the Division of Christian Education of the National Council of
Churches of Christ in the USA and used by permission. Scripture quotations
marked (NIV) are from the Holy Bible, New International Version. Copyright
© 1973, 1978, International Bible Society. Used by permission of Zondervan
Bible Publishers.

British Library Cataloguing in Publication Data

A catalogue record for this book is available from the British Library.

ISBN 0-86364-808-5

Printed in Great Britain by Mackays of Chatham PLC, Kent

To
My mother, Mary,
and
the memory of my father, Joseph,
who put Christ
in my name and in my life

Contents

Part Two: Land and Property Ethics

Part Three: Dependent Persons as Property

Abbreviations

AJS	*American Journal of Sociology*
BA	*Biblical Archaeologist*
BASOR	*Bulletin of the American Schools of Oriental Research*
BBB	Bonner biblische Beiträge
BDB	Brown-Driver-Briggs, *A Hebrew and English Lexicon of the Old Testament*
*BH*³	*Biblia Hebraica*, 3rd ed.
BHS	Biblia Hebraica Stuttgartensia
Bibl	*Biblica*
BWANT	Beiträge zur Wissenschaft vom Alten und Neuen Testament
BZAW	Beihefte zur Zeitschrift für die alttestamentliche Wissenschaft
CBQ	*Catholic Biblical Quarterly*
CH	Code of Hammurabi
ExpTim	*Expository Times*
FRLANT	Forschungen zur Religion und Literatur des Alten und Neuen Testaments
HAT	Handbuch zum Alten Testament
Heb.	Hebrew
HL	Hittite Laws
HSM	Harvard Semitic Monograph
HTR	*Harvard Theological Review*
HUCA	*Hebrew Union College Annual*
ICC	International Critical Commentary

IDB	The Interpreter's Dictionary of the Bible
IEJ	Israel Exploration Journal
ILR	Israel Law Review
JAOS	Journal of the American Oriental Society
JB	The Jerusalem Bible
JBL	Journal of Biblical Literature
JJS	Journal of Jewish Studies
JNES	Journal of Near Eastern Studies
JQR	Jewish Quarterly Review
JSOT	Journal for the Study of the Old Testament
JSS	Journal of Semitic Studies
JTS	Journal of Theological Studies
KJV	King James (or Authorized) Version
LE	Laws of Eshnunna
LXX	Septuagint
MAL	Middle Assyrian Laws
MT	Masoretic Text
NCBC	The New Century Bible Commentary
NEB	The New English Bible
NIV	New International Version
OTL	Old Testament Library
OTS	Oudtestamentische Studiën
PEFQS	Palestine Exploration Fund Quarterly Statement
PEQ	Palestine Exploration Quarterly
PRU	Le Palais royal d'Ugarit
RB	Revue biblique
RHPR	Revue d'histoire et de philosophie religieuses
RIDA	Revue international des droits de l'antiquité
RSV	Revised Standard Version
SBL	Society of Biblical Literature
SBT	Studies in Biblical Theology
SJT	Scottish Journal of Theology
TDOT	Theological Dictionary of the Old Testament
UT	Ugaritic Textbook
VT	Vetus Testamentum
VTS	Supplements to Vetus Testamentum
WMANT	Wissenschaftliche Monographien zum Alten und Neuen Testament
ZAW	Zeitschrift für die alttestamentliche Wissenschaften

Preface

"The first shall be last and the last first" is a statement which seems to apply to many more areas of life than one's membership in the Kingdom of God. This present work, although it is the latest of my efforts in the field of Old Testament ethics to be published, is actually the earliest in terms of origin. It is in fact a revised and updated edition of my doctoral dissertation, produced in Cambridge, U.K., and submitted in 1977. Various factors and reasons have delayed publication until now. It has been, however, the foundation for later reflection, application, and writing during the intervening years—especially for the lectures, seminars, discussion material, and articles which eventually coalesced to produce the survey of Old Testament ethics, *Living As the People of God* (Leicester: Inter-Varsity Press, 1983), published in the United States as *An Eye for an Eye* (Downers Grove: InterVarsity Press, 1983).

In recent years there has been a growing awareness of the need for in-depth sociological analysis of the biblical materials, which, when related to contemporary social realities, can provide a basis for a sound biblical ethics. Norman K. Gottwald's exhaustive treatment of the earlier period of Israel (*The Tribes of Yahweh: A Sociology of the Religion of Liberated Israel, 1250–1050 B.C.E.* [Maryknoll, N.Y.: Orbis, 1979]) has been the most thorough-going example of this approach, though some others—published and unpublished—are mentioned in the Introduction. On a smaller scale, and from a different theological perspective, the new journal, *Transformation: An International Dialogue on Evangelical Social Ethics,* is committed to including this kind of work. This present work is a study of one particular dimension of Israel's society—the economic structures concerning land, property, and dependent persons within the family. Since this involves close study of the laws, institutions, and social customs of Israel, the work is mainly descriptive and exegetical. However, in the conclusions to each of the three main parts there are some pointers to the range of wider application that could be made when this material is brought into the field of Christian social ethics. It will be found that these pointers link up and, in some respects, overlap with the more applied approach of *Living As the People of God / An Eye for an Eye.*

The Introduction describes the early steps in the research underlying this work. But it is worth mentioning here, by way of acknowledgment, that the original impetus toward the study of Old Testament ethics came from an invitation to give a course of lectures on Christian ethics at the Belfast Bible College, which led to the immediate discovery of the acute shortage of any significant books on the Old Testament's contribution to the subject. I am grateful to the principal, Mr. Victor Reid, for the direction which he unwittingly gave to my subsequent academic interests by that invitation.

My thanks are also due to the Rev. Dr. Ronald E. Clements, my supervisor in Cambridge for most of the period of research, as well as to other members of the Divinity School who helped me at several points along the way: Rev. John Sturdy, Rev. Dr. Anthony Phillips, and Rev. Dr. E. W. Nicholson. The resources and facilities of Tyndale House Library, Cambridge, provided invaluable help for the work itself, and I am grateful to the Wardens, successive librarians, fellow researchers, and members of the Tyndale Fellowship, who make Tyndale House such an oasis of academic thoroughness, Christian commitment, and warmth of fellowship. The revision of the thesis was a lengthy and intricate task, and I wish to thank Mrs. Sue Davis, who turned a heavily modified and much scribbled on typescript into a clear and accurate text for publication. Similarly, I am grateful to Peter Cousins and the Paternoster Press and Allen C. Myers of Wm. B. Eerdmans Publishing Co. for their patience and perseverance.

My wife, Elizabeth, who shouldered the burden of my research at a time when the demands of our small family were heaviest, deserves more thanks than words can express for doing so, so cheerfully, for so long.

It was my parents who first instilled in me a love for the Scriptures, by teaching and example. They also upheld my family and myself with material and spiritual support during the years of preparation of this work. In love and gratitude it is dedicated to them.

Christopher J. H. Wright
Ware, England

Introduction

A. AIMS

The thesis which forms the basis of this book was conceived when
a general interest in the ethics of the Old Testament was fertilized
by my supervisor's suggestion that I investigate the particular area
of property ethics. The process by which the thesis was brought to
birth, however, began with the discovery of a scarcity of scholarly
literature in either the general or the particular of the said fields of
interest. At the time of my research, only two scholars in the
previous forty years had produced what could be called major
monographs explicitly on Old Testament ethics,[1] and neither of

1. Johannes Hempel, *Das Ethos des Alten Testaments*. BZAW 67, 2nd ed.
[Berlin: Alfred Töpelmann, 1964]); and Hendrik van Oyen, *Ethik des Alten
Testaments*. Geschichte der Ethik, 2 (Gütersloh: Gerd Mohn, 1967). S. Y. Tang,
in Part I of his dissertation, "The Ethical Content of Job 31: A Comparative
Study" (Edinburgh, 1967), provides a useful survey and discussion of the
differing approaches that have been adopted to the ethical study of the Old
Testament—including historical, psychological, sociological, and theological
approaches. Since the writing of my dissertation, two substantial monographs on
Old Testament ethics have appeared: Walter C. Kaiser, Jr., *Toward Old Testament
Ethics* (Grand Rapids: Zondervan, 1983), which is largely an exposition of the
Decalog principles; and my own *Living As the People of God/An Eye for an Eye*,
in which ch. 4 deals with the land and economic issues and is closely related to
the material in the present work.

them devoted much space to the details of property ethics. There
have, of course, been many smaller contributions to ethical aspects
of the Old Testament.[2] But one senses that a mood of introspective
questioning about identity, aims, and method has settled on Old
Testament ethics similar to that which has been apparent for some
time in the discipline of Old Testament theology, to which obviously
it stands in a closely dependent relationship.

In the particular field of ancient Israelite economic life, property
relationships, and institutions there have been, broadly speaking,
two kinds of scholarly approach. On the one hand, there is the
sociological approach of those who have set out to produce descriptive socio-economic histories of Israel in the Old Testament period[3]
(or selected parts of that period)[4] or who have examined in detail
the background and rationale of selected Old Testament institutions.[5] On the other hand, there is the *legal* approach, both of
historians of comparative ancient law[6] and of specialists in Old
Testament legal institutions.[7] Both these descriptive approaches
continue to be profitably pursued.[8]

2. E.g., R. Davidson, "Some Aspects of the Old Testament Contribution to the
Pattern of Christian Ethics," *SJT* 12 (1959): 373-87; V. A. Fletcher, "The Shape of
Old Testament Ethics," *SJT* 24 (1971): 47-73; James L. Crenshaw and John T.
Willis, eds., *Essays in Old Testament Ethics* (New York: Ktav, 1974); John Barton,
"Understanding Old Testament Ethics," *JSOT* 9 (1978): 44-64; and John Goldingay,
"The Old Testament as a way of life," pp. 38-65 in *Approaches to Old Testament
Interpretation* (Downers Grove: InterVarsity, 1981).

3. E.g., S. W. Baron, *A Social and Religious History of the Jews,* 2nd rev. ed.,
8 vols. (New York: Columbia University Press, 1952).

4. E.g., Edward Neufeld, "The Emergence of a Royal-Urban Society in Ancient
Israel," *HUCA* 31 (1960): 31-53; John Andrew Dearman, *Property Rights in the
Eighth-Century Prophets.* SBL Dissertation 106 (Atlanta: Scholars Press, 1988).

5. E.g., Robert G. North, *Sociology of the Biblical Jubilee.* Analecta Biblica
4 (Rome: Pontifical Biblical Institute, 1954); S. Herbert Bess, "Systems of Land
Tenure in Ancient Israel" (diss., University of Michigan, 1963).

6. E.g., David Daube, *Studies in Biblical Law* (1947; repr. New York: Ktav,
1969); Bernard S. Jackson, *Essays on Jewish and Comparative Legal History.*
Studies in Judaism in Late Antiquity 10 (Leiden: Brill, 1975).

7. E.g., the various writings of Friedrich Horst, including "Das Eigentum nach
dem Alten Testament" and others in *Gottes Recht. Gesammelte Studien nach dem
Alten Testament. Theologische Bücherei* 12 (1961).

8. They are combined, to some extent, in the relevant sections of Roland

What has not been done, however, in any adequate way is to integrate the findings of these approaches with the theological concepts and traditions of Israel's faith so as to produce a genuinely *ethical* perspective. Least adequate of all in this respect were the older attempts to explain Israel's religious and theological development in purely sociological and economic terms, in the belief that it was economic conflicts which produced Israel's distinctive monotheistic, ethical faith.[9] This approach has recently been revived in a much more comprehensive and analytical way by Norman K. Gottwald's massive sociological study of the premonarchic period.[10] This newer sociological approach is developing rapidly, with much argument both for and against its methodology, presuppositions, and (in the view of some) its ideological prior commitments.[11] From the opposite perspective, a number of smaller studies have sought to emphasize the influence of Israel's theological insights upon its social, economic, and legal life.[12] There is a

de Vaux, *Ancient Israel: Its Life and Institutions* (New York: McGraw-Hill and London: Darton, Longman & Todd, 1961).

9. This is explicitly argued by Louis Wallis, *God and the Social Process* (Chicago: University of Chicago Press, 1935); and *The Bible is Human* (1942; repr. New York: AMS, 1972).

10. *The Tribes of Yahweh: A Sociology of the Religion of Liberated Israel, 1250–1050 B.C.E.* (Maryknoll, N.Y.: Orbis, 1979).

11. Several recent contributions and critiques are helpfully collected in the symposiums, Norman K. Gottwald, ed., *The Bible and Liberation: Political and Social Hermeneutics* (Maryknoll, N.Y.: Orbis, 1983); and David Noel Freedman and David F. Graf, eds., *Palestine in Transition: The Emergence of Ancient Israel.* The Social World of Biblical Antiquity 2 (Sheffield: Almond, 1983). For a survey of sociological approaches to ancient Israel from 1880 to 1960, see Frank S. Frick and Norman K. Gottwald, "The Social World of Ancient Israel," pp. 149-65 in Gottwald, *The Bible and Liberation.* See also Robert R. Wilson, *Sociological Approaches to the Old Testament.* Guides to Biblical Scholarship (Philadelphia: Fortress, 1984); and Walter Brueggemann, "Trajectories in Old Testament Literature and the Sociology of Ancient Israel," *JBL* 98 (1979): 161-85 (repr. pp. 307-33 in Gottwald, *The Bible and Liberation.* For critique, see Gary A. Herion, "The Impact of Modern and Social Science Assumptions on the Reconstruction of Israelite History," *JSOT* 34 (1986):3-33; D. Jobling, "Sociological and Literary Approaches to the Bible: How shall the Twain Meet?," *JSOT* 38(1987):85-93; and the essays in Ronald E. Clements, ed., *The World of Ancient Israel.* SOTS Monograph (Cambridge: Cambridge University Press, 1989).

12. E.g., Alfred Bloom, "Human Rights in Israel's Thought," *Interpretation* 8

tendency in these, however, to deal in generalizations or abstract principles which, however true, are not sufficiently earthed in detailed study of the socio-economic sphere. There is also the danger of distortion by simplification in these approaches. The fact is that there does not exist, as far as I am aware, any major study devoted to Old Testament property *ethics*, in the sense defined above. The purpose of this book, therefore, is to seek to make some contribution towards removing that deficiency.

This study is not, therefore, yet another economic history or analysis of Israel, though obviously economic institutions must be examined. Nor is it purely an analysis of Old Testament laws relating to property, though important laws in that category do come in for detailed exegesis. Rather, it is an attempt to see how Israel came to terms with socio-economic facts of life in the light of its distinctive historical traditions and theological self-understanding. We are concerned with the interaction of a nation's life and faith— in short, with the raw materials of biblical social ethics.

B. RELEVANCE

Raw materials, however, exist in order to be used for profitable construction. What may the reader expect to be able to build from the raw materials found herein? This raises the very large question of the hermeneutical relevance of the Old Testament to Christian ethics, which cannot be fully dealt with in an introduction. There are, however, two major ways in which I believe the social and economic dimension of the Old Testament should be taken up into Christian ethical construction.

1. *Typological.* In New Testament theology the Christian Church, as the community of the Messiah, is the organic continuation of Israel. It is heir to the names and privileges of Israel, and

(1954): 422-32; Ḥayyim S. Naḥmani, *Human Rights in the Old Testament* (Tel Aviv: J. Chachik, 1964); B. Davie Napier, "Community under Law: On Hebrew Law and its Theological Presuppositions," *Interpretation* 7 (1953): 404-17; Moshe Greenberg, "Some Postulates of Biblical Criminal Law," pp. 5-28 in *Yehezkel Kaufmann Jubilee Volume,* ed. Menaḥem Haran (Jerusalem: Magnes, 1960).

therefore also falls under the same ethical responsibilities—though now transformed in Christ. Therefore the thrust of Old Testament social ethics, which in their own historical context were addressed to the redeemed community of God's people, needs to be directed first of all at the equivalent community—the Church. The New Testament concept and practice of fellowship, the local church community as a household or family, the principles of financial sharing and mutual support all have deep roots in the social and economic life of Old Testament Israel. This point is discussed further in the Conclusion to Part One.

2. *Paradigmatic.* The purpose of redemption is ultimately to restore the perfection of God's purpose in creation, that perfection which sin and the fall have corrupted. Israel, as God's redeemed community, was to have been a "light to the nations"—not just the vehicle of God's redemption, but an illustration of it in actual historical life. Israel's socio-economic life and institutions, therefore, have a paradigmatic or exemplary function in principle. It is not that they are to be simply and slavishly imitated, but rather that they are models within a particular cultural context of principles of justice, humaneness, equality, responsibility, and so forth which are applicable, *mutatis mutandis,* to all people in subsequent cultural contexts. This point is discussed at the end of Part Two.

So, on the one hand, Christians who are concerned for the renewal of the inner, social life of the Church as the community of God's people committed to living the life of the Kingdom of God and, on the other hand, Christians who are concerned for the mission of the Church in the world in its social aspect—especially those actively involved in working for economic justice, development, and human rights—will find it profitable to wrestle with the socioeconomic dimension of the Old Testament. And if we are keen to have a solid biblical foundation for both these aspects of Christian concern, then we must also make sure that our understanding of the relevant biblical material is authentic and accurate.

C. LIMITATIONS

It is inevitable that a study of a topic of such broad human interest as property and economic life has to be selective. The following limitations on the scope of this work should therefore be noted.

1. No attempt has been made to go beyond the Old Testament, culturally or chronologically. Thus, I have not ventured at any point to pursue the later developments of Old Testament property institutions into post–Old Testament Jewish literature. And while occasional reference has been made to comparable ancient Near Eastern law codes, this has been done only by way of illustration and not in order to substantiate an argument. This is not a comparative study.

2. Within the Old Testament itself further limitation was necessary—it being impossible to attempt an exhaustive survey of all that the Old Testament has to say on property and wealth. Thus, I have not dealt with the interesting themes surrounding these subjects in the Wisdom Literature and Psalms, though there are occasional excursions into these areas for other reasons.

3. This study is an attempt to elucidate Israel's understanding of its relationship with Yahweh with regard to the socio-economic dimension, and to show how socio-economic facts and circumstances in Israel's life were absorbed into and formed an intrinsic part of the experience and expression of that relationship. It is *not* concerned to define that relationship in any of its other aspects. Specifically, it is not intended to study, define, or comment on the "covenant" question; to do so would have resulted in an altogether different study. In view of the intensified scholarly debate at present on the meaning of the term $b^e r \hat{\imath} \underline{t}$ and on the question of when, whence, and by whom it was introduced into Israelite theological vocabulary, I have tended to avoid using the terms "covenant" and "covenant community" (except when in dialogue with scholars who do use them). When I do use the terms, however, they should be understood as convenient "shorthand" for Israel's relationship with Yahweh and the community who shared in its privileges and responsibilities. After all, the community and its relationship to God

were realities whether or not at any particular historical period or in any particular text the covenant concept and terminology were consciously in use. So I trust I may avoid the charge of critical anachronism on this issue!

In the conclusion of his dissertation on Israelite judicial institutions, J. M. Salmon makes the following remarks:

> There is a need for new attempts to deal with the sociological character of life in early Israel, and the ways in which this character of life helped to mold the theology and ethics of the OT. The inadequacy of the concept of the "nomadic ideal," for example, has become generally recognized, but this concept has not been replaced by any more adequate description of the moral influences operative in early Israel. . . . The conclusions to which we have come regarding the strength of familial patterns of social organization . . . should help delineate the institutional framework within which these broad questions must be considered.[13]

It is hoped that the following study goes some way towards meeting the need perceived by Salmon, and within the same familial framework whose importance he recognized.

13. "Judicial Authority in Early Israel" (diss., Princeton, 1968).

PART
ONE

The Centrality of the Family in the Social, Economic, and Religious Life of Israel

INTRODUCTION

Once we begin inquiring into the laws and institutions concerning property and wealth in the Old Testament, we very soon come up against the fact that property in ancient Israel was primarily a family affair. In order to understand this sphere of Old Testament ethics, we must therefore take account of the centrality of the family. When using the word "family" we must remember that in Israel the family unit was characteristically larger than the modern, Western nuclear family. It was "extended" to include several generations and several smaller two-generation families, as well as any slaves and other residential employees, all within one household. "Household," in this sense, is the term we shall tend to use.

The household, with its landed property, stood as the basic unit at the center of several spheres of Israel's life. *Socially,* it was the fundamental cell of the kinship structure of the nation, greater in social and practical relevance than the larger groups—the "clan" and tribe. *Economically,* it was the smallest, viably self-sufficient unit within Israel's system of land division and tenure; and since that system had a strong religious rationale, the household was an integral part of Israel's "land theology." Thus also *religiously,* the

1

household had a crucial role in maintaining the covenant relationship between the nation and God and in preserving its traditions
throughout succeeding generations.

Our purpose, then, in these first three chapters is to make
cross-sections through each of these spheres. We begin with the
theological realm and examine how Israel's theology of the land
was related to its other historical and covenant traditions. Then in
Chapters 2 and 3 we outline the economic and social aspects of the
household's importance within the same theological context.

1 | *The Land and Israel's Relationship to God*

INTRODUCTION: ISRAEL'S THEOLOGY OF THE LAND

All human wealth depends ultimately on what God has entrusted to us in the immeasurable riches of the earth's crust. Even yet we have hardly begun to touch the resources in and under the oceans, so that for the most part and for all of human history wealth has been based on land. "Where there's muck there's money!" goes the old "earthy" saying. This is true, inasmuch as all that we can count as material goods originates from what grows on, feeds on, or is dug out of the soil of our planet. Even in our modern industrial and highly technological world, we depend on the efficient use of well-maintained farmland to keep us fed and clothed while we go about our creation and consumption of wealth in other ways many steps removed from direct contact with the land.

In earlier societies, including the ancient (though already highly civilized) world at the time of Old Testament Israel, wealth was even more directly linked to land and to land ownership. For a nation of arable and pastoral farming like Israel, land was the only permanent possession. Crops and herds and habitations might be destroyed by drought or war, but the land would recover. But to be dispossessed of one's family land or, worst of all, to be driven out of the country into exile was unmitigated calamity.

So, for example, from the perspective of Deuteronomy, focused on the far side of the Jordan just prior to the Conquest, the material prosperity of the nation was as yet future and unrealized. It depended on the entry into the "good land" so graphically described and eagerly anticipated in Deut. 8:7-10. Once in there, Yahweh would give Israel the "power to get wealth" (v. 18).

The anticipation of the promised land in Deuteronomy, however, is but the culmination of a major theme running through the whole Pentateuch. The promise of land is a constituent part of God's covenant with Abraham; the Exodus is presented as God's first act in preparing to fulfill that promise; the law and covenant are given with a view to life in the land; the wilderness wanderings are "abnormal"—a punishment for cowardly failure to enter the land at the first opportunity. Beyond the Pentateuch, the land remains a primary theme: its capture and division in Joshua; the struggle to survive on it in Judges; the eventual complete control of the whole territory under David and Solomon; the prophetic protest at injustices perpetrated on the land; the Exile as divine judgment and the people's eventual restoration to the land as a token of a renewed relationship with God. And beside all this there are all kinds of laws, institutions, and cultic practices concerned with the use of the land.

All of this amounts to a complex mass of traditions and themes which can loosely be called Israel's theology of the land. But because this is an area which has aroused growing interest among scholars and because there is a great diversity of viewpoints, it is difficult to present a unified picture of the subject. However, we shall survey some of the more important work in the field and discern the main themes that emerge as indisputable factors in Israel's land theology. Our purpose will then be to see how this theology of the *land* fits in with the broader and fundamental Old Testament theology of Israel's unique *covenant* relationship with Yahweh, their God.

A. HISTORICAL AND CULTIC CONCEPTIONS OF THE LAND

In the opening paragraph of his 1943 essay on the land,[1] Gerhard von Rad comments that in spite of the preponderance and importance in the Hexateuch (Genesis–Joshua) of the concept of the land, promised to the patriarchs and granted to their descendants, a thorough examination of the idea had never been made.[2] His own study (which he describes as "only a quite brief rough survey of the subject") was therefore both pioneering and also, as the number of studies on the subject since has shown, seminal.

Von Rad's main argument is to distinguish two conceptions of the land—historical and cultic. The *historical* conception comprises both the promise to the patriarchs (which, following Albrecht Alt,[3] von Rad regards as an original feature of patriarchal religion and among the oldest traditions of the Pentateuch) and its fulfillment in the Conquest. The linking of these two themes of promise and fulfillment and the insertion of the Egyptian captivity, the Exodus, and wilderness wanderings to form a historical sequence is regarded by von Rad as the work of the so-called Yahwistic editor, known to critical scholars as J (pp. 83ff.). The *cultic* conception, on the other hand, is basically the belief that the land was owned by Yahweh—Yahweh's land, as distinct from promised land. The clearest expression of this is in Lev. 25:23: "The land shall not be sold in perpetuity (NIV 'permanently'), for the land is mine." The

1. "The Promised Land and Yahweh's Land in the Hexateuch," pp. 79-93 in *The Problem of the Hexateuch and Other Essays* (1966; repr. Philadelphia: Fortress and London: SCM, 1984); first published in German in *Zeitschrift des Deutschen Palästinavereins* 66 (1943): 191-204.

2. There had been, however, the word study of Leonhard Rost, "Bezeichnungen für Land und Volk im Alten Testament," analyzing the usage of *ᵃdāmâ* and *'ereṣ*; pp. 125-148 in *Festschrift Otto Procksch zum sechzigsten Geburtstag* (Leipzig, 1934), repr. pp. 76-101 in *Das kleine Credo und andere Studien zum Alten Testament* (Heidelberg, 1965).

3. "The God of the Fathers," pp. 65-66 in *Essays on Old Testament History and Religion* (Garden City: Doubleday, 1968); translation of "Der Gott der Väter," *BWANT* 48 (Stuttgart: Kohlhammer, 1929), repr. *Kleine Schriften zur Geschichte des Volkes Israel* 1 (Munich: C. H. Beck, 1953, ³1964).

context of the statement is the Sabbatical Year, which Alt considers to have been the occasion when "the true and sole ownership of Yahweh is brought once again into prominence."[4] Von Rad also includes within this conception all the cultic laws concerning the firstfruits, tithes, gleanings, and so forth which,

> in so far as they fall within the context of Yahwistic religion, are certainly to be interpreted in the light of the belief that Yahweh is the real owner of the land and therefore claims "a recognition of his right of ownership" from human beings.[5]

Von Rad rejects the suggestion that this cultic conception was derived from Canaanite Baal worship, believing rather that it belonged to earliest Yahwism before the emergence of syncretism (p. 88).

Von Rad's article also examines some of the land terminology—in particular showing the distinctiveness of Deuteronomy's use of $nah^a l\hat{a}$ to signify the *whole* land as the inheritance of *all* Israel and not merely, as elsewhere, the portions of tribes or clans (the significance of this is discussed below, pp. 19 and 20).

The interest in Israel's land theology is reflected in the number of dissertations on the subject appearing in the 1960s. In the United States, W. Malcolm Clark began his study of "The Origin and Development of the Land Promise Theme in the Old Testament"[6] with a detailed critique and rejection of the position of Alt, von Rad, and Martin Noth regarding the originality of the land promise theme as an authentic part of patriarchal religion. According to Clark, the promise of land to the patriarchs "is the result of the projection into the patriarchal period of a tradition which originated elsewhere. This projection was first executed by the J. source on a systematic basis" (p. 95). Clark examines two possible original life settings for the land promise form: the covenant and military institutions. He rejects the former, arguing that all connection between the promise

4. "The Origins of Israelite Law," p. 165 in *Essays on Old Testament History and Religion*; translation of "Die Ursprünge des israelitischen Rechts," *Berichte über die Verhandlungen der Sächsischen Akademie der Wissenschaften zu Leipzig. Philologisch-historisch Klasse* 86/1 (1934), repr. *Kleine Schriften* 1.

5. "Promised Land," p. 87.

6. Diss., Yale, 1964.

of land and the covenant concepts and forms is secondary and purely literary (pp. 145-169). He concludes that the land promise was originally part of the war oracles to individual clans and tribes attacking cities or small areas of land. The idea of a promise of the whole land was a secondary expansion with no historical life setting, analogous to the combination into a single story of the many diverse Conquest traditions (pp. 179-205).[7]

S. Herbert Bess[8] analyzed the historical development of the Israelite economy and the relevance of theological concepts—in particular that of Yahweh as principal owner of the land. Arthur Mason Brown[9] produced a detailed study of the terms *nāḥal* and *yāraš* in both their socio-economic and theological applications. He sought also to relate the concept of Yahweh as owner and giver of the land to the system of inheritance as well as to the relationship between Yahweh and Israel. (More detailed reference to these last two dissertations is made below.)

In 1969 Georg Christian Macholz contributed, in "Israel und das Land,"[10] a comparison between the Priestly work and the Deuteronomistic history. Although both of these accounts were composed in the situation of the Exile, they nevertheless stood in

---

7. It is impossible to embark here on a detailed critique of Clark's thesis, but three points may be made:

a. He does not explain why the land promise form must have originated in *either* the covenant setting *or* a military setting, when it is possible that it may have had early connections with both. See below, pp. 72-76, for the views of some scholars who see a military aspect in Israel's covenant traditions from the earliest times.

b. Clark does not convincingly establish his rejection of a promissory covenant involving land. "Particularly as applied to the patriarchs," he says, "one may doubt whether this was a *real* covenant" (p. 169, italics mine). But he has nowhere defined a "real" covenant or stated criteria for this view.

c. Although critical of Alt's exposition of patriarchal religion, he accepts uncritically Alt's view of the settlement of the tribes in Palestine to form Israel (cf. pp. 46, n. 3 and 206). Since Clark's theory of a development of the land promise from a localized war oracle to a national tradition depends on Alt's reconstruction, it is open to the same questions and reservations as the latter.

8. "Systems of Land Tenure in Ancient Israel" (diss., University of Michigan, 1963).

9. "The Concept of Inheritance in the Old Testament" (diss., Columbia, 1965).

10. (Habilitationsschrift, Heidelberg, 1969).

diametrical opposition as regards their estimate of the theological
worth of the land and Israel's relationship to it. To the Priestly mind,
Israel was constituted through the historical events from Abraham
to Sinai. For its theological existence Israel was therefore bound
neither to the land nor to the temple; Israel remained the people of
Yahweh wherever they found themselves—in the wilderness, in the
land, or in exile. The Deuteronomistic historians, by contrast,
believing Israel to be constituted by the gift of the land and by the
law as regulative of life in the land, regarded Israel as essentially
bound to the land (p. 166). The loss of the land was thus the end of
the people's existence as Israel in the theological sense. "The gifts
which made Israel's existence possible were no more. The last word
of Yahweh was, 'No-more-time for No-more-Israel' " (p. 182).

In 1972 Peter Diepold published his dissertation, *Israels
Land*,[11] which surveys both the geographical and theological conceptions of the land in four related areas of Old Testament literature:
Deuteronomy,[12] Jeremiah, the Deuteronomic portions of the book
of Jeremiah, and the Deuteronomistic history. Here Diepold criticizes Macholz's sharp distinction between the Deuteronomistic
history and the P source. Diepold's basic conclusion is that for all
four works residence in the land was a *sine qua non* of Israel's
existence as the people of God (pp. 187-88).

As its title indicates, W. D. Davies' *The Gospel and the Land*[13]
is mainly concerned with the concept of the land in the New
Testament and early Christianity, but Davies also devotes the 158
pages of Part I to a survey of "The Land in Israelite Religion and

---

11. BWANT 95.
12. On the land theme in Deuteronomy, see also Josef Georg Plöger, "Aus-
sagen über *'ereṣ* und *'adāmāh* im Deuteronomium," pp. 121-29 in *Literarkritische,
formgeschechtliche und stilkritische Untersuchungen zum Deuteronomium*. BBB
26 (1967); and Patrick D. Miller, Jr., "The Gift of God: The Deuteronomic Theology
of the Land," *Interpretation* 23 (1969): 451-465, which utilizes Plöger's study. On
the land theme in general, see Walter Brueggemann, *The Land*. Overtures to Biblical
Theology (Philadelphia: Fortress, 1977); and Elmer A. Martens, *Plot and Purpose
in the Old Testament* (Leicester: Inter-Varsity, 1981), published in the United States
as *God's Design: A Focus on Old Testament Theology* (Grand Rapids: Baker, 1981).
13. *The Gospel and the Land: Early Christian and Jewish Territorial Doctrine* (Berkeley: University of California Press, 1973).

Judaism." On the Hexateuch, Davies reiterates and amplifies von Rad's historical/cultic distinction. On the general attitude of the prophets to the land, Davies comes independently to the same conclusions as Diepold in the latter's more restricted study of Jeremiah; he finds that Israel and the land were so inseparably bound together that if they were to be deprived of the land (whether in prediction or actuality), it would be an abnormal existence. After a chapter of "cautionary considerations," in which he discusses a number of factors that modify an otherwise too simple assessment of Israel's land theology, Davies concludes:

> There was no one doctrine of the land, clearly defined and norma-
> tive, but, as is usual in Judaism, a multiplicity of ideas and
> expectations variously and unsystematically entertained. It should
> be clearly recognized that there were currents which would temper
> any concentration on the land, but belief in the promise of the land
> to Israel by Yahweh, to whom it belonged, also persisted. Among
> many Jews the certainty of the ultimately indissoluble connection
> between Israel and the land was living and widespread in the world
> within which Christianity emerged. (p. 157)

Within this "multiplicity of ideas," however, three cardinal concepts stand out as fundamental and persistent and as together forming the essence of what may properly be called a "theology of the land" in the Old Testament:

1. The land was given by Yahweh in fulfillment of the promise to the fathers—the historical tradition;

2. Nevertheless, Yahweh was still the ultimate owner of the land, a fact which was to be acknowledged in various legal and cultic ways;

3. Israel and its land were bound together in what Davies rather aptly described as an "umbilical" relationship, that is, a relationship determined by the nature of Israel's own relationship to God.

These are the three main themes that will occupy us for the rest of this chapter.

B. DIVINE GIFT AND DIVINE OWNERSHIP

We have seen how Gerhard von Rad drives a wedge between the *historical* concept of the land of promise and gift, produced by the Yahwist's fusion of patriarchal and settlement traditions, and the *cultic* concept of the land as owned by Yahweh.[14] One suspects, however, that he has driven his wedge too deeply; rather, these two concepts should be seen as the two sides of one coin. Theologically, the land could be viewed from two angles. From Israel's point of view it was the land of promise and gift—the major theme of their historical traditions. From Yahweh's point of view it was the land which belonged in a unique sense to him, and his prior ownership of it must be acknowledged by Israel in cultic and legal institutions. These are complementary, not "basically quite distinct viewpoints" (p. 89). Two considerations may be advanced in support of this point.

1. It would seem obvious that Yahweh's giving of the land presupposes in itself his prior ownership of it—that is, that as owner it was in Yahweh's authority and power to give the land. Von Rad counters this by referring to Yahweh's *dispossession* of the *former* owners of the land.

> In no single instance is the land which is promised to the patriarchs and apportioned by Joshua referred to as "Yahweh's land". On the contrary, it is the land which formerly belonged to other nations, and has now been given by Yahweh to his people in the course of a series of historical events. (p. 85)

Even if we concede von Rad's exclusion of Josh. 22:19, 25-27 from the case, on the grounds of the difficulty of dating the parts of that chapter (pp. 87-88), an explicit link between Yahweh's ownership of the land and the historical land gift tradition of Israel's possession by conquest is to be found in Exod. 15:13-17. From the perspective

14. "Driving a wedge" is not an exaggerated metaphor. Referring to Lev. 25:23, a "prooftext" of Yahweh's ownership of the land, von Rad speaks of a "new realm of ideas" with "nothing in common with that promise of possession of the land" (p. 85). ". . . This notion is of a totally different order from that of the promise of the land to the early patriarchs. It is a wholly cultic notion, as compared with the other which may be characterised as the historical conception" (p. 88).

of the song (cf. v. 17), the dispossession of the nations is as yet
future, yet the land is described as the *present* possession of
Yahweh, in such terms as "thy holy abode" (v. 13), "the mountain
of your inheritance" (v. 17, NIV), and so forth. Studies of this and
related passages by Ronald E. Clements[15] have shown how these
terms were representative of the whole land, and "expressive of the
belief that the whole land of Canaan now belonged to him. Thus the
land was Yahweh's to give to his people Israel."[16] Clements links
this song to Mt. Zion, agreeing with those scholars who date it in
the United Monarchy. Others have argued for an earlier, premonarchic date, on linguistic grounds.[17] In either case, however, the song
is evidence for the complementarity of the two ideas—cultic and
historical, ownership and gift—at a period earlier than the generally
accepted critical date of the earliest pentateuchal source.

We are presented here, at the beginning of the monarchy period,
with a welding of the two ideas into one. Yahweh's choice of
Mount Zion, signifying his ownership of the land of Canaan, is
shown to have come about through the conquest of that land by
the Israelites who were redeemed out of Egypt.[18]

2. Von Rad included within the cultic concept of Yahweh's
ownership of the land the laws concerning the harvest, firstfruits,
tithes, gleanings, and so forth (p. 87). Are these regulations therefore excluded from the allegedly quite distinct realm of the land

---

15. Ronald E. Clements, "Temple and Land: A Significant Aspect of Israel's
Worship," *Transactions of the Glascow University Oriental Society* 19 (1961–
1962): 16-28, esp. pp. 20ff.; and *God and Temple* (Oxford: Blackwell and Philadelphia: Fortress, 1965), pp. 51ff. In addition to the literature cited in these works on
the Canaanite background to these concepts, see also Richard J. Clifford, *The
Cosmic Mountain in Canaan and the Old Testament.* HSM 4 (Cambridge, Mass.:
Harvard University Press, 1972).
    16. *God and Temple,* p. 52.
    17. Most recently, David A. Robertson, *Linguistic Evidence in Dating Early
Hebrew Poetry.* SBL Dissertation Series 3 (Missoula: Scholars Press, 1972),
presents a linguistic case for dating Exod. 15 in the twelfth century. For the range
of critical arguments and literature on this poem, cf. Brevard S. Childs, *The Book
of Exodus.* OTL (Philadelphia: Westminster and London: SCM, 1974), pp. 240-253.
    18. Clements, *God and Temple,* p. 54.

gift, settlement tradition? Von Rad implies as much by saying that Deut. 26:1ff., which explicitly relates the offering of firstfruits to God's gift of the land, does so *"quite exceptionally"* (p. 87, n. 16). This seems quite irreconcilable with his earlier statement: "It is surely inherent in the logic of early Israelite belief that thanksgiving for the harvest should stand side by side with, and indeed be contained within, thanksgiving for deliverance from bondage and for the gift of the promised land."[19] And is Deut. 26:1ff. in fact "exceptional"? On the contrary, the same form of words, apart from the Deuteronomic repetition and expansion, is found in Lev. 23:10 (the sheaf of firstfruits) and Lev. 25:1 (the Sabbatical Year). It is hard to imagine how an Israelite, once settled on the land, could have brought his offerings to the sanctuary in acknowledgment of Yahweh's ownership of the land without at the same time reflecting, in the light of the strong settlement traditions to which he was heir, on the fact that the land whose harvest he had just reaped was God's gift to Israel, the fulfillment of his promise to the fathers, and the climax of the redemptive acts of Yahweh on Israel's behalf. The two ideas must have been correlative and complementary.

We may conclude, therefore, that, although von Rad was undoubtedly right to make a useful *conceptual* distinction between the two ideas, they cannot be regarded as *independent*, originally unrelated concepts. The importance of having established this point is twofold.

(1) Crucial areas of Israel's property law and ethics, which we shall be examining, are dependent on the belief in God's ownership of the land. It is important to see at the outset that this belief is integrally related to the historical, "covenant" tradition of redemption and land gift. This dual context of Israel's property ethics will be a recurring theme hereafter.

(2) Another theme will be the way in which some aspects of Israel's relationship with Yahweh are illuminated by further insights into Israel's socio-economic life and practice. One way of expressing that relationship was the concept of Israel as Yahweh's son and heir. The fact that Israel receives as a gift (in Deuteronomic language, as

---

19. "The Problem of the Hexateuch," p. 4 in *The Problem of the Hexateuch*.

an inheritance) the land that Yahweh owns certainly has a bearing on the meaning of Israel's sonship. (We return to this below, pp. 15-22.)

C. SINAI AND SETTLEMENT

Emphasis upon the bond between Israel and their land is found prominently in the prophetic literature, almost always within the context of Israel's relationship with Yahweh.[20] When that latter relationship was broken by Israel the people suffered first judgment in the land and then expulsion from it. Before there could be a return to the land, there had to be a return to Yahweh, a renewed and restored relationship with him.

This fusion of ideas—Israel and the land: Israel and Yahweh—implies that the historical land gift tradition, including especially the Exodus and settlement, was closely identified with the belief in the existence of a covenant relationship between Yahweh and Israel which imposed obligations and conditions, sanctioned by threats of judgment. That is, the land gift tradition had close affinities with the traditions associated with the Sinai event and its constitutive significance for Israel as Yahweh's own people. This, of course, is precisely the unified conception of the two themes presented to us in the completed Pentateuch. The Exodus leads to the giving of the law and sealing of the covenant at Sinai, and it is then from Sinai that Israel moves on to the (eventual) conquest of the land.

However, at this point we have to take account of widespread scholarly disagreement. There has been much study on the major themes of the Pentateuch, and the question here is: Did these two themes—the historical (Exodus-Settlement) tradition and the Sinai covenant-law tradition—originate and develop together, or were they originally separate both in historical terms (i.e., as the historical legends of different groups that later merged to form Israel) and in traditio-historical development (i.e., as stories preserved and handed down by different groups within Israel)?

20. Davies, ch. 3, provides a useful documentation of the biblical and scholarly material on the land theme in the prophets.

Again, the initiating voice in the debate was Gerhard von Rad. His form-critical and traditio-historical investigations led him to regard the Sinai complex of traditions as originally quite separate from the Exodus-settlement traditions. The former he regarded as the cult legend of the covenant festival at Shechem, the latter as the recurring sacral validation of the actual system of land settlement, possibly originally connected with Gilgal. According to von Rad, it was the original work of the Yahwist (J) to combine the two traditions by inserting the Sinai complex *en bloc* between the Exodus and the Conquest as the central event of the intervening wilderness period.[21]

Many scholars, however, have not accepted the proposed separation of the two traditions. The arguments on both sides in the ensuing debate and the relevant literature (by now of considerable bulk) have been recently summarized and need not be rehearsed here.[22] In my view, the case presented by the opponents of the separation is convincing and Ernest W. Nicholson, for example, is right to conclude that "von Rad's view that the so-called settlement tradition was originally quite independent of the Sinai tradition must be rejected" (p. 27).

However, since so much of the rest of the argument in this book depends on the assumption of a close, organic connection between Israel's land theology and its covenant theology, this judgment needs to be supported by more detailed argument. But in order not to detain the reader at this point, these arguments will be found in the Appendix to this chapter, and may be summarized here as follows:

Von Rad argues that the combination of the settlement and Sinai traditions was the work of J. As a novel and purely literary combination, it did not affect the living transmission of the two traditions which, according to von Rad, remained separate until exilic and

21. "The Problem of the Hexateuch."
22. J. Philip Hyatt, "Was there an Ancient Historical Credo in Israel and an Independent Sinai Tradition?" pp. 152-170 in *Translating and Understanding the Old Testament,* ed. Harry Thomas Frank and William L. Reed (Nashville: Abingdon, 1970); Ernest W. Nicholson, *Exodus and Sinai in History and Tradition* (London: Blackwell and Richmond: John Knox, 1973).

postexilic times. But in fact there are preexilic texts which present the two traditions closely interwoven. In reverse historical order these include eighth-century prophets (Amos 2:6ff.; Hos. 13:4-6; Mic. 6); Exod. 33:1-3, 12-16; the epilogue of the Book of the Covenant (Exod. 23:20-33); very early Hebrew poetry (Ps. 68:7-8; Deut. 33:2-5). The poetic texts in particular are, respectively, contemporary with and earlier than the commonly accepted critical dating of J (tenth century), and thus they constitute strong evidence that the two themes were related and complementary from the start.

When these exegetical considerations (see the Appendix to this chapter) are combined with the other arguments marshalled by J. Philip Hyatt and Nicholson, we may confidently proceed in the view that Israel's land gift tradition (with its great sweep of promise and fulfillment) must be understood and interpreted alongside and in the light of the belief in the covenant relationship established at Sinai (with its demands and sanctions). Each is indispensable to the other.

Establishing this conclusion at a traditio-historical level, however, leaves us with a problem of a theological nature. This concerns the apparent discrepancy between, on the one hand, the unconditional promises involved in the historical land gift tradition and, on the other, the imperatives and conditions imposed on Israel's secure possession of the land that are involved in the demands of their relationship with Yahweh. If the two themes were as closely integrated as we have sought to demonstrate, how is this tension to be understood? What kind of relationship can it have been to produce this duality in which the indicative of God's grace is explicitly unconditioned yet requires Israel's obedience and response? The answer, it seems, is to be found in the relationship of Israel's "sonship of Yahweh," which is expressed in many parts of the Old Testament. As a living, personal relationship, Israel's "sonship" involved this organic tension or duality by its inherent nature.

D. ISRAEL'S SONSHIP AND THE LAND

The conception of Israel's relationship to Yahweh in father-son terms was very ancient. Probably the earliest reference to this relationship is to be found in Deut. 32, now regarded generally as a very ancient poem, from a period not later than the eleventh century.[23] Here Yahweh's fatherhood of the nation of Israel is explicitly referred to several times: Deut. 32:5, 6, 18, 19. In the historical tradition, the assertion that Israel is Yahweh's firstborn son precedes the Exodus (Exod. 4:22), a fact of which Hosea was aware (Hos. 11:1). Similar references to Yahweh's fatherhood and Israel's sonship are found in other pre- and postexilic prophets (Isa. 1:2; 30:1-9; 43:6; 63:16; 64:8; Jer. 3:14, 19, 22; 31:9, 20; Mal. 1:6; 2:10), as well as in two other places in Deuteronomy (Deut. 8:5; 14:1).[24] Analysis of this material reveals two levels in Israel's sonship.

1. The *national* level. Israel as a nation is described as Yahweh's son, in the singular, or Yahweh is spoken of as the father of the people as a whole. This includes Exod. 4:22; Hos. 11:1; Deut. 32:6, 18; Jer. 31:9. The point here is that Israel owes its national existence to the creative or "procreative" action of Yahweh. In this respect, the use of the adoption analogy is somewhat suspect, since the texts speak rather of sonship by birth. Marie-Joseph Lagrange pointed this out clearly:

> Yahweh was father and Israel was his son because he had brought them into existence. . . . It is a question of national existence, of

23. This date was argued by Otto Eissfeldt, *The Old Testament: An Introduction* (New York: Harper & Row and Oxford: Blackwell, 1965), p. 227; and, in greater detail, in *Das Lied Moses*. Berichte über die Verhandlungen der Sächsischen Akademie der Wissenschaften zu Leipzig 104/5 (1958). Eissfeldt's arguments were accepted and added to by William F. Albright, who had previously dated it much later; see Albright, "Some Remarks on the Song of Moses in Deuteronomy xxxii," *VT* 9 (1959): 339-346. The judgments of both these scholars have since been corroborated by the linguistic research of Robertson, *Dating Early Hebrew Poetry*.

24. In a stimulating monograph (*Fatherhood and Motherhood in Israelite and Judean Piety* [Leiden: Brill, 1974]), P. A. H. de Boer points also to other less direct evidence for the fatherhood of Yahweh, namely, the use of the term "father" for persons of status or authority in the nation who could be seen to derive their position from the fatherly authority of God. For example, a prophet is called "father" because "he is a 'man of God', *'is ha-elohim*, in whom the deity appears. Calling him 'father' is acknowledging the Fatherhood of the God of the prophet." Likewise, "a king, a royal steward, a priest, a prophet, a wise man—all of them are outstanding people. Their title 'father' appears to be derived from the divine authority behind their position" (pp. 20-21).

the creation of a particular people. . . . As van Hoonacker clearly put it: "The status of sonship is *presupposed* in Israel"; it was as old as the nation itself. Israel did not become a son by adoption, being already a nation and then subsequently chosen by Yahweh; it was Yahweh who brought them into being, and for that reason he is their father.[25]

Arthur Mason Brown probably overstates his case, therefore, in his use of adoption practices and formulae from the ancient Near East to illumine the father-son relationship between Yahweh and Israel and its particular relevance to Israel's inheritance.[26] But, on the other hand, the subject of adoption is very hazy in the Old Testament and, as P. A. H. de Boer points out, ideas derived from the practice (in particular as related to inheritance) may exist in contexts far removed from its precise juridical meaning, so that perhaps the distinction between birth and adoption should not be too rigidly drawn.[27]

What is clear is that it was not by Israel's choice or action that they are Yahweh's son, nor does the status and privilege involved

25. M.-J. Lagrange, "La paternité de Dieu dans l'Ancien Testament," *RB* 5 (1908): 482-83. He quotes Albin van Hoonacker, *Les douze petits prophètes*. Études bibliques (Paris: Gabalda, 1908), p. 104, commenting on Hos. 11:1.

26. "The Concept of Inheritance," pp. 309-324. Brown outlines possible evidence for adoption in the Old Testament and then examines selected patterns of adoption in the ancient Near East. He offers three observations on the latter: (1) An adopted son could be given the rights of the firstborn. (2) A slave could be adopted by being set free. (3) "Adoption carried with it conditions and obligations which had to be carried out in order for the adoptee to receive the security of a family relationship and the inheritance of family land and property" (p. 325). Brown then applies these points to Israel's early history.

However, regarding (1) the Old Testament does not suggest that Israel had to be adopted in order to receive the rights of the firstborn, but simply that Israel *was* Yahweh's firstborn, and therefore entitled to the inheritance. Nor, as regards (3) was it only upon adopted sons that there lay obligations, for obedience was required of *all* sons, under sanction of the death penalty. Point (2) is undoubtedly true, but it cannot be inverted to suggest that by being set free a slave was *ipso facto* adopted; thus the mere fact of Israel's release does not "equal" adoption to sonship. In any case, the declaration of sonship preceded the Exodus. We are not here disputing the valid points that Brown makes regarding the significance of Israel's sonship, but only his couching of the whole issue in an adoption framework.

27. De Boer, p. 24.

derive in any sense from Israel's own action or merits. In this respect, Israel's sonship is a *datum* which corresponds entirely with the unconditional, indicative *datum* of their election. Israel is the firstborn son of Yahweh for no other reason than that Yahweh brought them as a nation into existence, just as they are the people of Yahweh for no other reason than that he "set his love upon" them and chose them for himself (Deut. 7:6-7).

2. The *individual* level. The Israelites are addressed as sons or children of Yahweh, in the plural. In such contexts the relationship expresses the Israelites' responsibility before Yahweh to manifest the loyalty and obedience required of sons. Thus, Deut. 14:1 invokes the relationship as grounds for exhortation to holiness. "Just as Israel, as a result of its relationship with Yahweh, is a holy nation, so these sons of Yahweh must be holy."[28] Most of the prophetic passages cited above appeal to this relationship by way of accusing Israel of failing in *obedience*. They are "rebellious" (Isa. 1:2), "faithless" (Jer. 3:22), "lying sons" (Isa. 30:9). "The demand thus becomes apparent that faithfulness is required of those who truly deserve the title of son of Yahweh" (Lagrange). This second aspect of Israel's sonship, therefore, clearly involves an imperative, in the demand for filial obedience upon all individual members of the nation.

Thus we find within one and the same relationship that both poles of the promise-obedience duality are to be found in the natural, inherent tension arising from the givenness of the filial relationship (the indicative) and the demands it imposes (the imperative). The significance of this for our purpose in this chapter also has two aspects.

(1) As noted above (p. 6), Yahweh's ownership *and* gift of the land have great import in the light of the Deuteronomic description of the whole land as the inheritance of *all* Israel. Gerhard von Rad, in drawing attention to this distinctive and almost unique Deuteronomic usage, did not dwell at any length on its significance, but in the present context its implications are considerable. For in describing the land

28. Lagrange, p. 485.

as Israel's *inheritance*,[29] Deuteronomy must regard Israel as *Yahweh's son*. In the light of the prominence of the gift of the land in Deuteronomy, the sonship of Israel consequently has a much more central place in the theology of this book than one might deduce from the sole direct reference (Deut. 14:1) and the more figurative references (1:31; 8:5). Furthermore, this Deuteronomic usage corresponds precisely with the unconditional givenness of Israel's sonship, for that is exactly what Deuteronomy stresses again and again as regards the gift

29. The word *naḥⁿlâ* is, of course, widely used throughout the Old Testament and is indeed the keyword of a rich cluster of ideas concerning Yahweh, Israel, and the land. For that reason, it has already been subjected to thorough study. F. Dreyfus saw it as a term used to emphasize the permanence of Israel's relationship to Yahweh, on the basis of what he considered to be very early texts—Exod. 34:9; Deut. 32:9 ("Le thème de l'héritage dans l'Ancien Testament," *Revue des sciences philosophiques et théologiques* 42 [1958]: 28-30). Dreyfus also noted the interesting triple use of *naḥⁿlâ*, namely, for the relationship of Israel to Yahweh (Ps. 33:12; 78:71; 1 Kgs. 8:51ff.), of the land to Yahweh (Exod. 15:17; Ps. 68:7-10; 79:1; Jer. 2:7; 12:7-9), and of the land to Israel (Deuteronomy, passim; Ps. 105:11; 136:21-22). As a common term in this triangular relationship, it has close links with the similar socio-theological position of the family vis-à-vis Yahweh, land, and nation (cf. below, p. 105). Friedrich Horst's word study ("Zwei Begriffe für Eigentum (Besitz): נַחֲלָה und אֲחֻזָּה," pp. 135-156 in *Verbannung und Heimkehr. Festschrift Wilhelm Rudolf*, ed. Arnulf Kuschke [Tübingen: Mohr, 1961]) emphasizes the word as a term for Yahweh's lordship over both people and land. Brown's dissertation has already been mentioned (see above, p. 17).

Most recent is Harold O. Forshey's dissertation, "The Hebrew Root *NHL* and Its Semitic Cognates" (Harvard, 1973). Forshey argues that it is mistaken to interpret *naḥⁿlâ* primarily in terms of familial inheritance. Rather, the term originally signified possession by virtue of military victory. If he were right, our argument above would obviously suffer, but there are two major weaknesses in Forshey's case.

(1) Forshey relies heavily upon the Old South Arabian texts, which speak only of feudal grants of land to loyal servants, and markedly plays down the evidence from Mari, where—as he admits—*nāḥal* can "reasonably be interpreted in inheritance terms" (p. 232). Yet sociologically Mari has far closer links with the Israelite tribal structure of society than does South Arabia, which was so different from Israel that Horst judged the material from there to be irrelevant to Israelite land tenure ("Zwei Begriffe," p. 152, n. 19). (On the Old South Arabian material, see most recently C. H. J. de Geus, *The Tribes of Israel*. Studia Semitica Neerlandica 18 [Assen: van Gorcum, 1976], pp. 150-56.)

(2) Forshey must resort to a very severe use of the literary-critical knife to support his contentions (a) that there is no evidence for a tribal sense of *naḥⁿlâ*

of the land to Israel. It emerges, therefore, that the gift of the land, as a historical indicative which owes nothing to the action or merit of Israel, is directly related to the same unconditional feature of Israel's sonship; it is because Israel is Yahweh's firstborn son that the land is given as an inheritance. The bond between Israel's land theology and the status of the people's unique relationship with Yahweh is here seen at its closest—the one being, as it were, the tangible manifestation of the other.[30]

(2) The second aspect of Israel's sonship, the "imperative," is also present in Deuteronomy. This has been pointed out by Dennis J. McCarthy,[31] who argues that "love" in the relationship between Israel and Yahweh involves much more than filial or paternal affection (though it includes that). Context and usage show that such love involves primarily faithfulness and obedience, exercised within the *discipline* of the father-son relationship. A pointer to this is the fact that it was a love which could be *commanded* and therefore was more than an emotion.

> . . . The very ancient Israelite concept of Israel as Yahweh's son . . . was conceived in terms which correspond to the definition of covenantal love as found in Deuteronomy. . . . The normative idea, the one which can be documented through a wide range of the Israelite tradition including Deuteronomy itself, was that the

---

before the Monarchy (ch. 6) and (b) that the association of *nah^{a}lâ* with the land gift is not Deuteronomic (seventh century) but Deuteronomistic (exilic) (ch. 4). I found neither argument sufficiently convincing to threaten the accepted familial/inheritance sense of *nah^{a}lâ* or our argument above.

30. This connection between sonship and the gift of land is illustrated externally by Moshe Weinfeld from the formulas of adoption and grants of land in the ancient Near East ("The Covenant of Grant in the Old Testament and in the Ancient Near East," *JAOS* 90 [1970]: 184-203). He relates them particularly to the accounts of the Davidic empire and dynasty. Not only David, however, but also Israel is called by God "my first-born son" (Exod. 4:22; Jer. 31:9). Also, "as the adoption of David is aimed to legitimize the inheritance of nations, i.e., the Davidic empire, so is the adoption of Israel by God aimed to validate the gift of the land" (p. 194). We may quibble over the term "adoption" (cf. above, n. 26), but it remains a valid point in the light of the Deuteronomic usage discussed above that Israel's sonship is a very important factor in their having received the land from Yahweh.

31. "Notes on the Love of God in Deuteronomy and the Father-Son Relationship between Yahweh and Israel," *CBQ* 27 (1965): 144-47.

father-son relationship is essentially one of respect and obedience. . . . Deuteronomy sees nothing incongruous about basing
a law (*sc.* Deut. 14:1) safeguarding the essential relationship to
Yahweh on an appeal to the father-son relationship. (pp. 145-46)

McCarthy concludes that in Deuteronomy the father-son relationship and the covenant relationship were more or less synonymous,
the common or mutual factor being "love" (in the sense defined
above).

In the light of our own study hitherto we would want to modify
this proposition by saying that the covenant and Israel's sonship are
not exactly co-extensive. Rather, the demands of the Sinai covenant
express *one* aspect of Israel's sonship—namely, the imperative of
loyalty and obedience and the threat of discipline. There was
another aspect, as we have seen—the indicative, unconditional
status of Israel as Yahweh's firstborn son, tangibly experienced in
the inheritance of the land and stressed as such by Deuteronomy.
Nor is Israel's sonship co-terminous with the Sinai covenant. In the
narrative the declaration of sonship preceded the Exodus, and it
remained to be invoked even after the judgment of the Exile on the
nation's disobedience as the basis for a fresh redemption and a
restored relationship (Hos. 11:1ff.; 1:10; Jer. 31:9, 20; Isa. 43:6;
63:16; 64:8). On Jer. 31:9 in particular, McCarthy comments:

. . . The restoration of Israel is the restoration of the father-son
relationship. This is in the context governed by 31:1, that is, by
the proclamation of a new and better union between Yahweh and
Israel based on a new covenant. Thus, in the mind of Jeremiah the
covenant relationship and the father-son relationship were not
incompatible, they were essentially the same thing. (p. 147)

We may note as well, from our point of view here, that the context
in Jer. 31:9 also speaks of restoration to the *land.* Brown also speaks
of this aspect of Israel's sonship. He sees "the father-son relationship having within it the human ingredient of hope transcending the
inevitable outcome of judgment that followed a broken covenant.[32]

32. P. 329.

Similarly, Harold O. Forshey finds an optimism in the Deuteronomistic use of inheritance language, describing Israel as
Yahweh's inheritance: "Thus, Israel's relationship to Yahweh can
continue to be affirmed despite her alienation from her land. Thus,
the perspective of the deuteronomic circles in the exilic community
may not be as bleak as it is usually portrayed by contemporary
German scholars."[33]

We may note in passing that the apostle Paul's handling of this
issue likewise asserts the priority of the promise and the relationship
of sonship established by God's grace through faith. The giving of
the law (Sinai covenant) did not affect this principle (Gal. 3:17),
nor did the "failure" of that covenant nullify the promise or frustrate
God's purpose. Rather, as that purpose had always been, in the
Messiah the blessing of Abraham extends to the Gentiles by way of
"inheritance" (Gal. 3:28). This inheritance is understood as the
promise of the Spirit (Gal. 3:14), whose precise purpose it is to
witness to the given status of sonship enjoyed by the redeemed (Gal.
4:5-7). We shall return later to the matter of the link between the
land as the promise to Abraham and inheritance of Israel in the Old
Testament, and the work of the Holy Spirit in the New Testament.

Thus we conclude that it is Israel's sonship which unites the
indicative and the imperative, as they are reflected respectively in
the historical land gift and the demands of Israel's relationship with
Yahweh. We find, therefore, at a theological level the same degree
of integration of the two themes that was argued, on textual grounds,
in section C above.

CONCLUSION

We began by pointing out the centrality of the land to a study of
Israel's property laws and ethics. In the course of this chapter we
have seen that the theology of the land, with its twin themes of

---

33. "The Construct Chain *nah^{a}lat YHWH/ ^{e}lōhîm*," *BASOR* 220 (1975): 53
and n. 18. The criticism of the last sentence is probably aimed in particular at Georg
Christian Macholz (see above, pp. 7-8) and Martin Noth.

divine ownership and divine gift (and particularly the historical tradition associated with the latter) is inseparable from Israel's consciousness of their unique covenant relationship with Yahweh. This has the important consequence that our ensuing examination of the socio-economic, legal, and ethical aspects of property and related issues in Israel cannot at any point be isolated from the theological dimension of that relationship. Because of its explicit links with the land traditions, the relationship between God and Israel was thoroughly "earthed" in the socio-economic facts of life—shaping and being shaped by them, and at times threatened by developments in that realm.

The focal point of this "earthing" process in Israel was the *family*. It thus becomes our next task to examine the role of the family (a) relative to the actual tenure of land and its theological rationale (Chapter 2), and (b) in its social and religious importance in the community, from both national and individual standpoints (Chapter 3).

APPENDIX   *Yahweh of Sinai and the Gift*
                 of the Land

The multiplicity of arguments against Gerhard von Rad's thesis can
be followed up in the literature cited in footnote 22 above. There is,
however, one point in von Rad's case which, as far as I am aware,
has not been subjected to critical examination.

In attributing to the Yahwist the credit for combining the two
hitherto independent traditions, von Rad argued that this was
nevertheless a novel and purely literary combination which for a
long time did not affect the living form of the transmission of the
settlement tradition, in which the events of Israel's redemption
history were recounted without reference to Sinai.

> Only in the exilic Ps. CVI, and in the prayer of Neh. IX, does the
> Sinai episode appear as an event of the redemption story. It can
> only be that the association of the two traditions was of recent
> origin, not something which the Yahwist found ready-made, since
> even at a time later than that of the Yahwist it had not taken root
> in the traditional account of the history of redemption. It is in fact
> to the Yahwist himself that we owe the fusion of the Sinai tradition
> with the Settlement tradition, and it was a long time before the
> pattern became fully accepted; only at about the time of the Exile
> did the association of the two win popular approval. Had this
> association taken place in the pre-literary phase, should we not
> have expected the two traditions to be rather more tightly and
> organically interwoven than they are?[34]

Now the logic of the last sentence implies that if the two
traditions were to be found "organically interwoven" in the preexilic period, then it could be argued that they were already closely
combined *before* the supposed literary work of J.[35] Furthermore,

34. "The Problem of the Hexateuch," pp. 53-54.
35. It is possible that von Rad later inclined to a pre-J date for the combination
of the traditions. Perhaps this is implied in his preface to the English translation of
his work where he asks that the essay on the Hexateuch be read in conjunction with
Martin Noth's more recent *Überlieferungsgeschichte des Pentateuch* (1948; Eng.

pursuing the same logic, the earlier they are found to be thus "interwoven," the stronger becomes the case for saying that in fact they never were independent. Accordingly, our investigation proceeds from some passages in preexilic prophets back to early poetic texts contemporary with or earlier than the Yahwist.

1. Eighth-Century Prophets

In three passages with formal similarities in Amos, Hosea, and Micah the historical land gift tradition is integrally related to the demands of the relationship between Israel and Yahweh. All three (Amos 2:6ff.; Hos. 13:4-6; and Mic. 6) are oracles of judgment and are widely accepted as authentic. Some doubts are expressed about the Mican passage, but there are no convincing grounds for rejecting it. We shall take Hos. 13:4-6 first because it presents the most succinct integration of the themes; then we shall see how its formal and functional characteristics (italicized) are paralleled in Amos and Micah.

a. Hos. 13:4-6

4   *"But I am the* LORD *your God, (who brought you) out of Egypt.*
    You shall acknowledge no God but me, no Savior except me.
5   *I cared for you in the desert, in the land of burning heat.*
6   *When I fed them, they were satisfied; when they were satisfied,*
    they became proud; then they forgot me. (NIV)

The external form of this passage is a *first person* résumé by *Yahweh* (as distinct from a credal confession by Israel) of the historical tradition, including the *Exodus* (Hos. 13:4a), the *wilderness* period

---

trans. *A History of Pentateuchal Traditions* [1972; repr. Atlanta: Scholars Press, 1989]). While Noth endorsed von Rad's separation of the two traditions (cf. Noth, pp. 59-62), he did not accord to the Yahwist the "versatile, epoch-making role in the history of traditions" (p. 41) for having joined them. Rather, they had already been combined in the fixed *Grundlage* of traditions which Noth saw behind the literary work of J and E (p. 40).

(v. 5), and the enjoyment of their *setting,* the land (v. 6a). But the internal point of the oracle is the *accusation* that, in spite of Israel's unique *relationship* with Yahweh (v. 4b), they have forgotten him (v. 6b). And its function in its present context is to link the grounds of the accusation—Israel's *sin* of idolatry (v. 2)[36] with the threat of *judgment* (vv. 7ff.). The two traditions are mutually dependent.[37]

b. Amos 2:6ff. and Mic. 6

That the same pattern of complementarity is to be found in these passages may be seen from the following analysis.

	Amos 2	Micah 6
First person	vv. 6, 9, etc.	vv. 3, 4
Exodus	v. 10a	v. 4a
Wilderness	v. 10b	v. 5a

36. The explicit presence of idolatry in the context has led many commentators to see in v. 4b a deliberate allusion to the First Commandment, and in v. 4a an echo of the preface to the Decalog. Wilhelm Rudolph, for example, citing this and other texts in the prophet (e.g., Hos. 3:1; 4:2; 6:7-9; 7:1, 10; 8:1-4; 12:9), described Hosea's essential message as based on the belief that Israel's relationship to Yahweh was grounded *both* on their historical traditions (Exodus-Settlement) *and* on the Sinai covenant (*Hosea.* Kommentar zum Alten Testament 13/1 [Gütersloh: Gerd Mohn, 1966], p. 254). Essentially similar views are expressed by Hans Walter Wolff, *Hosea.* Hermeneia (Philadelphia: Fortress, 1974), p. xix; Gerhard von Rad, *Old Testament Theology,* 2 (New York: Harper & Row and Edinburgh: Oliver & Boyd, 1965), p. 142; James Luther Mays, *Hosea.* OTL (1969), p. 174; Roland de Vaux, *The Early History of Israel* (Philadelphia: Westminster and London: Darton, Longman & Todd, 1978), 1:410-19.

However, on the need for caution in speaking of "covenant" themes in the eighth-century prophets, in the light of recent scholarly debate on the covenant, cf. below, n. 39.

37. This Hosean passage has many similarities, conceptual and verbal, with Deut. 8:11-20 (cf. Rudolph, p. 243, and in greater detail Moshe Weinfeld, *Deuteronomy and the Deuteronomic School* [Oxford: Clarendon, 1972], pp. 367-68). The latter passage also concerns idolatry resulting from prosperity, and into it too is woven the theme of Yahweh's saving acts.

One wonders why von Rad ignored Deuteronomy in his assertion that the two themes are not found "interwoven" before the Exile. For Deuteronomy in every respect—form, content, language—presents a complete fusion of the land gift/Settlement traditions with the obligations of the Sinai/Horeb covenant.

Setting	vv. 9, 10c	v. 5b ("Shittim to Gilgal" implying the invasion across the Jordan)
Accusation	v. 6a	v. 2
Relationship	cf. 3:2a	v. 2 ("his people"), v. 3 ("my people")
Sin	vv. 6b-8	vv. 10-12, 16a
Judgment	vv. 13-16	vv. 13-15, 16b

The common *purpose* of all three passages, therefore, is the accusation of Israel and the proclamation of imminent judgment. Both of these, however, presuppose a known tradition of a special relationship between Israel and Yahweh involving obligations and sanctions[38]—that is, basic factors in what was, or was to become, the covenant conception.[39] And the common *method* of all three is to set this accusation in the context of the Exodus-wilderness-Conquest tradition. The rhetorical value of this juxtaposition is obvious: it places the sin of Israel in stark contrast with "the saving acts of Yahweh." But it is equally arguable that the arrangement was *historically* conditioned in that the relationship with Yahweh was

38. "Behind Amos we must recognize the existence of a standard of covenant law, and its acceptance by the people. . . . Amos's appeal to the law pre-supposes that the law represents the will of Yahweh" (Ronald E. Clements, *Prophecy and Covenant.* SBT 43 [London: SCM and Naperville: Allenson, 1965], p. 76, referring to Amos 2:6b-8).

39. Clements has since considerably modified his view of the prophetic use of the covenant tradition in the light of subsequent scholarship (see *Prophecy and Tradition* [Oxford: Blackwell and Atlanta: John Knox, 1976], ch. 1). He does, however, still maintain that even if "we cannot reconstruct a consistent covenant theology as a distinctive coherent tradition underlying the preaching of the prophets . . . we can see that the traditions which the prophets inherited and used had a place in the emergence of a distinctive covenant ideology in Israel" (p. 23).

The whole question of the originality or otherwise of the references to covenant in "pre-Deuteronomic" prophetic literature (particularly Hosea) is one of the issues in the whole area of covenant study, at present *sub judice*. In view of this I have not included in the main argument other texts in Hosea where the covenant and land are closely linked, notably 4:1-3 (the land mourns) and 8:1-3; 9:8, 15, where the land is symbolically described as the "house of the LORD." On the association in these texts, cf. Rudolph, *Hosea,* p. 162; and Norbert Lohfink, "Hate and Love in Osee 9:15," *CBQ* 25 (1963): 417.

known to have been constituted in the course of the Exodus-Settlement period and was therefore, traditio-historically, part of that tradition. Certainly both themes are inseparable, intrinsic to their contexts and essential to the meaning of the oracles in question. Since this pattern is found in both northern and southern prophets, it must reflect a tradition already widespread and well-established before the eighth century, a tradition in which the twin themes of the salvation history and the covenant relationship with Yahweh were historically and theologically integrated and betray no sign of separate origin or development.

2. Exod. 33:1-3, 12-16

1 Then the LORD said to Moses, "Leave this place, you and the people you brought up out of Egypt, and go up to the land I promised on oath to Abraham, Isaac and Jacob, saying, 'I will give it to your descendants.' "

2 I will send an angel before you and drive out the Canaanites, Amorites, Hittites, Perizzites, Hivites and Jebusites.

3 Go up to the land flowing with milk and honey. But I will not go with you, because you are a stiff-necked people and I might destroy you on the way."

. . . .

12 Moses said to the LORD, "You have been telling me, 'Lead these people,' but you have not let me know whom you will send with me. You have said, 'I know you by name and you have found favor with me.'

13 If I have found favor in your eyes, teach me your ways so I may know you and continue to find favor with you. Remember that this nation is your people.'

14 The LORD replied, "My Presence will go with you, and I will give you rest."

15 Then Moses said to him, "If your Presence does not go with us, do not send us up from here.

16 How will anyone know that you are pleased with me and with your people unless you go with us? What else will distinguish

*me and your people from all the other people on the face of the
earth?" (NIV)*

The literary-critical and redactional questions in this chapter are part
of the wider issue of the whole block, Exod. 32–34, concerning
which no commanding critical consensus has yet emerged.[40]
However, while source analysis has produced divergent views at
many points—and at some points has been abandoned altogether—
the position most widely taken by critical scholarship still views the
chapters as based mainly on J, though including numerous smaller,
independent units of tradition, and as owing their present shape to
the pre-Deuteronomic JE redaction.[41] We are on fairly safe critical
grounds, therefore, in assuming a comparatively early date for the
passage under consideration. This is not made doubtful by the
contents of the story itself, which centers on Moses as mediator—a
function which belongs to his role in the earliest Sinaitic traditions.[42]

In 33:1-3 Yahweh declares his intention to fulfill his promise
to the patriarchs by granting possession of the land of Canaan to
their descendants, whom he has brought up out of Egypt. But
because of their apostasy (described in ch. 32) his presence, which
would be a continual threat, would not accompany them. After
parenthetical sections (33:4-6, 7-11) we find Moses engaged in
intercession with Yahweh for the second time (the first being
32:11-12), the outcome of which is that Yahweh pardons the people.
Chapter 34 describes the renewal of the covenant.

In 32:11ff. Moses appealed to the *promises* to the patriarchs in
order to avert Yahweh's intended destruction of the people for
breaking the covenant just concluded at Sinai. But in 33:12-16 he
appeals to the *relationship* established by the *Sinai* covenant in

40. A comprehensive survey of the relevant literature, the critical questions,
and proposed solutions for these chapters is provided by Childs, pp. 553-562. For
a comprehensive discussion of the theology of these chapters, see R. W. L. Moberly,
At the Mountain of God. JSOT Supplement 22 (Sheffield: JSOT, 1983).

41. Nicholson (p. 75) feels that there may be a much greater degree of
Deuteronomic influence in the shaping of Exod. 32 than is usually allowed for.

42. Cf. Nicholson, p. 79.

order to prevent a merely formal and physical fulfillment of that with the patriarchs, which lacked the spiritual reality of the presence of Yahweh. This is the unmistakable intention of the emphatic exclamation of v. 13b: "Look! It is *your* people, this nation" (author's translation). It is reinforced by the repetition of "*your* people" in the rest of the comparatively brief intercession (v. 16a, b). If the presence of Yahweh did not accompany Israel, then they would lose all claim to be his special, distinct people (v. 16), and the whole prospect of conquest and settlement—even in the delectable land of promise (vv. 1-2)—would become empty and meaningless. They might as well stay in the wilderness (v. 15).

The clear implication of this section is that the relationship established between Israel and Yahweh at Sinai was the indispensable "heart and soul" of the historical Exodus-Settlement tradition. Without it, that tradition was an empty shell. Not even its grand motifs of election and redemption, promise and fulfillment could give it a validity of its own. The historical events of this tradition could only have meaning and value for Israel if they were in fact the people of Yahweh—witnessed to by his real presence in their midst—and that was only possible on the basis of the relationship established at Sinai. The separation of the two traditions, therefore, fails to take into account all the evidence and also results in theological distortion.[43] It is somewhat ironical that the possibility of separating the historical sequence of events (from the Exodus to the land) from the relationship established at Sinai was precisely what Moses is represented here as pleading should *not* happen!

3. *Exod. 23:20-33*

20 *See, I am sending an angel ahead of you to guard you along the way and to bring you to the place I have prepared.*
21 *Pay attention to him and listen to what he says. Do not rebel*

43. Cf. Artur Weiser's remark that the separation of the Sinai tradition from that of the redemption history was only achieved by means of "a certain forcible simplification" (*The Old Testament: Its Formation and Development* [New York: Association, 1961], p. 85).

against him; he will not forgive your rebellion, since my Name is in him.

22 *If you listen carefully to what he says and do all that I say, I will be an enemy to your enemies and will oppose those who oppose you.*

23 *My angel will go ahead of you and bring you into the land of the Amorites, Hittites, Perizzites, Canaanites, Hivites and Jebusites, and I will wipe them out.*

24 *Do not bow down before their gods or worship them or follow their practices. You must demolish them and break their sacred stones to pieces.*

25 *Worship the LORD your God, and his blessing will be on your food and water. I will take away sickness from among you,*

26 *and none will miscarry or be barren in your land. I will give you a full life span.*

27 *I will send my terror ahead of you and throw into confusion every nation you encounter. I will make all your enemies turn their backs and run.*

28 *I will send the hornet ahead of you to drive the Hivites, Canaanites and Hittites out of your way.*

29 *But I will not drive them out in a single year, because the land would become desolate and the wild animals too numerous for you.*

30 *Little by little I will drive them out before you, until you have increased enough to take possession of the land.*

31 *I will establish your borders from the Red Sea to the Sea of the Philistines, and from the desert to the River. I will hand over to you the people who live in the land and you will drive them out before you.*

32 *Do not make a covenant with them or with their gods.*

33 *Do not let them live in your land, or they will cause you to sin against me, because the worship of their gods will certainly be a snare to you. (NIV)*

It is widely argued that this epilogue to the Book of the Covenant was probably not originally part of the body of laws which precedes it. The main critical questions have therefore been concerned with the original milieu of its composition and the date of its redactional inclusion at this point—after the legal sections and before the ratification of the covenant, described in Exod. 24.

Its repetitious and parenetic style are reminiscent of Deuteronomic homily. Indeed, much of its content and language recur in Deut. 7, but there are differences of sequence and ideas which make direct *literary* dependence either way unlikely. Brevard S. Childs reckons that both derive from an early oral tradition.[44] In that case the Exodus passage would be the earlier literary manifestation of the tradition in sermonic form.

The occasion of the account's inclusion at the end of the Book of the Covenant is as uncertain as the redactional history of the Book of the Covenant itself.[45] Some think the passage was added at the stage of the literary fusion of the two distinctive parts of the Book (Exod. 21:1–22:16; 22:17–23:19) in order to provide a homiletical epilogue to the whole. On the other hand, it is noticeable that the epilogue does not explicitly refer back to a preceding body of laws and call for obedience to them (in contrast to this conspicuous feature of Lev. 26 and Deut. 28). Rather, the epilogue is concerned with the *land*—just as are a number of the injunctions in the *second* part of the Book immediately preceding the epilogue (e.g., Exod. 22:28-29; 23:10-11, 16-17, 19). This raises the possibility that the passage may have been added to that second section *before* the literary fusion with the casuistic material of the first part.

This passage is most interesting when compared with Exod. 34:11-26. Many of the laws in 34:18-26 are similar or identical to those in 23:10-19, the second part of the Book of the Covenant, and have a similar orientation towards the land. More significantly, the homily which precedes them (34:11-16) also has many points of comparison with this epilogue (23:23-33).

Note, for example:

The exhortation to obedience	23:21-22	34:11
The expulsion of the nations	23:23, 28	34:11

44. P. 461.
45. For a survey of the historical, literary, and redactional questions involved, cf. Childs, pp. 451-58.

The exclusion of other gods	23:24	34:14
The destruction of Canaanite cult objects	23:24b	34:13
The prohibition on making covenants with the inhabitants of the land	23:32	34:12, 15
The danger of the "snare"	23:33	34:12

Now if, as seems likely, 34:10-27 is to be regarded as substantially a unity, then the same may be held of 22:20–23:33. This would mean that the homiletical epilogue was originally and integrally part of the second division of the Book of the Covenant, rather than a "floating" piece of homily which has been appended to the whole Book in the final stages of its literary redaction.

With this possibility in mind we may not be quite so ready to grant, with Childs, that the passage "may well have functioned in a different setting originally."[46] He is, however, undoubtedly right in saying:

> It is fundamental to its proper understanding that its present role be not overlooked. It is hardly accidental that this passage concludes the Book of the Covenant and separates the laws from the sealing of the covenant in ch. 24. (p. 486)

The point is that, whatever the correct solution to the redactional problem, when the redaction was achieved this homiletical passage concerned with the *land* was felt to be wholly appropriate in a thoroughly *covenantal* context. Thus, right in the middle of the major Sinai narratives we find a short but very significant passage taken up with the themes of the conquest and settlement of the land, its extent, the conditions of blessing on it, and its protection, integrity, and purity. Von Rad's claim, therefore, that not "even the major elements" of the historical land tradition are to be found anywhere in Exod. 19–24[47] simply cannot be maintained.

We have not yet, however, exhausted the extent of the inter-penetration of the two themes in this passage. For even within this

---

46. Childs, p. 486.
47. "The Problem of the Hexateuch," p. 18.

"homily on the land"—indeed, as its focal point—we find what was the fundamental and undeniably original basis of the covenant relationship: the obligation to serve Yahweh alone (23:24-25, 32-33; cf. 34:14), coupled with obedience to his declared will. It is clear, therefore, that, within the traditions that lie behind this homily and its "cousin" in Exod. 34, the historical land gift and settlement theme and the basic requirements of the covenant relationship were closely bound together. This exegetically grounded conclusion surely renders untenable also von Rad's assertion that "no properly assimilated, integral harmonization of the materials existed" before J, and that J's achievement was only a literary interpolation which did not really knit the themes together.[48] On the contrary, as we have seen, the integration in this passage is both contextual and intrinsic.

4. Early Hebrew Poetry

If, finally, we take up von Rad's invitation to look at the "poetical variants of this Sinai tradition,"[49] we find a number of texts of greater significance to the issue than von Rad's brief reference to them would suspect. The main importance of the material about to be discussed lies in its antiquity. Most of it reached its written form well before the accepted critical dating of the earliest pentateuchal narratives and affords, in my view, the strongest possible grounds for believing the Sinai and Settlement traditions to have been united from the beginning.

a. Ps. 68:7-8 (Heb. 8-9)

7 *O God, when you went forth before your people,*
   when you marched through [from] the wilderness.[a]
8 *The earth shook, the heavens poured down rain,*[50]

48. "The Problem of the Hexateuch," p. 54.
49. "The Problem of the Hexateuch," p. 19.
50. Both here and in the yet more ancient Judg. 5:4 the Sinai theophany is accompanied by both earthquake and violent rainstorm. One wonders in passing if

> *at the presence of God, the One of Sinai,*[b]
> *at the presence of God, the God of Israel. (author's translation)*

   a. *bîšîmôn.* Comparison with Deut. 33:2; Judg. 5:4; and Hab. 3:3 suggests that the *beth* here may indicate movement "through and out of" the wilderness.
   b. *ᵉlōhîm zeh sînāy.* The suggestion of Franz X. Wutz (*Die Psalmen textkritisch untersucht* [Munich: Kösel & Pustet, 1925], p. 167) that this expression means "God—the one of Sinai" (cf. LXX *toû Sina*) is now widely accepted. Cf. NEB, "God the lord of Sinai."

Two critical problems relate to this Psalm: its unity (or otherwise) and its date. As regards the first, diametrically opposite views have been held. Umberto Cassuto regarded it as a unified and symmetrically structured prayer supporting faith in time of national danger.[51] William F. Albright, on the other hand, regarded the Psalm as a collection of "incipits"—i.e., first lines of independent poems, brought together in a purely literary exercise to form a sort of poetic montage.[52] Sigmund Mowinckel disagreed entirely and maintained that it is virtually a unity, with a cultic *Sitz im Leben* in the festival of Yahweh's enthronement.[53] As regards date, most scholars agree on dating the Psalm before the division of the kingdom. Mowinckel placed it in the time of Saul, on the grounds of the apparent hegemony of Benjamin (Ps. 68:27). Cassuto felt it could have been composed at the time of the Syro-Aramaean threat to David (2 Sam. 10:16-19). Albright dated his "incipits" to poems of the thirteenth–tenth centuries, and the whole composition to the reign of Solomon.

   (1) *Internal* examination of this stanza shows that the spectacu-

---

this does not render doubtful the literary-critical source analysis of Exod. 19 in which the earthquake is said to belong to one source (J) and the thunderstorm to another (E). Thomas W. Mann speaks of a "facile dichotomy of sources and traditions. . . . The fact that these images are interchangeable is evident in a wealth of material," e.g., Ps. 18:7-15 ("The Pillar of Cloud in the Reed Sea Narrative," *JBL* 90 [1971]: 16-17).
   51. "Psalm 68," pp. 241-284 in *Biblical and Oriental Studies* 1 (Jerusalem: Magnes, 1973); first published in Hebrew, *Tarbiz* 12 (1940): 1-27.
   52. "A Catalogue of Early Hebrew Lyric Poems (Psalm 68)," *HUCA* 23 (1950/1951): 1-39.
   53. *Der achtundsechztigste Psalm.* Avhandlinger utgitt av det Norske Videnskaps-Akademi i Oslo, 2, 1953/1.

lar phenomena of the Sinai theophany are integrally and syntactically[54] related to the military aspect of the wilderness march. Comparison with the virtually identical description in Judg. 5:4-5 confirms that the coming of Yahweh to, or on, Sinai is inseparable from
the coming of Yahweh *from* Sinai with his people in the wars of
conquest. The function of this ancient piece of poetry, therefore, was
not simply to recall the momentous theophany at Sinai, but to relate
it to Israel's military traditions—in the first place, to the original
conquest wars, but, as Judg. 5 shows, it could also be applied to the
later wars against the enemies of Yahweh and Israel. The connection
between Sinai and Israel's military traditions, in this and other
contexts, is strongly emphasized by Patrick D. Miller, Jr.:

> Here in Psalms 68 . . . the theophany is manifestly in terms of
> Yahweh's leading Israel. . . . In these verses the fusion of the
> cosmic and the historical . . . in the conceptions associated with
> Israel's sacral wars and particularly the wars of conquest, is
> transparent.[55]

Taken by itself, then, this text links Sinai to the wilderness theme,
and this inevitably involves the Exodus-Settlement tradition without
which the wilderness story lacks beginning, end, and meaning.[56]

(2) The *external* context of the stanza immediately confirms this
understanding of it. Most commentators regard Ps. 68:6b, in the
preceding stanza, as an allusion to the Exodus ("He leads forth[57]
captives to prosperity"), and to the perishing of the rebellious generation in the wilderness ("but rebels live in a parched land"). Even

54. Vv. 7-8 (Heb. 8-9) are in fact a single sentence, in which the wilderness
march is syntactically subordinate, in the form of two infinitive constructs
($b^e\bar{s}\bar{e}^{\prime}t^e k\bar{a}$ and $b^e \bar{s}a^{\cdot} d^e k\bar{a}$), to the description of the theophany in the main clause.

55. *The Divine Warrior in Early Israel.* HSM 5 (1973), pp. 106-7.

56. Cf. Noth's comment that the wilderness theme "presupposes in every
instance the themes 'guidance out of Egypt' and 'guidance into the promised land'
and depends on both of these" (*A History of Pentateuchal Traditions,* p. 58). Cf.
also, with particular reference to these themes in the Psalms, Johannes Kühlewein,
Geschichte in den Psalmen. Calwer Theologische Monographien 2 (Stuttgart:
Calwer, 1973), pp. 152ff.

57. The verb used, $y\bar{a}\bar{s}\bar{a}^{\cdot}$, is a technical term for the Exodus. See Kühlewein,
p. 137.

clearer, however, is the reference in the following stanza (vv. 9-10) to the settlement in the fertile, watered heritage of Canaan. The degree of integration is shown by the way vv. 7-8 are "keyed in" with their preceding and following contexts. Thus, note the references to the wilderness in both v. 6b and v. 7 and the references to rain in association with the presence of Yahweh in both v. 8 and v. 9a.

We have, therefore, in this psalm a recital of the major acts of the salvation history, albeit in an allusive, poetic form which lacks the sort of "credal" clarity found elsewhere. Within this recital the Sinai event is included and thoroughly integrated with the Exodus-Settlement tradition.

b. Deut. 33:2-5

There is a wide consensus that this chapter belongs to the earliest deposits of Hebrew poetry, particularly in view of its many similarities with the archaic Judg. 5. Frank Moore Cross, Jr., and David Noel Freedman regard the tenth century as the *terminus ad quem*, on orthographic grounds, for its being written down[58] but believe that its oral origins may be centuries earlier. Isaac L. Seeligmann considers it undoubtedly premonarchic.[59] There are also historical pointers to its antiquity in the body of the tribal blessings (see n. 61). It is regrettable that von Rad's discussion of this reference to Sinai is so brief and, one must add, misleading. He quotes only Deut. 33:2a and 4, seeing in them "a loosely worded allusion to the Sinai tradition" which involves "only a theophany, and the imposition of the divine commandments by which God takes possession of the nation."[60] He thus excludes from the reckoning the difficult, but important, vv. 2b-3a, as well as the whole of the context of the rest of the song.

(1) The Context

The context of this reference to Sinai is relevant whether one considers the tribal blessings (vv. 6-25) to be part of the original song

58. "The Blessing of Moses," *JBL* 67 (1948): 191-210.
59. "A Psalm from Pre-regal Times," *VT* 14 (1964): 75-92.
60. "The Problem of the Hexateuch," p. 20.

or, as is commonly held, that what is now the framework (vv. 2-5, 26-29) was originally a unified hymn into which the tribal blessings have been inserted.[61] Either way, the context is clearly the Conquest and Settlement and praise for the good gifts of the land (in the blessings, vv. 13-17, 21; in the framework, vv. 27-28). Once again, therefore, we find the Sinai theophany tradition and the historical land settlement tradition side by side. No separation is possible except on an unjustifiably fragmentary handling of the text.[62]

(2) Verses 2b-3a

2b *With him [Yahweh] were myriads of holy ones;[a]*
    At his right hand, heavenly warriors,[b]
3a *Yea also, the purified ones[c] of the peoples.[d] (author's transla-*
    tion)

The translation of these verses is extremely difficult. That offered here follows mainly the lines of Cross and Freedman; and Patrick D. Miller, Jr., "Two Critical Notes on Psalm 68 and Deuteronomy 33," *HTR* 57 (1964): 249-43. Additional bibliographical information is available in Seeligmann.
a. See Cross and Freedman, pp. 193, 198-99.
b. See Miller, "Two Critical Notes," pp. 241-42.
c. See Miller, "Two Critical Notes," p. 243.
d. Or possibly, "of his people"; cf. BH^3 following LXX.

61. The latter position makes little difference to the date of the poem as a whole, for the evidence points to a roughly similar date for the blessings also. As well as linguistic and orthographical considerations, there are historical clues. The implied danger to Reuben and Judah would seem to reflect the Ammonite and Philistine incursions of the twelfth and eleventh centuries, respectively. There is no suspicion of the rift between Judah and the rest of Israel, which points to the pre-Solomonic era, as does also the reference to the supremacy of Joseph among the tribes (v. 16). This must antedate the hegemony of Judah under David. Cross and Freedman regard the reign of Saul as the *iterminus ad quem* (pp. 202-3, 205).

62. The same criticism of von Rad's treatment of this text has recently been made, from a different viewpoint, by Miller: "Von Rad has referred to Deuteronomy 33:2-4 but as an example of the separation of the Sinai tradition. The problem in this case is that von Rad has assumed that verses 2-5 are to be understood by themselves, ignoring the fact that we have here the beginning of a framework which finds its ending in verses 26-29. There most explicitly one is dealing with the march of conquest and the settlement in the land" (*The Divine Warrior in Early Israel*, p. 169).

Even if not every point of the textual reconstruction (which is neither radical nor extensive) is certain, it is sufficiently clear that the lines are describing the hosts of those accompanying Yahweh in his theophany and the matching hosts of his human people, assembled at Sinai, with the wars of conquest in prospect.

> The parallelism "warriors of the gods" // "pure ones of the peoples" (or "consecrated ones of the peoples") is exact in form and structure. The parallelism of meaning is also clear when it is recognized that "the consecrated ones of the peoples" must refer to those mustered and sanctified for war. The holy warriors of Yahweh's host and of Israel's host are pictured as marching forth to battle under the command of Yahweh, the conquest of Canaan being the ultimate goal, as the rest of the hymnic framework shows.[63]

From this it emerges that Sinai, far from being originally unconnected with the Conquest, was in fact conceived of as its very starting point in these early poetic traditions. In this regard it is interesting to note, as de Vaux points out,[64] that the narratives in Exodus only explicitly speak of the military expulsion of the Canaanites *after* Sinai (e.g., in Exod. 23). Previously (e.g., in Exod. 3:8), only the gift of the land is mentioned.

(3) Verses 3b-5

3b *All the holy ones are in your hand [? = possession, authority].*
    They bow before your feet;[a] —
    they uphold your instructions,
 4 *the law [which][b] Moses commanded us,*
    a possession for the assembly[c] of Jacob.
 5 *[Yahweh][d] became king in Jeshurun,*
    when the heads of the people were gathered together,
    the tribes of Israel together. (author's translation)

63. Miller, "Two Critical Notes," p. 243.
64. *The Early History of Israel,* 1:414.

a. For this translation, cf. Otto Komlós, "תַּכּוּ לְרַגְלֶךָ (Deut. 33:3)," *VT* 6 (1956): 436. The implied submission of the people underlies LXX, *hypò sé eisin,* followed by NIV.

b. On this view of the syntax, see below p. 42.

c. Frank Zimmerman suggested understanding the rare word not as "assembly" but, by comparison with the context of its only other occurrence in Neh. 5:7, as "reproof." Thus, he translated: "an inheritance for the *admonition* of Jacob" ("The Root *KAHAL* in Some Scriptural Passages," *JBL* 50 (1931): 312).

d. The view that Yahweh is the implied subject of the opening *wayyᵉhî* is certainly correct. It can hardly refer to Moses, who is nowhere referred to as a king in Israel, and the establishment of the monarchy lies quite outside the scope of the poem. Cf. Seeligman, pp. 82-83, 89.

Sinai in this hymn, however, was not merely the theophanic "launching pad" of the Conquest. These next few lines show that the Sinai event was the occasion of the establishment of a *relationship* between Yahweh and Israel, based upon the proclamation of Yahweh's will and the commitment of the people to obedience and submission to Yahweh's kingship.

Deut. 33:4-5, however, is regarded by some as not originally belonging here. Miller regards these verses as the "torso of an alternative ancient introduction to the blessings" of vv. 6ff., which has been inserted here at the secondary stage of the literary fusion of the blessings into the hymnic framework.[65] This "secondary stage," however, must still have been early, given the overall antiquity of the poem. And the lines themselves, if they were originally part of the tribal blessings, must be older than the date of their literary attachment to vv. 2-3. The significance of such a literary juxtaposition, if such it be, cannot be overlooked. It would demonstrate that at an early period the Sinai theophany, with its attendant military imagery and links with the land conquest traditions, was also associated with the tradition of a relationship having been established there on the basis of the law mediated by Moses.

However, the reasons for separating vv. 4-5 from their context are not wholly convincing, and a strong case can be made, it seems to me, for regarding them as an original and integral part of the

65. *The Divine Warrior in Early Israel,* pp. 82ff.

hymnic framework—vv. 2-5, 26-29. Cross and Freedman surely exaggerate the dislocation and difficulty of the lines when they do not even attempt a reconstruction because they feel that no coherent unity could be produced without a "drastic reworking" of the MT.[66] Miller points out the poor transition from the end of v. 5 into either the tribal blessings or the rest of the framework at v. 26. This difficulty, however, as Miller himself was aware,[67] was overcome by Seeligmann. Building on a suggestion of Cross and Freedman that v. 21b originally followed v. 5 as part of the original early hymn, Seeligmann inserted the verb *way^{e}tannû*,[68] producing the result:

> *and they* [the "assembled tribes" of v. 5c]
> *recounted* the righteous deeds that Yahweh has done, his acts of justice on Israel's behalf.

If this suggestion is on the right lines, then there is much stronger reason to keep vv. 4-5 as part of the hymn continuing naturally at v. 26 rather than assigning them as a preface to the tribal blessings, with which they have much less direct affinity.

Furthermore, a link may be discerned between v. 3b and v. 4 which makes it even less likely that they should be separated. Verse 3b refers to the twofold response of God's people, his "consecrated ones." (a) They (?) "follow in his steps," that is, they are committed to obedience to his will, which is then defined more precisely in v. 4 as the *tôrâ*. (b) They "receive of, or 'bear up' his instructions." In the context of v. 3a this probably refers to the people obeying the commands of Yahweh in a military sense; but, as Miller puts it, "judicial connotations are not far away"[69]—no further away, in fact, than v. 4, which can thus be seen to follow on quite naturally. Indeed, v. 4 can be taken as syntactically part of v. 3—namely, as a relative clause describing further the last word of v. 3. Thus, the LXX takes *tôrâ* in v. 4 as the direct object of *yiśśā'* in v. 3: *kaì*

---

66. P. 203.
67. *The Divine Warrior in Early Israel*, pp. 83-84.
68. Pp. 76ff., 83-86.
69. *The Divine Warrior in Early Israel*, p. 81.

edéxato apò tōn lógōn autoú vómon, hòn eneteílato hēmín Mōusḗs.
The NEB also takes it thus: "They . . . receive his instruction, the
law which Moses laid upon us" (cf. NIV). This syntactical reading
also nullifies another of the arguments for removing vv. 4-5—
namely, the change of subject from Israel to Moses,[70] for Moses can
now be seen as the subject of a subordinate clause. In any case, this
is an insubstantial argument, since changes of subject and person
are not uncommon in Hebrew poetry.

These arguments from context and syntax are supported by the
content. Seeligmann rejected v. 4 (though he retained v. 5) on the
grounds that "the whole conception of Moses as a lawgiver to the
congregation of Jacob is hardly in harmony with an ancient
poem."[71] But this a priori judgment is contradicted by the verdicts
of recent scholarship on the role of Moses in the early Sinaitic
traditions. Nicholson finds that in the Sinai theophany narratives in
Exod. 19 Moses has "an indispensable role as mediator between
Yahweh and Israel (which) . . . can in no way be regarded as
secondary. The narratives afford no hint of an earlier stage of
tradition in which Moses had no place or indeed even a less
significant place."[72] There can be no reason, therefore, why mention
of Moses' role should have been out of place in an "ancient poem."
Furthermore, Deut. 33:4 fits precisely into the pattern discerned by
Nicholson in the Exodus narratives in which "the theophany is not
simply presented for its own sake but in close association with the
communication of God's will to Israel through Moses. The
theophany leads up to and is followed by proclamation."[73] As
Weiser had earlier insisted, Sinai was not merely a theophany, but
"an encounter with God which leads up to the acceptance by the
people of the will of God proclaimed in the commandments."[74] This
is precisely the sequence we find in Deut. 33:2-5.

There are, then, good grounds for retaining verses 4-5 as an
original part of the hymnic framework of the song. This means that

70. See Seeligmann, p. 73; and Kühlewein, p. 140.
71. Seeligmann, p. 79.
72. P. 79. The same point is made by Hyatt, p. 167.
73. P. 79.
74. P. 86.

the association of traditions, otherwise attributable to secondary literary juxtaposition (above, p. 42), should be regarded as an "organic" and not a "synthetic" bond.

Thus in Deut. 33:2-5 we have textual evidence from well before the Monarchy for the unity of the traditions. Yahweh of Sinai was also Yahweh of the Conquest. The gift of the land and its historical settlement were regarded as having been launched with the theophany at Sinai; but Sinai was also the occasion when a relationship was established between Israel and Yahweh involving Israel's obedience to the law of Yahweh as king.

On the basis of all the material discussed in this appendix, therefore, we may first of all conclusively rule out von Rad's view that the two traditions were not connected before the literary work of J. But further, we may confidently agree with those who reject altogether the separation of Sinai from the Exodus-Settlement complex. On the contrary, all the passages—which include some of the earliest literary deposits in the Old Testament—indicate that the historical, land gift themes must be interpreted alongside and in the light of the belief in the relationship established at Sinai—each being indispensable to the other.

2 | *Land and Family*

INTRODUCTION: LAND DIVISION TEXTS

The task of ascertaining the relationship of the family to the land necessitates a study of the information that exists on the subject of land tenure in early Israel. This involves the texts relating to the earliest period of Israel's history in the land of Canaan. It lies well outside the scope of this thesis to enter into the complexities of this period or to venture judgments upon the differing scholarly reconstructions of it. However, an important fact that emerges from any reading of the Old Testament evidence, one which needs to be stressed at the outset, is that Israel's acquisition of the land was initially partial and the process of secure settlement lengthy and far from uniform. There was, therefore, no single system of land tenure "imposed" by Israel on the whole of Palestine. Not only were many Canaanite cities not conquered for a considerable time (Judg. 1), but even in those that were it appears that concessions were made to the existing forms of land tenure and commercial customs.[1] The provisions in the Jubilee legislation for city property can be interpreted in

1. It is usually assumed that the "Canaanite system" involved simple sale and

this light (but cf. below p. 125), and certain concessions made by
later monarchs to the Canaanite system of sale and purchase in land
show that it had continued to exist alongside the Israelite tribal

purchase of land as a commercial transaction unfettered by questions of inheritance
or inalienability. But there is a danger of oversimplifying the picture. S. Herbert
Bess ("Systems of Land Tenure in Ancient Israel," pp. 50-55), for example, simply
repeats the theories of Louis Wallis (*God and the Social Process,* pp. 8-10)
concerning the Canaanite *ba'alim (sic)* as both landed aristocracy and local deities.
But Wallis's theories and his whole understanding of the Canaanite society, my-
thology, and religion, as well as his sociological interpretation of the evolution of
Israelite culture were heavily criticized by Herbert G. May, "A Sociological Approach to Hebrew Religion," *Journal of Bible and Religion* 12 (1944): 98-106. For
more reliable information on Canaanite land tenure from the Ugaritic texts, see Jean
Nougayrol, "Textes Juridiques," in *Le Palais royal d'Ugarit,* ed. C. F.-A. Schaeffer
and Nougayrol, vol. 3: *Textes Accadiens des Archives Sud.* Mission de Ras Shamra
6 (Paris: Imprimerie Nationale, 1955), pp. 23-32; and Georges Boyer, "Étude
Juridique: La Place des Textes d'Ugarit dans l'Histoire de l'Ancien Droit Oriental,"
PRU 3: 283-299; T. N. D. Mettinger, *Solomonic State Officials,* Coniectanea Biblica, Old Testament 5 (Lund: Gleerup, 1971), pp. 104-6; Norman K. Gottwald, *The
Tribes of Yahweh,* pp. 389-484; J. A. Dearman, *Property Rights,* ch. 2.

Of course, the nature of the emergence of Israel in Canaan is itself an issue of
major dispute in Old Testament scholarship which is still far from settled. In the
wake of George E. Mendenhall's original "peasant revolt" suggestion and its further
development into a full-scale social model for the origins of Israel by Gottwald and
others (in ways which Mendenhall himself has disowned; see his "Ancient Israel's
Hyphenated History," pp. 91-103 in *Palestine in Transition,* ed. David Noel
Freedman and David F. Graf), there has been ongoing investigation of the precise
nature of Canaanite social and economic arrangements in the Amarna Age and the
Late Bronze Age and the changes produced by the emergence of Israel. See, e.g.,
Mendenhall, "Social Organization in Early Israel," pp. 132-151 in *Magnalia Dei:
The Mighty Acts of God.* Festschrift George Ernest Wright, ed. Frank M. Cross,
Werner E. Lemke, and Patrick D. Miller, Jr. (Garden City: Doubleday, 1976); the
symposium of articles on the subject by Alan J. Hauser, Thomas L. Thompson,
Mendenhall, and Gottwald in *JSOT* 7 (1978); Frank Anthony Spina, "Israelites as
gērîm, 'Sojourners,' in Social and Historical Context," pp. 321-335 in *The Word of
the Lord Shall Go Forth.* Festschrift David Noel Freedman, ed. Carol L. Meyers
and Michael P. O'Connor (Philadelphia: American Schools of Oriental Research,
1983); John M. Halligan, "The Role of the Peasant in the Amarna Period," pp. 15-24
in *Palestine in Transition;* Gottwald, "Early Israel and the Canaanite Socio-
economic System," pp. 25-37 in *Palestine in Transition;* Marvin L. Chaney, "Ancient Palestinian Peasant Movements and the Formation of Pre-monarchic Israel,"
pp. 39-90 in *Palestine in Transition;* Baruch Halpern, *The Emergence of Israel in
Canaan.* SBL Monographs 29 (Chico, Calif.: Scholars Press, 1983); Frank S. Frick,

system.[2] Notwithstanding the complexity of the general picture, however, it can be said that Israel did have a rationale of land tenure. This rationale may have been to some extent idealistic and schematic, but there is no reason to doubt that in those areas where Israel did establish effective control the ideal corresponded to reality. Norman K. Gottwald *(The Tribes of Yahweh)* would argue that the reality in fact resulted from the very deliberate application of the revolutionary ideal on which Israel as a community was founded, namely, social and economic egalitarianism in direct and conflicting contrast with the Canaanite pattern of oppression. Our knowledge of the Israelite system of land tenure is mainly dependent on the historical texts of Joshua and Judges, and in particular the accounts of the territorial divisions of the land into tribal allotments in Josh. 13–19, supplemented by the details of Num. 26.

Critical study of this material over the last half century has been built around and upon the work of Albrecht Alt[3] and its development by Martin Noth.[4] Alt distinguished two types of material in the lists in Joshua—lists of towns and tribal boundary lists—which, though

---

The Formation of the State in Ancient Israel. The Social World of Biblical Antiquity 4 (Sheffield: Almond, 1985); Herbert B. Huffmon, Spina, and A. R. W. Green, eds., *The Quest for the Kingdom of God.* Festschrift George E. Mendenhall (Winona Lake, Ind.: Eisenbrauns, 1983); John J. Bimson, "The origins of Israel in Canaan: an examination of recent theories," *Themelios* 15 (1989): 4-15; and the essays in Ronald E. Clements, ed., *The World of Ancient Israel.*

2. E.g., David's *purchase* of the threshing floor of Araunah the Jebusite (2 Sam. 24) rather than appropriating it by right of conquest, as he might have done after his capture of the city, appears to be a departure from the practice of the earlier period and an acceptance of Canaanite practices at least for those parts of the kingdom not traditionally Israelite. Also, cf. Omri's purchase of the hill from Shemer (1 Kgs. 16:24), which Bess describes as "a move towards the Canaanites, not merely geographically, but culturally, and the purchase of property according to Canaanite customs becomes a fitting symbol of it" (p. 160).

3. Alt contributed three major studies to these chapters: "Judas Gaue unter Josia," *Palästinajahrbuch* 21 (1925): 100-116, repr. *Kleine Schriften zur Geschichte des Volkes Israel* 2; "Eine galiläische Ortslist in Jos. 19," *ZAW* 45 (1927): 59-81; "Das System der Stammesgrenzen im Buche Josua," pp. 13-24 in *Beiträge zur Religionsgeschichte und Archäologie Palästinas.* Festschrift Ernst Sellin (Leipzig: A. Deichert, 1927), repr. *Kleine Schriften* 1.

4. Noth's work on the subject is incorporated in his commentary, *Das Buch Josua.* HAT 7 (Tübingen: Mohr, 1938), pp. 47-95.

separate in origin and function, have been conflated by the editor
of the book to fill out the narrative of the land allotment. This basic
distinction proposed by Alt has been very widely accepted by
scholars, though differences in detail over date and background
have been advanced.

1. The town list of Judah (Josh. 15), which Alt held to be the
provincial administrative system of the Judean state under Josiah,
has been thought by other scholars to be more fittingly related to
earlier periods of Judah's history. Frank Moore Cross and George
Ernest Wright, for example, put forward a case for seeing the lists in
their present state as a revised edition of the Judahite province list
made in the reign of Jehoshaphat, but based on the administrative
division of the kingdom which they argue was the work of David.[5]

2. As regards the tribal boundary descriptions, there is much
wider agreement with Alt that these are premonarchic and authentically reflect real conditions during the period of the tribal alliances:[6] "One could scarcely deny that the original text of such a
detailed list did represent a real geographical-historical situation. It
could hardly have served any other purpose than that ascribed to it
in the Bible, viz. the exact delineation of the tribal boundaries."[7]
We are justified, therefore, for the purpose of this discussion, in

5. "The Boundary and Province Lists of the Kingdom of Judah," *JBL*
75 (1956): 202-226. Other contributions regarding this problem include: Zechariah
Kallai-Kleinmann, "The Town Lists of Judah, Simeon, Benjamin and Dan," *VT*
8 (1958): 134-160; Yohanan Aharoni, "The Province-list of Judah," *VT* 9 (1959):
225-246; Kallai-Kleinmann, "Note on the Town Lists of Judah, Simeon, Benjamin
and Dan," *VT* 11 (1961): 223-27.

6. The question whether the lists are the end product of a lengthy period of
tribal immigration and settlement (broadly the position of Alt and Noth) or the
deposit of an original act of allotment after early military victories (the view of John
Bright) also lies beyond our scope here. The only relevant fact for our purpose,
which is agreed on both sides, is that the lists did at some point in the early history
of Israel correspond roughly to territorial reality.

7. Yohanan Aharoni, *The Land of the Bible* (Philadelphia: Westminster and
London: Burns & Oates, 1967), p. 231. Cf. also the comments of John Bright:
"These border lists were based no doubt upon the actual holdings of the tribes (plus
territory claimed in theory) in earliest times" ("The Book of Joshua, Introduction
and Exegesis," *The Interpreter's Bible* [Nashville: Abingdon, 1953] 2:544); and of
Roland de Vaux: "The description of the apportioning territories to the tribes in

regarding these lists, with Alt and almost all scholars, as authentic and reliable evidence from ancient sources for the division of land in the premonarchic period.

A. THE "KIN GROUP" (mišpāḥâ)

The most obvious fact which emerges from a study of this material is that the land in Israel was divided and owned on a tribal basis.[8] It is, however, the subtribal groups which are of greater interest and importance for our purpose. It is recorded repeatedly in all the passages concerned with land division that the tribes received their allotments *lᵉmišpᵉḥōṯām* (Josh. 13:15, etc.; Num. 33:54). The common translation "according to their families" is misleading, since the *mišpāḥâ* was not a single family but a grouping of several family units into a largely self-sufficient and self-protective organism. It is also better to avoid the word "clan," often used by scholars as a translation for *mišpāḥâ,* for the reasons given by Gottwald:[9] in common anthropological and sociological terminology "clan" usually designates the "exogamous" clan (i.e., where marriage must be *outside* one's own clan), with communal land ownership and strongly centralized power. That kind of "clan" was not part of Israel's social structure. Gottwald uses the phrase *"protective association of extended families"* to describe the *mišpāḥâ.* Nevertheless, the word "clan" is likely to continue to be used as a convenient shorthand for this intermediate social layer between tribe and

---

Jos 13-19 reflects a real situation" (*The Early History of Israel,* 2:738). For criticism of the view that the lists are the idealistic work of the exilic Priestly school, see Bright, p. 546; and J. Alberto Soggin, *Joshua.* OTL (Philadelphia: Westminster and London: SCM, 1972), pp. 12-13.

8. "The usage of terms in the Hexateuch leaves no room for doubt about the existence of a firmly-based concept of tribal territory, נחלה ... the tribe was the trustee of the נחלה, and held the ultimate title to the land over and above the family" (Gerhard von Rad, "The Promised Land and Yahweh's Land in the Hexateuch," p. 86). The Old Testament, however, does devote more concern to the preservation of the *family's* title to the land. The question whether tribal ownership implied communal ownership will be discussed in the Appendix below, pp. 66-70.

9. *The Tribes of Yahweh,* pp. 301-5.

family, provided its specifically Israelite nature is borne in mind. With these issues in mind and in the interest of precision, I prefer in the discussion at hand to render *mišpāḥâ* by the neutral yet semantically appropriate designation "kin group."

The sociological importance of the "kin group" was very great, even if precise definition of its extent and composition is impossible owing to a certain degree of terminological fluidity in the Old Testament.[10] Its primary significance lies (a) within the *kinship* structure of the nation, as being the intermediate group between the household (the *bêt-ʾāḇ*) and the tribe (the *maṭṭeh/šēḇeṭ*) and for all practical purposes the most important social unit to which the individual Israelite belonged. As C. H. J. de Geus notes, "That the mišpāḥā *(sic)* was the most important form of organization and the most important way of living in the social context in Ancient Israel was and is agreed on all sides. . . ."[11] But as the use of the word as a technical term in the land division texts shows, the "kin group" was also (b) a *territorial* unit with a key role in the system of land tenure.

> It seems beyond doubt, that, in terms of possession, the clan played a much more significant part in the society of Israel than the *šēbheṭ/maṭṭeh*. . . . The *mišpāḥāh* is the primary social unit as far

10. On the terminology, see Johannes Pedersen, *Israel: Its Life and Culture*, 1-2 (London: Oxford, 1926), pp. 46-50 (though Pedersen exaggerates the fluidity of usage; other scholars have shown that the term is used with a fair degree of technical precision, in view of the nontechnical nature of most of the Old Testament). See also C. Umhau Wolf, "Some Remarks on the Tribes and Clans of Israel," *JBL* 65 (1946): 45-49; "Terminology of Israel's Tribal Organization," *JQR* 36 (1945/1946): 287-295; Roland de Vaux, *Ancient Israel*, pp. 19-23. For an excellent study of the "kin group" in Israelite nomenclature, see Francis I. Andersen, "Israelite Kinship Terminology and Social Structure," *Bible Translator* 20 (1969): 29-39; C. H. J. de Geus, *The Tribes of Israel*. Studia Semitica Neerlandica (Assen: van Gorcum, 1976), pp. 135-150; Gottwald, *The Tribes of Yahweh*, pp. 257-284, 293-341. Gottwald's is by far the most comprehensive and analytical treatment. For a helpful survey of recent scholarship see James D. Martin, "Israel as a Tribal Society," pp. 95-117 in Clements, *The World of Ancient Israel*.

11. De Geus, p. 137. See also Andersen; and George E. Mendenhall, "The Relation of the Individual to Political Society in Ancient Israel," pp. 89-108 in *Biblical Studies in Memory of H. C. Alleman*, ed. J. M. Myers, O. Reimherr, and H. N. Bream (Locust Valley, N.Y.: J. J. Augustin, 1960).

as territorial holding is concerned; *mišpāḥāh* is a technical term in hereditary land tenure.[12]

Francis I. Andersen's study of nomenclature demonstrates that this territorial nature of the "kin group" meant that the inclusion of a person's "kin group" in his full name served practically as a geographical address.[13] This would have been all the more so when, in the process of settlement, "kin groups" became identified with villages or groups of villages—a process which is apparent in the occasional interchangeability of "kin group" names with those of villages (e.g., Mic. 5:2; 1 Chr. 2:50-51; 4:5, etc.) and in the absorption of pre-Conquest Canaanite towns into the tribal structure of Israel as "kin group" names (e.g., Shechem, Tirzah, and Hepher, which were Caananite cities [Gen. 34; Josh. 12:17, 24], are later listed among the "kin groups" of Manasseh [Josh. 17:2-6]).

This dual nature of the "kin group" as both a large *kinship* group and also a *territorial* unit in the system of land tenure removes the discrepancy between those scholars who regard the division of districts in Josh. 15 as basically administrative and those who take it as ethnic. The latter position is argued by Yeḥezkel Kaufmann:

> . . . In Joshua, the description of the tribal territories follows ethnographic, not administrative, lines. Similarly, the division into *districts* of the portion of Judah—Simeon—Benjamin is to be understood, in fact, not as an administrative division, but as a distribution to *families* and clans. The truth is that these are not administrative *districts* but clan portions.[14]

The truth probably is that they were both. Since there are good grounds for regarding the administrative division of Judah as the

---

12. W. Johnstone, "Old Testament Technical Expressions in Property Holding: Contributions from Ugarit," *Ugaritica* 6 (1969): 313. Johnstone points to Ugaritic use of the word *šph* which supports his view of the meaning of *mišpāḥâ* in Hebrew. In *PRU* V:62 (*UT* 2062) it is associated with "realm"; in Keret II:24-25 (*UT*, p. 250) it is parallel to "heir."

13. P. 36.

14. *The Biblical Account of the Conquest of Palestine* (Jerusalem: Magnes, 1953), p. 21 (his italics).

work of David,[15] it is very likely that David, with his known desire to retain the institutions of the tribal federation and the friendship of the tribal leaders,[16] would have based such an administrative system on the already existing natural kinship divisions of the "kin group" structure. Thus, an area originally settled as the portion of a "kin group" would, after a period in which the "kin group" became identified with the villages and towns in its area, have made a natural unit in the political division under the monarchy.

Corroboration, from the *kinship* angle, for this process is found in the accounts of the Simeonite inheritance. The lists of towns given for the tribe of Simeon in Josh. 19:2-8 is also found, with minor differences, in 1 Chr. 4:28-32. The Chronicler reports that the list describes the pre-Davidic settlement of the tribe (v. 31), and there seems to be no reason to question this statement.[17] Now, Josh. 19:1, 9 point out how the Simeonite inheritance was within the territory of Judah, and accordingly most of the towns listed in the two explicitly Simeonite lists in Josh. 19 and 1 Chr. 4 also turn up as a group among the towns of the Negeb province of Judah in the Judahite list in Josh. 15:26-32. Aharoni's comparison of the lists leads him to conclude that "the term 'Negeb of Judah' as used in the time of David was actually identical with the tribal area of Simeon."[18] In this case, therefore, a locality originally settled as a kinship unit later forms a self-contained part of an administrative territorial division.

The *territorial* importance of the "kin group" has also been confirmed by archaeological discovery, namely, the Samaria ostraca.[19] Among these sixty-three inscriptions, which record dis-

---

15. See the arguments and archaeological evidence adduced by Cross and Wright and Kallai-Kleinmann, "Town Lists" (1958).

16. The distribution of booty to "the elders of Judah, who were his friends," in 1 Sam. 30:26-31 is a good example of this aspect of David's policy.

17. It is accepted by Cross and Wright, pp. 214-15; Yohanan Aharoni, "The Negeb of Judah," *IEJ* 8 (1958): 31; Shemaryahu Talmon, "The Town Lists of Simeon," *IEJ* 15 (1965): 235-241; Kallai-Kleinmann, "Town Lists" (1958), pp. 159ff. For further discussion of the literary history of this passage, see H. G. M. Williamson, *Israel in the Books of Chronicles* (Cambridge: Cambridge University Press, 1977), pp. 76-81.

18. "The Negeb of Judah," p. 31.

19. Details of publication and a tabulated translation of the inscriptions,

patches of oil and wine, are to be found the names of seven districts which correspond to "kin group" names of the tribe of Manasseh as recorded in Num. 26:30-33; Josh. 17:2-3; and 1 Chr. 7:14-19, namely, Shemida, Abiezer, Helek, Asriel, Schechem, Hoglah, and Noah. The precise date of the ostraca is a matter of some uncertainty, but they are most probably to be assigned to the first half of the eighth century and the reigns of Joash and Jeroboam II. They are therefore very valuable evidence that the ancient "kin group" divisions had retained their identity and integrity into the late Monarchy. This fact is the more impressive if it is correct that the ostraca should be connected with the royal estates in the vicinity of Samaria,[20] since it would show that they were able to preserve their identity even under the expansion of the royal domain. It has been suggested that the classification according to clans or "kin groups" in the second group of ostraca, which probably come from the reign of Jeroboam II,[21] may reflect the census carried out by that king (1 Chr. 5:17). This would indicate the continuance of the earlier practice of carrying out censuses according to "kin groups" (Num. 1:26),[22] and would further confirm the importance of the "kin group" in the administrative structure of the nation under the Monarchy.

The "kin group" was a major constituent in the Israelite system of land tenure, and its primary function was economic. It existed to protect and preserve the viability of its own extended families through such mechanisms as the redemption of both land and persons that

---

together with comprehensive bibliographical and topographical information, are provided by Aharoni, *The Land of the Bible,* pp. 315-327. See the important discussion and bibliography in Dearman, pp. 117-123. Dearman reinforces the view advanced here that the Samaria ostraca are important evidence of the village/clan social structure of Israel during the Monarchy.

20. This was suggested by Martin Noth, "Das Krongut der israelitischen Könige und seine Verwaltung," *Zeitschrift des Deutschen Palästina-Vereins* 50 (1920): 211-244, repr. *Aufsätze zur biblischen Landes- und Altertumskunde* 2 (Neukirchen-Vluyn: Neukirchener Verlag, 1971); cf. also Albrecht Alt, "Der Stadtstaat Samaria," *Berichte über die Verhandlungen der Sächischen Akademie der Wissenschaften zu Leipzig,* Phil.-hist. Klasse 101/5 (1954), repr. *Kleine Schriften* 3 (Munich: C. H. Beck, 1959); and Mettinger, p. 91.

21. See Aharoni, *The Land of the Bible,* p. 324; and Mettinger, p. 91.

22. Kallai-Kleinmann regards the Simeonite list as a fragment of the Davidic census of 2 Sam. 24; "Town Lists" (1958), pp. 159-160.

were in danger of passing—or had already passed—out of the hands of the kinship group. This function can be seen in Lev. 25. It did not own land collectively in its own name, nor did it apparently have any coercive power over its family units. Rather, it was a restorative and protective organism—a "protective association," as Gottwald calls it. The military functions of the "kin group" are described below.

B. THE "FATHER'S HOUSE" (bêt̠-ʾāb̠)

The "kin group," then, as a large, subtribal, kinship grouping was of major importance in Israelite land tenure. But the "kin group" was itself composed of smaller familial units, the "fathers'-houses," each of which also had its portion of land within the territory of the "kin group." Again, the evidence is not altogether precise as to the extent and composition of the "father's house,"[23] but most likely it comprised all the living descendants of a single living ancestor— the rō'š-bêt̠-ʾāb̠—with their families, servants, and so forth. The rō'š or *paterfamilias* could well be the "head" of three generations below his own, so that clearly a single "father's house"—under average conditions of fertility, and even if practicing monogamy— could comprise quite a number of smaller, two-generation families and be numerically quite substantial.

Sociologically, the "father's house" was the most important *small* unit in the nation—as is apparent from the role and functions of the heads of fathers' houses, which will be discussed later. It was also the primary group within which the individual Israelite found identity and status, as the inclusion of the "father's house" names in formal nomenclature shows. As George E. Mendenhall notes, "There is little doubt indeed that it was the smallest political unit, not the largest, that conferred status upon the individual by giving him its protection and educating him in his obligations to society."[24]

It is to be expected, therefore, that the "father's house" had an

23. In general, see the works referred to in note 10 above, especially Gottwald, *The Tribes of Yahweh*, pp. 285-292.

24. "Relation of the Individual," pp. 92-93. Cf. also Andersen, p. 34.

important role in the ownership of land within the "kin group," and this in fact is confirmed by a number of texts:

1. Judg. 6:11ff. Although Gideon was a married man with children (8:20), the land on which he lived and worked belonged to his father Joash, the head of Gideon's "father's house" (6:15).[25]

2. Judg. 21:24. In speaking of the return of the people of Israel after the Benjaminite war, this verse describes each one returning to his tribe *(lᵉšibṭô)*, to his "kin group" *(lᵉmišpaḥtô)*, and thence to his inheritance *(lᵉnaḥᵃlāṭô)*. Placed in such a descending order, the third must refer to the inheritance of the "father's house" as the smallest territorial unit to which a person belonged. The same typical pattern is found in Mic. 2:2.

3. Deut. 25:5. The law of levirate marriage is introduced here by the phrase "if brothers are living together." This is taken by most scholars to mean that they are residing on the same land, that is, the ancestral family estate, in which case it is an example of the whole "father's house," including adult married sons, constituting a single unit of land tenure.

There are, however, a number of questions concerning this preface to the law of levirate which prevent our building upon it too precise a picture of family land tenure. Was the father still alive or deceased? The latter would seem more probable in view of the lack of reference to any part that he might have been expected to play in the matter. In that case, was the brothers' co-residence and sharing of the inheritance normal practice on a father's death, so that the mention of the fact is simply meant to describe some typical circumstances in which the law applied? Most scholars rather prefer the view that it was *not* normal or typical, and that the opening phrase is intended to define *exclusively* the conditions in which the levirate was to be practiced and so, in effect, to restrict it.[26] This would mean that the

25. This passage also illustrates the authority of the "father's house" over even its adult members (v. 27) and the general responsibility of the *paterfamilias* for the members of the household (v. 30). These are themes to which we will return later.

26. For a recent thorough survey of these questions and the scholarly debate thereon, see the published dissertation of Donald A. Leggett, *The Levirate and Goel Institutions in the Old Testament* (Cherry Hill, N.J.: Mack, 1974), esp. pp. 42-48. Eryl W. Davies discusses the matter further, pointing out comparative ancient Near

more normal procedure was for surviving sons to divide the ancestral
inheritance, each setting up his own "father's house" and thus ceasing
to "live together." A few texts do point in this direction. It may be that
the otherwise somewhat pointless phrase in Judg. 8:29 that Gideon
"went and dwelt in his own house" (RSV) refers to Gideon setting up
his own "father's house" after the death of his father, Joash. It is
immediately followed by reference to the size of his family—his
many wives and seventy sons. In Gen. 31:14 (Laban's daughters) and
Judg. 11:2 (Jephthah), the term "father's house" appears to denote an
area of land, that is, the estate which was to be divided up as a
patrimony between the heirs on the father's death.[27] In view of Gen.
36:6-7, where Jacob and Esau cease dwelling together only because
of the excess size of their possessions, the practice of *non*-division of
the ancestral estate referred to in the phrase "when brothers live
together," probably reflects ancient, semi-nomadic customs. If it is
this practice which is being so warmly praised in Ps. 133, it may be
that, even after the Settlement, it was still regarded as something of
an ideal, even if it had become uncommon in practice.

Having analyzed the role of the extended family unit in Israel's
land tenure and social system, Gottwald summarizes it thus:

> The *bēth-'āv* (*sic*) was the basic economic unit in the Israelite
> social system. It formed a self-sufficient unit in the sense that it
> produced the basic means of subsistence for all its members and
> consumed all, or nearly all, of what it produced.[28]

C. INALIENABILITY

Mention of the levirate institution leads us to a fundamentally
important aspect of Israelite land tenure, namely, the inalienable
character of the land. That the land should be held in the form of

---

Eastern laws, and agrees that the Deuteronomic law intended to limit the conditions
in which the levirate duty applied ("Inheritance Rights and the Hebrew Levirate
Marriage," *VT* 31 [1981]: 138-144, 257-268).
27. Cf. Mettinger, p. 75.
28. *The Tribes of Yahweh,* p. 292.

patrimonies which should not pass out of the family was a cherished ideal in Israel that was protected by legislation and theologically justified and sanctioned. It is therefore clearly of importance in any study of Israel's property ethics. The practical outworking of the concept is discussed in Chapter 4; here we are simply concerned with it as a basic factor in Israel's rationale of family land tenure.

Although admittedly an argument from silence, it is nevertheless an impressive fact that the whole Old Testament provides not a single case of an Israelite voluntarily selling land outside his family group. In those cases of land transfers which are recorded, various factors are present which show that they are not exceptions to this statement—factors such as kinsman-redemption (as with Jeremiah and Ruth), or sale by non-Israelites (as in the cases mentioned in note 2), or the nonvoluntary sale or mortgage of land for debt (as in Neh. 5:3).

This silence of the text is matched by the absence as yet of any inscriptional evidence from Palestine of Israelite sale and purchase of land, though there is abundant evidence of such transactions from Canaanite and surrounding societies. There do exist two cuneiform tablets from Gezer which record the sale of estates, including houses, fields, and slaves.[29] The tablets can be dated (eponymously) to 651 and 649 B.C., late in the reign of Manasseh, when Assyria was at the peak of its influence over Judah. The witnesses, seals, and language are all Assyrian, which points to the existence of an Assyrian garrison or colony as the dominant class in Gezer at the time. Hence these tablets cannot be taken as evidence of normal *Israelite* conveyance of real estate. There is no evidence either that "disguised sales," such as are known at Mari, took place in Israel— that is, where a sale or transfer of land was fictitiously or symbolically presented as an inheritance with a ceremony of adoption.[30]

This complete lack of evidence is consonant with the lack of any legal provision in the Old Testament for the sale of land. Apart

29. See T. G. Pinches, "The Fragment of an Assyrian Tablet Found at Gezer," *PEFQS* (1904): 229-244 (cf. pp. 207-8, 355-56, 400-402); and C. H. W. Johns, "The New Cuneiform Tablet from Gezer," *PEFQS* (1905): 208-210 (cf. p. 185).

30. "Mari society devised various methods of evading this rule (inalienability) . . . ; but these very same legal subterfuges clearly indicate the existence of the principle evaded" (Abraham Malamat, "Mari and the Bible," *JAOS* 82 [1962]: 149).

from inheritance within the family, there was "no other legal method devised whereby (an Israelite) might come into permanent possession of landed property and there was therefore no proper way in which to dispose of property except to apportion it to his legal heirs."[31] The hypothetical case in Lev. 27:22-24 at first sight appears to be an exception to this, but it is not. Here a man dedicates a field which was not "a part of his possession by inheritance." But the purchase did not effect a permanent transfer, for in the Jubilee the land is to revert to the one whose original property it had been before coming into the possession of the one who dedicated it.

Legal and institutional protection of the inalienability of the land applied both to the "father's house" and to the "kin group." As regards the former, although the family's land is not explicitly mentioned in Deut. 25:5-6, it is generally regarded as certain that part of the purpose of the levirate marriage was to prevent the property of the deceased brother passing out of the family.[32] This is implicit in the phrase "(he) shall succeed to the name" (Heb. *yaqûm 'al-šēm*), and is explicit in the account of a levirate type of marriage in Ruth. Ruth 4:10 states Boaz's intention to "perpetuate the name of the dead *in his inheritance*." Preservation of the family's land is also a major part of the purpose of the Jubilee provisions in Lev. 25:10, 28 (see below, pp. 123-25). Concern for the integrity and preservation of the land of the "kin group" as a whole is shown (a) in the redemption provisions in Lev. 25:24ff. (see below, pp. 119-121), and (b) in the legislation arising from the case of Zelophehad's daughters (Num. 27:1-11; 36:1-12), which specified that where daughters inherited (in the absence of sons) they must marry only within the "kin group" of their father. In this way, tribal territory also would not be diminished. Thus it can be seen that the principle of inalienability applied throughout the whole system of land tenure, from the largest to the smallest units.

The concept and practice of inalienability of land in Israel would clearly come into conflict with the idea that the whole land was held in common ownership and periodically redistributed within the tribes, a notion formerly held by some scholars and one

31. Bess, p. 91.
32. Cf. Leggett, p. 52; and E. W. Davies.

which still occasionally makes an appearance. This theory is discussed and rejected in the Appendix to this chapter.

D. DIVINE OWNERSHIP (LEV. 25:23)

The theological rationale of the system of land tenure, and especially of the principle of inalienability, is found most succinctly stated in Lev. 25:23, a key passage in which the assertion of God's ownership of the land is formally associated with the inalienability of family land.

> The land must not be sold permanently, because the land is mine and you are but aliens and my tenants.

Understanding of Lev. 25 is bound up, of course, with the literary-critical and redactional problems of the so-called Holiness code, of which it is a part. Unfortunately, scholarly research on H appears to be moving further than ever from a consensus. In Lev. 25 Henning Graf Reventlow finds three independent units combined;[33] Rudolf Kilian traces four chronological stages of its development;[34] Karl Elliger discovers possibly eight.[35] When this divergence on ch. 25 alone is added to the fact that regarding H as a whole "in recent scholarly work practically all varieties of view possible are represented,"[36] one may be excused for suspending judgment on the literary-historical issue.

Fortunately, however, there is wider agreement that any literary solution to the present form of the text would not by itself determine the sociological date of the contents,[37] and that both H and P incorporate laws and institutions of great antiquity. The prohibition

33. *Das Heiligkeitsgesetz formgeschichtlich untersucht.* WMANT 6 (Neukirchen-Vluyn: Neukirchener Verlag, 1961), pp. 139ff.
34. *Literarkritische und formgeschichtliche Untersuchung des Heiligkeitsgesetzes.* BBB 19 (1963), pp. 130ff.
35. *Leviticus.* HAT 4 (1966), pp. 347ff.
36. Otto Kaiser, *Introduction to the Old Testament* (Minneapolis: Augsburg, 1975), p. 115.
37. This fact was recognized as early as 1880 by John Fenton, *Early Hebrew Life* (London: Trübner, 1880). In his preface he distinguishes between the procedure

on permanent sale of land, linked as it is to the ancient belief in Yahweh's ownership of the land, was undoubtedly just such an ancient law. Thus, Elliger, who regards this verse as belonging to Ph₁ (the primary Priestly redaction of the holiness material—to which he did not accord an existence independent of its inclusion in P),[38] sees in it the preservation of very ancient Israelite land tradition.

Since this verse is central to Israel's rationale of land tenure, we shall examine it in detail.

1. "The Land Shall Not Be Sold in Perpetuity" (hā'āreṣ lō' ṭimmāḵēr liṣᵉmiṭuṭ)

Found only here and in v. 30, the word liṣᵉmiṭuṭ is connected with the root ṣmṭ, "to exterminate or annihilate,"[39] and so implies here the sort of sale which involves a destruction—presumably of the seller's right to recover the land thereafter. Thus J. E. Hogg understood it to mean sale "in derogation of the seller's right of redemption."[40] A parallel with a recurring phrase in Ugaritic real estate transactions was noted by J. J. Rabinowitz, who regarded this as evidence of the antiquity of the formulation of the prohibition in Leviticus.[41]

2. "For the Land Is Mine" (kî-lî hā'āreṣ)

This central statement of the verse both explains the preceding prohibition and gives meaning to the following description of the Israelites' status. To discover the significance of this affirmation of divine ownership of the land, we may approach it from several possible angles.

---

and findings of literary criticism and of sociological research: "It is not possible to infer immediately from the literary date of a custom to its sociological date" (p. xiii).

38. P. 165.

39. Cf. BDB, p. 856.

40. "The Meaning of לצמתת in Lev. 25:23," *American Journal of Semitic Languages and Literatures* 42 (1925/1926): 208-210; this article includes a detailed discussion of the word in the ancient versions. See also, in agreement, Friedrich Horst, "Eigentum nach dem Alten Testament," p. 220; and Elliger, p. 354.

41. "A Biblical Parallel to a Legal Formula from Ugarit," *VT* 8 (1958): 95. The link is accepted by Mettinger, p. 109, n. 55.

a. Yahweh's Ownership of the Land: As a Cultic Conception?

We have already referred to Gerhard von Rad's insight on this and
its development (see above pp. 5-9). The point must again be
emphasized, however, that this cultic aspect cannot stand independently. The cult only had meaning within the context of Israel's
relationship with God, and it is in *that* context that God's ownership
of the land has to be set. In the Old Testament we find that "direct
relationship between Yahweh and the land of Canaan is specifically
stressed as a fulcrum in the relationship between Yahweh and
Israel."[42] Furthermore, this relationship was grounded in Israel's
historical traditions, specifically the Exodus–land gift tradition. As
regards our understanding of Lev. 25:23, it is therefore very significant that this key text for the "cultic" tradition of Yahweh's ownership of the land occurs in a chapter where the "historical" theme is
referred to four times (vv. 2, 38, 42, 55).

> [In the Old Testament] we have a vitally significant combination of
> the concept of divine ownership of the land, a view held by other
> Near Eastern cultures and particularly evident in Ugaritic literature,
> with the more specifically Hebraic concept of Yahweh's involve-
> ment in history. This involvement was the existential vehicle for
> expressing Yahweh's relationship with Israel, and the land of Canaan
> was the focal point around which that history was enacted.[43]

What of the Canaanite background to this as a cultic idea?
While von Rad was probably right in denying that Israel simply
derived their cultic concept of divinely owned land from the
Canaanites,[44] it remains true that the idea does have parallels with
Canaanite cultic concepts concerning the relationship between gods
and land. This is particularly so as regards the idea of the land as
the *abode* of the god, and of a mountain, temple, or both as
representative of the whole land.[45] Ronald E. Clements makes very

---

42. Arthur M. Brown, "The Concept of Inheritance," p. 182.
43. Brown, "The Concept of Inheritance," p. 190.
44. "Promised Land," p. 88.
45. On this particular contribution of Ugaritic studies to Old Testament concepts,
see Richard J. Clifford, *The Cosmic Mountain in Canaan and the Old Testament*.

effective use of these parallels to illuminate the link between the temple of Mt. Zion and the land of Yahweh, a link which is found in some Psalms and prophetic passages (e.g., Ps. 23:6; 27:4; 61:4; 78:54; Isa. 11:9; 57:13).[46] Worshipping in the temple (which represented the whole land) was connected with dwelling in the land.

> An Israelite who participated in the worship of Yahweh on Mount Zion was maintaining his obligations and responsibilities as one who dwelt on Yahweh's land. He was rendering due homage to the one to whom the whole land belonged and who held the right to give or withhold the land from its inhabitants. When therefore, the poet proclaimed, "Who shall dwell on thy holy hill?" (Ps. 15:1), not only was the right to enter the temple at stake, but through that the right to continue as an Israelite; to be one of Yahweh's "GĒRÎM" (Ps. 39:[12]13, Lev. 25:23) and to dwell on Yahweh's land.[47]

Clements then invokes Lev. 25:23 as "an instructive testimony to this idea that lies behind the Psalms."

This is an insight which is clearly helpful in understanding the poetic texts in question. It shows that the belief in divine ownership of the land had a pervasive influence in realms not directly concerned with the land itself as an economic commodity. It does not, however, serve to illuminate "in reverse," as it were, the meaning of Lev. 25:23 in its own context. For nothing in that context is concerned with worship in the temple or on Mt. Zion. The insights derived from Canaanite cultic parallels, helpful no doubt in other areas, are therefore of no assistance for our purpose here.

b. Yahweh's Ownership of the Land: As a Politico-territorial Concept?

Another factor in the idea of divine ownership of land which was quite common among Israel's neighbors was that it emphasized the national and territorial claims of a particular god. This deity was the god of the

46. "Temple and Land: A Significant Aspect of Israel's Worship," *Transactions of the Glasgow University Oriental Society* 19 (1961–1962): 16-28; and *God and Temple*, pp. 52ff.

47. Clements, "Temple and Land," p. 23.

land he owned and of the nation who lived there. Frequently this was connected with the "divine right" of the king, whose title and authority over the land were granted by the god who owned the land. The land therefore belonged to the king as the appointee of the god.[48] Lev. 25:23, however, cannot be explained in these terms, for nothing in its context is concerned with either (1) the exclusive recognition of Yahweh as the national deity or (2) the title of a human king.

(1) Exclusive nationalism.

This idea fails to fit with the context of the situation (sc. in Lev. 25). The prohibition against sale is concerned to preserve the claim of every Israelite to his own land, whereas the exclusive recognition of Yahweh as national god would be just as well verified if a few Israelites held title to all the land. *Such an explanation might show why the land should not be sold to aliens . . . but not why it should not be sold to Israelites in perpetuity.*[49]

We may add, with regard to the last point in italics, that there does seem to have been concern for the protection of the integrity of the land by preventing it from passing into the hands of foreigners or reverting to the ownership of the original inhabitants. This may have been a factor in the warnings against covenants and marriages with such groups (Exod. 23:32; 34:15-16; Deut. 7:2ff.).[50] But it is notable that Yahweh's ownership of the land is *not* adduced to support such concern. It is not invoked in defense of a national policy to protect the national territory, and that is certainly not the purpose of the statement in Lev. 25:23.

48. Detailed surveys of the occurrences of the concept of divine ownership of the land in ancient Near Eastern cultures, with particular reference to Ugaritic material, are provided by both Brown, pp. 83ff.; and Bess, pp. 87ff. On royal land ownership outside Israel, see Mettinger, pp. 101-9, and the extensive literature there cited.

49. Bess, p. 85 (his italics). The same point is made by Robert G. North, *Sociology of the Biblical Jubilee,* pp. 159-160, whom Bess is quoting in part.

50. Cf. F. Langlamet, "Israël et 'l'habitant du pays': Vocabulaire et formules d'Ex. 34:11-16," *RB* 76 (1969): 338-341; and Götz Schmitt, *Du sollst keinen Frieden schliessen mit den Bewohnen des Landes.* BWANT 91 (1970): 13-24 (on Exod. 23:32 and Deut. 7) and ch. 3 (esp. pp. 97-101, on the protection of the land as a motive for prohibition of covenants and marriages with Canaanites).

(2) The title of a king. The belief in Yahweh's ownership of the land is certainly older than, and not dependent on, the rise of monarchy in Israel. But more important, far from being used as a justification for a feudal system with the king as ultimate owner of the national territory, this belief appears to have been a factor in *resisting* such a development in Israel.

> In contrast to the Egyptian sovereign, and probably also to the Ugaritic one, the Israelite king was not regarded as the ultimate owner of the national territory, a fact which is intimately linked with the idea of the Lord as the proper owner of the land. . . . In Israel, the "feudal" conceptions had been transferred to the theological plane.[51]

c. Yahweh's Ownership of the Land: As a Theologico-economic Concept?

When the statement is interpreted in the light of its immediate context in Lev. 25, it becomes clear that Yahweh's ownership of the land is affirmed to ensure the security of *individual families* by preventing permanent alienation of *their land*. It is not simply a grand statement of national belief about the national territory, but the theological sanction of an *internal* economic system of land tenure. The primary feature of this system was the preservation of multiple family holdings in relative equality and freedom. The *theological* force of the belief in divine ownership of the land is thus brought to bear at the *economic* level and focused, in its practical effects, on the *family*.

> The proper concept of this divine ownership appears to be that every Israelite proprietor was to regard his holding as deriving from God himself as though it had been apportioned to him from God. . . . There existed the consciousness of an intrinsic equality among the Hebrews before God . . . which was expressed, among other ways, by each head of a family holding his land as from God.[52]

51. Mettinger, p. 109.
52. Bess, pp. 85-86. Cf. also the remarks of von Rad on this, "Promised Land,"

3. "For You Are Guests and Residents with Me" (kî-gērîm wᵉtôšābîm 'attem 'immādî)

In the light of the foregoing discussion, this final phrase of the verse must be interpreted positively—not taken as "minimizing" Israel's rights on the land. As Clements points out from many poetic passages, to be one of Yahweh's *gērîm* was to have the *right,* as a member of his people, to continue to dwell on his land.[53] The additional word *'immādî* may well have here the connotation "under my protection,"[54] just as the *gēr* enjoyed the security of the household in which he resided. Far from being an expression of the "timid piety" of postexilic Judaism,[55] it affirms the *security* of Israelites on the land because they are residing on it by God's authority and under *God's* protection, not at the arbitrary pleasure of some human king or landlord. It is an affirmation, not a denial, of rights—the rights of families to a share in the land. This third phrase, therefore, immediately brings us back again to the fact of Israel's relationship with God. As his "dependents," Israel stood under the protection of Yahweh. This protective aspect of the relationship applied not only to the nation as a whole but, *with much greater social and practical relevance,* to each individual family and its land.

---

p. 85; and Walther Eichrodt's comment: "The basic idea of this law constitutes a consistent and energetic attempt to guarantee the independence and liberty of each individual Israelite" (*Theology of the Old Testament,* 1. OTL [1961], p. 97). One would only want to modify this statement by saying that the law was really more concerned with the *family,* without which the individual could enjoy neither liberty nor equality.

53. "Temple and Land," p. 23.

54. For this use of the word see Horst Dietrich Preuss, "'ēt ['ē th], 'im," *TDOT* 1 (1977), p. 450; and cf. below, p. 102.

55. A phrase of W. Robertson Smith: "the idea that the Israelites are Jehovah's clients, sojourning in a land where they have no rights of their own, but are absolutely dependent on His bounty, is one of the most characteristic notes of the new and more timid type of piety that distinguishes post-exilic Judaism from the religion of old Israel" (*Lectures on the Religion of the Semites,* rev. ed. [London: Adam and Charles Black, 1894], p. 78).

CONCLUSION

The link which was established in Chapter 1 between Israel's relationship with Yahweh and Yahweh's ownership of the land now emerges into a sharper definition, inasmuch as we have seen that the most explicit assertion of divine land ownership in the Old Testament is made for the sake of protecting the *family* and its *land*. The proposition may therefore be advanced at this point, to be developed in the next chapter, that these family-plus-land units had a basic role and importance in Israel's understanding of their relationship with Yahweh. When therefore economic changes and human greed later combined to attack and destroy large numbers of such small family landholdings, certain prophets were moved to denounce this, not merely on the grounds of social justice but because it represented an attack upon one of the basic socio-economic pillars on which Israel's relationship with Yahweh rested—the family and its land.[56]

56. On this socio-economic aspect of the prophets, see below, pp. 105-9.

APPENDIX   *Was Tribal Territory Subject to Communal Ownership and Periodic Reallotment?*

Over the past century a variety of scholars have advanced the theory that the tribal structure of ancient Israelite society and its allegedly nomadic origins must have meant that land was the property of whole tribes, in the sense that it was held in collective ownership and periodically redivided to members of the tribe for cultivation. According to a comparatively recent proponent of the theory, for example, we must note as the basis of Israelite land tenure

> . . . the existence of *communal land*. . . . Communal land must have been the primitive practice. A given area would be occupied by a tribe, or part of a tribe, and then divided by lot and, or, measured out, each family . . . being allotted a section. The whole area would remain none the less "common" property to be re-divided by lot when occasion demanded.[57]

The use of the terms "must have" and "would" betray the hypothetical status of this view.

As a theory this position has a long history. It arose in the last century as part of a widespread assumption among early anthropologists and sociologists of primitive mankind that communal ownership was the general rule in early societies—especially tribal societies—whereas private property was a late development with the rise of individualism and commerce. This notion was then imported (along with many other similar assumptions of the pioneers of anthropology and sociology) into the history of Israelite society, for since the Hebrews were (according to the then prevailing state of knowledge and opinion) a "primitive" people their land practices must have been communal.[58] Thus M. J. Lauré, dominated entirely by this presupposition, could assert, concerning *Israelite* property ideas:

57. K. H. Henry, "Land Tenure in the Old Testament," *PEQ* 86 (1954): 9.
58. See, e.g., M. Lurje, *Studien zur Geschichte der wirtschaftlichen und sozialen Verhältnisse im israelitisch-jüdischen Reiche.* BZAW 45 (1927): 5-6.

Private property in the primitive horde is almost unthinkable, since it presumes a highly developed and clearly defined idea of the individual. . . . In the primitive horde the individual was merged in the group. The horde was the unit. The notion of personality was hazy and vague.[59]

Even as applied to truly primitive peoples this is an unverifiable and questionable assumption; applied to Israel (as Lauré does) at any period of their known Old Testament history, it is absurd. Yet Lauré describes[60] the evolution of the Hebrews from a "primitive horde" with communal ownership (reflected in the Book of the Covenant[61]—Exod. 22:5-6; 23:10 notwithstanding), through a stage of kinship ownership (reflected in the Naboth incident), to a commercialized nation suffering the ills of capitalism (reflected in the prophetic denunciation of private property)—all in the space of two or three centuries!

Henry Schaeffer believed that communal tribal property as a feature of nomadic life survived in Israel even when, after the Settlement, an "internal sense of ownership" developed.[62] He found evidence of this in the Jubilee, which as the "logical development of the old tribal system" he considered very ancient.[63] But perhaps the baldest statement of the theory was Chester C. McCown's: "Nearly all peoples show evidence of having at some period practiced communism in the holding of tribal lands."[64] This comes in a chapter evocatively called "The Dawn of Democracy," on Israel's "nomadic ideal."

Precisely this assumption, however, had been challenged from

59. M. J. Lauré, *The Property Concepts of the Early Hebrews*. Bulletin of the State University of Iowa. Studies in Sociology, Economics, Politics and History 4/2 [N.S. 91] (1915): 89.

60. Pp. 48-54.

61. P. 52.

62. *The Social Legislation of the Primitive Semites* (New Haven: Yale University Press and London: Oxford University Press, 1915), pp. 228ff.

63. *Hebrew Tribal Economy and the Jubilee as Illustrated in Semitic and Indo-european Village Communities* (Leipzig: J. C. Hinrichs, 1922), p. 1.

64. *The Genesis of the Social Gospel* (New York and London: Alfred A. Knopf, 1929), p. 119.

the early days of the theory by other anthropologists. Particularly trenchant criticisms were made by Numa D. Fustel de Coulanges (1) of the confusion of terms and concepts caused by a loose use of a so-called "comparative method" ("National communism has been confused with the common ownership of the family; tenure in common . . . with ownership in common; agrarian communism with village commons";[65] and (2) of the political and doctrinaire considerations that were prejudicing proper enquiry. Some writers had accepted from Jean-Jacques Rousseau the idea "that property is contrary to nature, and that communism is natural. . . . Minds under the influence of this idea . . . will always prefer to *assume* that there must first have been a period of communism."[66] This assumption, Fustel de Coulanges maintained, had never been proved by any satisfactory evidence. E. Ginzberg made a similar criticism, in the biblical field, noting that "emotional interests in modern schemes for social reform interfered gravely with the clear vision of many a student."[67]

Sociologist Thorstein B. Veblen also disputed the assumption on psychological and social grounds:

> The idea of communal ownership is of relatively late growth and must by psychological necessity have been preceded by the idea of individual ownership. . . . Corporate ownership is quasi-ownership only; it is therefore necessarily a derivative concept and cannot have preceded the concept of individual ownership of which it is a counterfeit.[68]

If the theory in general may be said to rest on dubious assumptions rather than evidence, as applied to the Old Testament in

65. *The Origin of Property in Land* (London: Sonnenschein, 1891 and New York: Charles Scribner's, 1892), p. 150.

66. P. 150.

67. "Studies in the Economics of the Bible," *JQR* 22 (1932): 392. For more recent and more detailed exposure of the fallacies and excesses of that era of anthropology and sociology of religion, and their continuing legacy in this century, see, E. E. Evans-Pritchard, *Theories of Primitive Religion* (London: Oxford University Press, 1967).

68. "The Beginnings of Ownership," *AJS* 4 (1899): 358.

particular it runs up against several serious obstacles which must lead us to reject it.

1. The theory is partly based on the postulation of nomadic origins and culture of the Israelite tribes. But there is an increasing accumulation of evidence casting doubt both on the extent of true nomadism in ancient Semitic races and on the simple equation of primitive tribalism and nomadism. A recent study by C. H. J. de Geus finds that the attribution of so much of Israel's social and economic ethos to nomadic origins has produced serious misunderstandings.[69] Gottwald's thorough study of the matter comes to the same conclusion.[70]

2. Another factor was the fundamental principle of inalienability. We have seen that this applied not only to the land of the whole tribe, but much more emphatically to the land of individual families. The protection of family land by institutions such as inheritance, levirate marriage, and the Jubilee would be inexplicable and pointless if the whole tribal territory were periodically redistributed to different families.

3. There was a very strong family attachment to the land, connected with the ancestral burial place.[71] The significance of this bond, and the importance for the sake of the ancestors of the continuance of the family on its own land, have been thoroughly examined by Herbert C. Brichto.[72] The evidence he presents makes it impossible to imagine a regular redistribution of this ancestral land, with its burial places.

4. Some of the earliest laws (e.g., Exod. 22:5-6; 23:10) already

---

69. *The Tribes of Israel.* In his summary of conclusions, de Geus speaks of "communal ownership," but in the corresponding portion of text he appears to mean by this not collectivism, in the sense of the theory outlined above, but the identity of the "clan" with its own territory—i.e., the kinship/territorial dimensions of the "kin group"—with which, of course, we agree. Cf. also, Norman K. Gottwald, "Were the Early Israelites Pastoral Nomads?" pp. 223-255 in *Rhetorical Criticism.* Festschrift James Muilenburg, ed. Jared J. Jackson and Martin Kessler. Pittsburgh Theological Monograph 1 (Pittsburgh: Pickwick, 1975).

70. *The Tribes of Yahweh,* pp. 435-463.

71. A point noted in passing by von Rad, "Promised Land, p. 85.

72. "Kin, Cult, Land and Afterlife—a Biblical Complex," *HUCA* 44 (1973): 1-54. This article is more fully discussed in Chapter 5.

presuppose a settled individual possession of land. If such a radical upheaval as a periodic redivision of all tribal land (every seven years, according to some scholars)[73] did take place, it is very odd that it has left no trace whatever in any of the legal codes. On the contrary, the law seeks to preserve the ancient boundaries, with the sanction of the curse (Deut. 19:14; 27:17).

There is, of course, the evidence of Ps. 16:5-6 and Mic. 2:5[74] that *some* redivision of *some* land did take place. It is very probable that not all the land in a tribal or "kin group" territory was divided into inalienable family patrimonies. Other terms for land such as *migraš* and *śāḏeh* may describe common land, either divided up for cultivation or used for pasturage.[75] This kind of mixed economy—a combination of private ownership and common use—has been observed in modern Palestine[76] and may well have obtained in ancient Israel.[77] But there simply is not enough evidence to be dogmatic. At any rate, these two texts (both of which occur in poetic passages, with possibilities of figurative overtones) cannot alone support the weight of a theory of collective ownership and regular redistribution of all tribal lands, a theory which is accordingly to be rejected.

73. E.g., Robert H. Kennett, *Ancient Hebrew Social Life and Culture as Indicated in Law, Narrative and Metaphor* (London: Oxford University Press, 1933), pp. 73ff.

74. Cf. Albrecht Alt, "Micha 2, 1-5 ΓΗΣ ΑΝΑΔΑΣΜΟΣ in Juda," pp. 13-23 in *Interpretationes ad Vetus Testamentum pertinentes*. Festschrift Sigmund Mowinckel, ed. Arvid S. Kapelrud. Norsk teologisk Tidsskrift 56 (Oslo: Forlaget Land og Kirke, 1955), repr. *Kleine Schriften* 3.

75. This was suggested by Fenton, pp. 36ff.

76. Cf. S. Bergheim, "Land Tenure in Palestine," *PEFQS* (1891): 191-99; North, p. 164.

77. This is substantially the position adopted by Bess, pp. 56-58. Cf. also F. P. W. Buhl, "Some Observations on the Social Institutions of the Israelites," *American Journal of Theology* 1 (1897): 731-33.

3 | *The Family and Israel's Relationship to Yahweh*

INTRODUCTION

Having examined both the link between Israel's relationship with God and God's ownership of the land (Chapter 1) and also the centrality of the family in Israel's rationale of land tenure (Chapter 2), the purpose of this chapter is to develop the proposition (made above, p. 65) that the landholding household units constituted the basic social fabric through which Israel's relationship with God was "earthed" and experienced. We shall approach the subject from two angles: first, examining the role of the family in certain areas of Israel's life where that relationship had a particular practical, moral, or religious effect; second, seeing how membership of a landowning household was important for the individual as regards his or her standing within the religious community.

A. THE IMPORTANCE OF LANDOWNING HOUSEHOLDS IN THE NATIONAL CONTEXT

1. The Military Sphere

That war played a large part in the history of early Israel needs no argument. It is equally clear that, at least in the early period, before the organization of professional and standing armies under the monarchy, the military levy was based on the natural units of society—"kin groups" (or "clans") and households. The term *'elep* was used for the military contingent of a *mišpāḥâ* and was the basic unit of tribal levies. In some military narratives the terms appear to be synonymous.[1] An *'elep* was the *"kin group-at-arms"*—the complement of troops provided by a "kin group" for the tribal levy. In addition to providing combatants, the "father's house" also seems to have had a function in the enrollment and leadership of these units.[2]

It seems likely that there was some connection between the division and tenure of land on the one hand and military capability and obligations on the other. The census lists of Num. 1 and 26 are specifically and repeatedly related to *military* capacity, but in the latter case the allotment of *territory* is said to be based also on the same analysis of tribes, clans, and households. This suggests that the holding of land involved liability for military service. S. Herbert Bess made a study of this question, in which he examined fiefholding practices in Babylonia and, more particularly, at Mari.

> The Mari kings are known to have censused their subjects with the purpose of acquiring soldiers and other servants for the crown, and . . . land grants were given in fief to these subjects in compensation for their services. Possession of such land obligated a

---

1. E.g., Judg. 6–7; 1 Sam. 10:19; 17:18; 22:7; 2 Sam. 18:1. On the terminology and social basis of the army, see Roland de Vaux, *Ancient Israel*, pp. 214ff. and bibliography.

2. E.g., 1 Chr. 7; 2 Chr. 26:11-12; and the military census lists of Num. 1 and 26. On these last see George E. Mendenhall, "The Census Lists of Numbers 1 and 26," *JBL* 77 (1958): 52-66. The military role of the "kin group" is discussed, with further comment on the work of Mendenhall, by Norman K. Gottwald, *The Tribes of Yahweh*, pp. 270-76.

person to service, and the census was renewed periodically to insure that such land was in the hands of those who were capable of rendering the required services.[3]

Bess then suggested that a similar conception of landholding may have existed in Israel, but as related to *Yahweh* as king, not to the Israelite kings. Yahweh was the ultimate owner; the people held the land as by grant from Yahweh. In Babylonia, Bess noted, land which was held in fief from the king was inalienable, and this compared well with the fact that in Israel the inalienability of the land was based upon Yahweh's ultimate ownership of it and the Israelites' tenure of it as his *gērîm weтôšāḇîm,* "guests and residents." These terms, when used in a nonliteral sense (as, e.g., in Lev. 25:23), have been given by some scholars a "feudal" interpretation which accords with the view just expressed: that is, as referring to Israel as Yahweh's "feudal tenants," holding land from him, residing under his protection, and obligated in various ways in return.[4] Such obligations of the land-holder toward Yahweh would include engaging in warfare for or under him. Num. 32:22 indicates that, for the Reubenites, Gadites, and the half-tribe of Manasseh, participation in warfare with the other tribes was the condition of their proper and secure possession of the land east of Jordan. Fulfillment of this obligation would leave them "free" *(noqî)* to occupy their allotted land.

Such a dimension of Israel's obligations to Yahweh would be doubly significant for our purpose in that (1) it is directly linked to the tenure of land and (2) it is based upon the units of landholding households—that is, precisely the pattern which we are trying to elucidate.

It must be admitted, of course, that this is a picture which to a large extent is built on inference and analogy, and that it is difficult to bring forward evidence of a generally acceptable historical nature showing this concept in actual operation. Two problems in partic-

3. "Systems of Land Tenure in Ancient Israel," p. 111.
4. See, e.g., Hans Wildberger, "Israel und sein Land," *Evangelical Theology* 16 (1956): 417-18. Cf. also T. N. D. Mettinger's comments on Israel's transference to the theological plane of feudal concepts found in surrounding cultures (*Solomonic State Officials,* p. 109).

ular as regards the early period prevent a clear historical picture
being presented: on the one hand, scholarly disagreement on how
far it is legitimate to speak of "Israel" as such in the premonarchic
period; and on the other, what was the nature of the warfare
undertaken at that time by the groups to whom the name was
attached. Both the "amphictyony" theory of Martin Noth[5] and the
"holy war" theory of Gerhard von Rad,[6] which once seemed securely established, have come in for increasing scholarly criticism
and dissent. Some reject the concept of amphictyony altogether;[7]
others retain it but reject the concept of holy war as an "amphycty-
onic institution."[8]

In the face of this present uncertainty, it might be thought
pointless to argue for the kind of relationship outlined above between Yahweh and the landholding households of Israel in the realm
of military obligation and action. The picture is not, however, totally
blank. Certain basic facts and features of the period may be asserted
as undoubtedly historical, and as such they provide a minimum but
sufficient ground for our proposition to be tenable.

It is certain that wars and battles did take place and that tribal
and subtribal groups engaged in them. It seems equally certain, from
the primary witness of the Song of Deborah, that the name of
"Israel" was used by these groups (even though it was not a case of
a twelve-tribe "amphictyony" acting in concert). It seems certain
also that this "Israel" considered themselves to be the "people of

5. *Das System der zwölf Stämme Israels.* BWANT 52 (1930; repr. 1966).

6. *Der heilige Krieg im alten Israel.* Abhandlungen zur Theologie des Alten
und Neuen Testaments 20 (1951; repr. Göttingen: Vandenhoeck & Ruprecht, 1965).

7. E.g., with a survey of critical literature on the subject, A. D. H. Mayes, *Israel
in the Period of the Judges.* SBT, 2nd ser. 29 (1974); C. H. J. de Geus, *The Tribes
of Israel*; and most recently Gottwald, pp. 345-386.

8. E.g., Rudolf Smend, *Yahweh War and Tribal Confederation* (Nashville:
Abingdon, 1970). Gwilym H. Jones adopts Smend's viewpoint on the nature of
Yahweh war, but leaves open the question of the existence or otherwise of an
amphictyony (" 'Holy War' or 'Yahweh War'?" *VT* 24 [1975]: 644). Cf. also the
recent discussion of the subject by Barnabas Lindars, "The Israelite Tribes in
Judges," pp. 95-112 in *Studies in the Historical Books of the Old Testament,* ed.
J. A. Emerton. *VTS* 30 (1979). See also Millard C. Lind, *Yahweh Is a Warrior*
(Scottdale, Pa.: Herald, 1980); and H. Eberhard von Waldow, "The Concept of War
in the Old Testament," *Horizons in Biblical Theology* 6/2 (1984): 27-48.

Yahweh" and that the battles were thought of as waged by Yahweh, with the help of the people, against his enemies. There did exist therefore, notwithstanding the confused and fragmented circumstances, an "Israel consciousness" and a "Yahweh consciousness" among the tribal groups. The former manifested itself in the "cry for help" (the $ṣ^{e\cdot}āqâ$) to neighboring clans and tribes which led to the local levies and alliances formed to meet immediate dangers.[9] The latter is apparent in the concept of the war being Yahweh's, of fighting *for* Yahweh as being a duty such that failure to fulfill it merited censure or the curse (cf. Judg. 5:16-17, 23). Furthermore it is certain that these wars were fought, not by a wealthy military aristocracy, but by those who lived on the land—peasant farmers in the open country. Thus, Judg. 5:11b equates the "righteous deeds (or 'acts of vengeance') of Yahweh" ($ṣid^{e}qôṯ\ YHWH$; author's translation) with the "righteous deeds of his peasant farmers (NIV 'warrior') in Israel" ($ṣid^{e}qōṯ\ pirzōnô\ b^{e}yiśrā^{\cdot}ēl$)—the possessive suffix surely indicating the relationship between Yahweh and the country-dwellers, the landowning households, of Israel.

Thus, even from this minimum of knowledge, one can discern the kind of pattern described above—an awareness of mutual obligation in military action among the kinship groups living on the land, arising from a common obligation to Yahweh. This much can be affirmed without involving an elaborate theory of amphictyony or an institutionalized covenant concept. There are some scholars who maintain that whatever tenuous degree of unity Israel had at this period was based upon a covenant which had been in existence before the Settlement[10] and which had strong military

9. Smend attaches considerable importance to this intertribal $ṣ^{e\cdot}āqâ$: "This cry for help to the neighbor . . . and the results achieved by it are the most unquestionable, the most essential, and the most vital manifestation of Israelite unity which is known to us from that time. . . . The levy is determined by the actual military requirement; that it affects the groups that also worship the god Yahweh . . . , is self-evident by the character of this war" (p. 21).

10. E.g., George W. Anderson: "It seems natural, therefore, to look for the establishing of this unity, not in the emergence of an amphictyony . . . but rather . . . in the period before the settlement, and, more specifically, in the establishment of the Sinai covenant between Yahweh and the Israelite tribes" ("Israel: Amphictyony: ʿAm; Ḳāhāl; ʿĒḏâh," p. 149 in *Translating and Understanding the Old Testament.*

aspects.[11] Although such a position would obviously support our argument here—and is the position I personally hold—our case is not dependent on such a covenantal coloring.[12] It can be asserted with reasonable historical confidence that Israelite families on the land responded to military challenges out of a consciousness of common "Israelhood." This common bond included a relationship with and obligation to Yahweh as the God of Israel and giver of the land—*whether or not* this relationship and its obligations were *then* conceived of in covenant terminology.

The role and importance of the family in the military sphere therefore overflows into the theological realm, for its obligations were not only loyalty and assistance to fellow tribes and tribal leaders (Judg. 5:15) but also to "come to the help of the LORD" against his enemies (v. 23). This latter obligation, if Bess's conjecture is correct, may indeed have been consciously involved in the very tenure of land from Yahweh, its true owner.

2. The Judicial Sphere

Another area of Israelite life which was permeated by a sense of responsibility to Yahweh was the realm of judicial principles and practice. Obedience to the will of Yahweh was basic to the relationship from the beginning and had a practical effect on the whole of life. The role of the family in this sphere had two equally vital aspects: internal, domestic jurisdiction, and external, public administration of justice.

a. Internal Jurisdiction

In some matters the Israelite household was virtually a "law unto itself," in the sense that the head of the household had authority to

Festschrift Herbert G. May, ed. Harry Thomas Frank and William L. Reed [Nashville: Abingdon, 1970]).

11. Cf. particularly the work of Patrick D. Miller, Jr., cited in Chapter 1, n. 12.

12. It is important to stress this, in view of the present state of scholarly debate on the covenant and how early it may be said to have been in use as a term to describe Israel's relationship with Yahweh. The remarks in the Introduction (p. xix) should be borne in mind.

act judicially without reference to any outside legal authority.[13] Respect for this independence of heads of households in the exercise of their jurisdictional rights can be seen in the degree of inviolability apparently enjoyed by the household. Members of a household under the authority of its *paterfamilias* could not simply be seized on suspicion (Deut. 24:10-11; Judg. 6:30-31; 2 Sam. 14:7). Only a fool allows such a thing to take place without preventing it (Job 5:4). It was also fully expected that this internal authority should be exercised (1 Sam. 2:22-36; 8:1-5). The procedure for dealing with the rebellious son (Deut. 21:18-21) explicitly presupposes that internal family action has been taken. Only because this has failed does the problem then become a matter for public concern and action.[14]

The "father's house," therefore, was the primary framework of judicial authority within which the Israelite found himself, and to which he remained subject for a considerable period of his life. In this context, the Fifth Commandment, "the first commandment with promise" (Exod. 20:12), takes on a particular significance. The promise attached involves long life in the land—that is, the permanence, security, and enjoyment of the relationship between Yahweh and Israel in the land he had given them. This is made conditional upon the maintenance of respect and obedience of children to their parents—which includes submission to the jurisdictional authority of the *paterfamilias*. The rationale behind this particular association of commandment and promise supports our argument in this chapter, namely, that the national relationship with

13. Anthony Phillips, "Some Aspects of Family Law in Pre-exilic Israel," *VT* 23 (1973): 349-361, a study of this internal jurisdiction, perhaps goes too far in postulating a distinct category of law consciously recognized and applied as such by Israelite families—though the term is useful for *our* classificatory purposes. J. M. Salmon, "Judicial Authority in Early Israel," is a very thorough examination of Israelite judicial institutions which particularly emphasizes their familial basis (see esp. pp. 19-59). See also Anthony Phillips, "Another Example of Family Law," *VT* 30 (1980): 240-45.

14. Restrictions on the authority of the *paterfamilias,* particularly as regards the right of life and death over his dependants, are dealt with below in Chapter 7 and need not be listed here. On Deut. 21:18-21 see further Elizabeth Bellefontaine, "Deuteronomy 21:18-21: Reviewing the Case of the Rebellious Son," *JSOT* 13 (1979): 13-31.

God was vested in the family units living on their portions of land, and therefore its continuance depended on the survival and stability of these units. This in turn depended on the maintenance of a healthy authority structure within the family itself.

In this light, the various laws which prescribe the death penalty for any form of open disrespect for parental authority can be seen in a new and more positive perspective. They are not relics of a harsh *patria potestas* or an arbitrary, authoritarian patriarchy. They are in fact safeguards of the *national* well-being. For violation of parental authority—rejection of the domestic jurisdiction of the head of the household—was a crime against the stability of the nation inasmuch as it was an attack upon that on which the nation's relationship with God was grounded—the household. It was thus as justly liable to the sanction of capital punishment as the more blatant forms of apostasy or idolatry. The treatment of the rebellious son in Deut. 21:18-21 shows most clearly how seriously this was taken. If the circumstances were sufficiently grave, the stability and well-being of the *household* were to be reckoned of greater importance than the life of one of its members. The *national* significance of the situation is reflected in the phrase "all Israel will hear of it and be afraid" (v. 21).[15]

b. The Administration of Justice

As well as being responsible for domestic jurisdiction, heads of households functioned in public judicial action at the local level. This was probably their main civic function, as elders,[16] in the daily life of the community. Even with Jehoshaphat's reform of the judicial

15. Further discussion of the Fifth Commandment and related issues is undertaken in Chapter 5, Section B.

16. The elders were the mainstay of Israelite community life throughout the whole Old Testament period. Though their role and influence varied, their connection with the law and judicial activity was a constant factor. For the chronological distribution of the usage of the term $z^e q\bar{e}n\hat{i}m$, see Günther Bornkamm, "πρέσβυς," in *Theological Dictionary of the New Testament*, ed. Gerhard Friedrich (Grand Rapids: Wm. B. Eerdmans, 1968) 6:655-661. For a comparative survey of their functions, see John L. McKenzie, "The Elders in the Old Testament," *Bibl* 40 (1959): 522-540 (esp. pp. 526ff. on the judicial functions). See also J. Conrad

system and creation of an official, royally appointed body of judges (2 Chr. 19:4-11), the role of the heads of households was not greatly diminished. The panel of "appeal judges" in Jerusalem consisted of Levites, priests, and *heads of fathers' houses*—the first two no doubt for their presumed detailed knowledge of the law, the third for their practical experience in actual local cases and disputes. It is probably to this last group that "certain of the elders of the land" belong, who in the *ad hoc* trial of Jeremiah (Jer. 26) play a significant—and apparently official—part alongside the presiding officials *(śārîm)* in defending Jeremiah from a capital charge (v. 17). The presence of this nonroyal, popular element in judicial proceedings in Jerusalem even in the very late Monarchy indicates "a considerable degree of continuity between these royal courts and the institutions of the local assemblies, since the officials would have been largely drawn from the heads of the most important families."[17]

It is also very probable that the judges appointed by Jehoshaphat in the cities were local elders, now given official status and royal authority.[18] They are spoken of as "living in their cities" (2 Chr. 19:10). In any case the royal appointments were confined to the fortified cities (v. 5), so the processes of justice at the lowest level, in the village assemblies, must have continued virtually unaffected. J. M. Salmon observes: "From the pre-monarchic period until the end of Old Testament times, then, the local assembly of elders and citizens in the gate remained one of the mainstays of the administration of justice in Israel."[19] The nature of their task would also have been largely unaffected.[20]

---

and G. Johannes Botterweck, "zāqēn," *TDOT* IV (1980), pp. 122-131; and cf. de Geus, pp. 139ff.

17. Salmon, pp. 335-36.

18. Contra Anthony Phillips, *Ancient Israel's Criminal Law* (Oxford: Blackwell and New York: Schocken, 1970), p. 18, who believes that the royal appointments "abolished the local jurisdiction of elders." Cf. also William Foxwell Albright, "The Judicial Reform of Jehoshaphat," p. 76 in *Alexander Marx Jubilee Volume*, ed. Saul Lieberman (New York: Jewish Publication Society, 1950); and Phillips on the historicity of the reform.

19. P. 427.

20. On the functioning of judicial assemblies, cf. Ludwig Köhler, "Justice in the Gate," pp. 127-150 in *Hebrew Man* (Nashville: Abingdon and London: SCM,

Now it is probable, though the evidence is not very explicit, that the main qualification for eldership and the exercise of its judicial rights was the possession of landed property and family. In spite of the wealth of references, the Old Testament gives no very clear information on what qualified one as an elder. It has been argued that all adult males were elders and sat in local assemblies.[21] Against this is the fact that the terms "elders" and "inhabitants" or "men of" are not *always* interchangeable (cf. Josh. 8:10; 9:11; Isa. 3:14; and Ruth 4), though they *sometimes* appear to be (e.g., Josh. 24:1-2; Judg. 8:14). Preferable is the view that the elders were the senior, authoritative, constituent, and sometimes representative element of the local assemblies, neither identical with nor entirely distinct from the whole body of citizens.[22] The most natural identification of elders in *this* sense is with the heads of fathers' houses—that is, the *senior* male member of each household, who would also therefore have been the owner of the family land and property.[23] Job 30, for example, shows clearly how Job's *loss* of property and family utterly destroyed his status in the local judicial assembly, in stark contrast to Job 29's informative picture of his prominent part in it. In this respect, Anthony Phillips is correct in emphasizing the disastrous consequences arising for an Israelite from the dispossession of home and property.[24] Apart from the obvious economic disabilities, it

---

1956); Donald A. McKenzie, "Judicial Procedure at the Town Gate," *VT* 14 (1964): 100-4; Hans-Jochen Boecker, *Law and the Administration of Justice in the Old Testament and Ancient East* (Minneapolis: Augsburg, 1980), pp. 27-52. Deuteronomy provides a wealth of examples of the kind of judicial matters which were dealt with by elders: Deut. 16:18-20; 17:2-13; 19:11-13; 21:1-9, 19-20; 22:13-21; 25:5-10.

21. C. Umhau Wolf, "Traces of Primitive Democracy in Ancient Israel," *JNES* 6 (1947): 98-108.

22. See further Robert Gordis, "Democratic Origins in Ancient Israel—the Biblical '*ēdāh*," pp. 384-85 in *Alexander Marx Jubilee Volume*; J. P. M. van der Ploeg, "Les Anciens dans l'Ancien Testament," pp. 175-191 in *Lex tua veritas*, Festschrift Hubert Junker, ed. H. Goss and F. Mussner (Trier: Paulinus, 1961); J. L. McKenzie, "Elders," pp. 538-39; Geoffrey Evans, " 'Coming' and 'Going' at the City Gate," *BASOR* 150 (1958): 28-33; Salmon, pp. 403ff.

23. Cf. Phillips, *Ancient Israel's Criminal Law*, p. 17.

24. His attempt, however, to make this the criminal offense against which an alleged original form of the Tenth Commandment was directed rests on very shaky

meant loss of standing and participation in a sphere of social life where the obligations of the relationship with God impinged most closely on the practical realities of society—the local administration of justice. The removal of large numbers of people from this status by dispossession, and the consequent monopolizing of judicial administration by a corrupt plutocracy,[25] was one of the factors which threatened the stability and survival of the nation before God, a factor in the degenerative process referred to above (p. 78).

Thus again we find family and land together at the heart of basic Israelite institutions. If anything can be said to have been crucial to the relationship between Israel and Yahweh, it was the requirement of justice and the integrity of those who administered it. Both of these depended upon the maintenance of the social fabric of free, landholding households. Given such a social pattern, the administration of justice could have, at least ideally, a democratic and theocratic character. But the spread of judicial corruption that accompanied the breakup of that social fabric could not be halted even by the judicial reforms, royal decrees, and appointments of a Jehoshaphat—as is clear from the prophetic preaching of the century following his reforms.

3. The Continuity of the Relationship with God

We move back again to a closer look at the internal role of the family as a vehicle of continuity for the faith, history, and traditions of Israel. This was arguably its most important function in the maintenance of the nation's relationship with Yahweh.

a. Didactic Function

The family had a major role in the preservation of the legal traditions through the didactic duty of the father. He was to teach his children

---

ground indeed (Phillips, *Ancient Israel's Criminal Law,* pp. 151ff.). On this, see below, pp. 138-39.

25. Cf. Köhler, pp. 142-43; J. L. McKenzie, p. 539; Erling Hammershaimb, *Some Aspects of Old Testament Prophecy from Isaiah to Malachi* (Copenhagen: Rosenkilde og Bagger, 1966), pp. 30-33.

the precepts of Yahweh, both as a solemn obligation of parenthood and as a condition of prolonged enjoyment of life in the land.

> Lay to heart all the words which I enjoin upon you this day, that you may command them to your children, that they may be careful to do all the words of this law. For it is no trifle for you, but it is your life, and thereby you shall live long in the land which you are going over the Jordan to possess. (Deut. 32:46-47)

We note yet again the connection between continued life in the land and the authority of the family. This matter of teaching the law within the family is particularly prominent in Deuteronomy (Deut. 6:7; 11:19), but it must reflect very ancient family custom. In this respect, Erhard S. Gerstenberger has emphatically drawn attention to the influence of the ancient tribal and patriarchal structure of early Israel and their ancestors upon the form and development of Israelite law. Gerstenberger's work is not without its weaknesses and its critics,[26] but he has highlighted the role of the household and the "kin group" in Israelite law. As a didactic force throughout succeeding generations, the family stood at the center of the twin relationships between Israel and Yahweh and between Israel and their land (as stressed in Deut. 32:47).

26. Detailed criticisms of some aspects of his work are made in Herbert B. Huffmon's review article, "Law and Wisdom," *Interpretation* 22 (1968): 201-4. As regards his form-critical procedure, cf. William McKane, *Proverbs*. OTL (1970), pp. 5-6. His attempts to find the *origin* of the "prohibitive" (a term Gerstenberger prefers to "apodictic," for its broader scope) form of Israelite law in nomadic *Sippenethos* (clan ethic) cannot, in my view, be regarded as successful. Apart from the doubtfulness of the "nomadic" theory (cf. Appendix to Chapter 2, nn. 69 and 70), it is a confusion of functions. That the family provided a *vehicle* for the perpetuation of the laws is not the same thing as, and certainly does not prove, that the laws themselves *originated in* family ethics and paternal instruction. Against this is the strength and antiquity of Israel's belief in the law as something "given" and connected both with particular events and with the figure of Moses as lawgiver (cf. Otto Kaiser, *Introduction to the Old Testament*, p. 62, on the necessity of allowing historical weight in some degree to the tradition of Moses in the origins of Israel's law). Gerstenberger does not account for the force of these beliefs, but rather sidesteps them, to my mind, by calling them a "secondary cultic setting of the 'family ethos' " ("Covenant and Commandment," *JBL* 84 [1965]: 51; this article is only a précis of his major work, *Wesen und Herkunft des "Apodiktischen" Rechts*. WMANT 20 [1965]).

b. Catechetical Function

A second aspect of this role of the family in the continuity of the national relationship was the catechetical duties of the father. This is related not so much to the law itself (like the didactic function) as to certain cultic institutions or memorials of historical events, the significance of which a father is required to explain to his inquiring children ("When your son asks you . . . you shall say. . ."). Hence the term "catechetical."

The term was proposed by J. Alberto Soggin in his form-critical discussion of the five occasions where a particular event, institution, or memorial is the object of a question and answer sequence between father and son: Exod. 12:26-27; 13:14-15; Deut. 6:20-24; Josh. 4:6-7, 21-23.[27] Soggin sees here a liturgical form. He is probably right, but this would not preclude the use of such catechesis at a domestic, family level. Nor is this made unlikely by Soggin's fair observation that the questions hardly arise from "the normal curiosity of a child,"[28] for no catechism was ever devised to meet childish curiosity, but rather to "prime" the child with questions as a "springboard" for the teaching of specific religious history and belief. In these particular Old Testament examples, the catechesis covers the events of the Exodus, the conquest and gift of the promised land, and the receiving of the law—themes which were central to Israel's understanding of their relationship with Yahweh. The family's role in preserving the knowledge of this relationship was therefore correspondingly central.

In the example of the form in Deut. 6:20-24, the catechesis is intended to give historical justification for the observance of the law. It is notable that this catechesis *presupposes* a knowledge of the law in the son, for he asks, "What do these laws mean?" It must therefore arise within the context of the didactic function of the family in providing such knowledge. The cases in Exodus strongly support the idea of a family catechesis—the first being part of the

27. "Cultic-Aetiological Legends and Catechesis in the Hexateuch," pp. 72-77 in *Old Testament and Oriental Studies*. Biblica et Orientalia 29 (1975). Cf. J. Philip Hyatt, "Ancient Historical Credo," pp. 160-65.
28. "Legends and Catechesis," p. 76.

recurring family festival of the Passover, the second being related
to that uniquely important event in the life of an Israelite family—
the birth of the first son. This latter rite has particular significance
for our purpose and requires closer attention.

c. The Consecration of the Firstborn

The requirement to devote to Yahweh the firstfruits of the earth,
firstlings of flock and herd, and the firstborn of mankind is found
frequently throughout the Pentateuch. The texts referring to the
human firstborn are:[29] Exod. 13:2, 12-15; 22:29; 34:1-20; Num.
3:11-13; 8:16-18;[30] 18:15.

1   *The* LORD *said to Moses,*
2   *"Consecrate to me every firstborn male. The first offspring of
    every womb among the Israelites belongs to me, whether man
    or animal."*

. . . .

11 *"After the* LORD *brings you into the land of the Canaanites and
    gives it to you, as he promised on oath to you and your
    forefathers,*
12 *you are to give over to the* LORD *the first offspring of every
    womb. All the firstborn males of your livestock belong to the
    LORD.*
13 *Redeem with a lamb every firstborn donkey, but if you do not*

29. Apart from the redactional position of the rite in Exod. 13 and its
theological significance there (discussed below), the literary-critical source assign-
ment of these texts does not materially affect our understanding of the rite, since
the basic requirement and the historical and theological explanation of it remain
more or less constant throughout.

30. Num. 3:11-13 and 8:16-18 are in the context of the Levites being "taken"
by Yahweh as "his own" instead of the firstborn. This is most commonly viewed
by commentators as an explanatory justification of the special position of the
Levites. It did not imply that the requirement to dedicate and redeem the firstborn
was thereby rescinded, for the practice is envisaged as continuing in Num. 18:16.
Rather, the story in Num. 3, with its elaborate genealogy and precise numbering,
appears to record what was believed to have been a unique event, affecting only a
single generation—that of the wilderness period.

> *redeem it, break its neck. Redeem every firstborn among your*
> *sons.*
> 14 *"In days to come, when your son asks you, 'What does this*
> *mean?' say to him, 'With a mighty hand the* LORD *brought us*
> *out of Egypt, out of the land of slavery.*
> 15 *When Pharaoh stubbornly refused to let us go, the* LORD *killed*
> *every firstborn in Egypt, both man and animal. This is why I*
> *sacrifice to the* LORD *the first male offspring of every womb*
> *and redeem each of my firstborn sons.'*
> 16 *And it will be like a sign on your hand and a symbol on your*
> *forehead that the* LORD *brought us out of Egypt with his mighty*
> *hand."*
>
> (*Exod. 13:1-2, 11-16, NIV*)

It is widely accepted that the practice of dedicating or sacrificing
the first produce of land and beast had pre-Israelite origins and
was probably already a part of the cultus of Israel's ancestors
before the Exodus. The same can be said for the Feast of Unleavened Bread, which is closely associated with the rite of the
firstborn both in Exod. 34 and Exod. 13, even though there was
probably no connection between them in their pre-Israelite
origins. However, neither the fact that the firstborn rite was in
ultimate origin older than and unconnected with the Exodus, nor
the lack of any connection at that stage between it and whatever
agricultural festival or rite lies behind the Feast of Unleavened
Bread and the Passover, alters the fact that as *Israelite* cultic
practices in the only form in which they appear to us from the Old
Testament they are both related historically and theologically to
the Exodus and the events immediately preceding it. From the
point of view of Israel's faith, therefore, the origin of the rite of
the redemption of the firstborn can truly be said to have been the
Exodus,[31] and the juxtaposition with the Passover in Exod. 13 and

31. Similarly, from the perspective of the Christian faith, the festival of
Christmas can truly be said to have its historical and theological origin in the birth
of Jesus Christ, even though its original roots and some of the practices associated
with it are pre-Christian or pagan.

34 is therefore not "only literary connections,"[32] "probably er-
roneously"[33] made, but, again from the perspective of Israel's
faith, historically and theologically valid.

Two points relevant to our purpose may be made concerning
this rite.

1. It was a symbolic declaration of the nature of the relationship
between Israel and Yahweh—namely, one of *complete belonging* to
Yahweh as his possession, and that on the basis of the deliverance
from Egypt. What Yahweh had redeemed from death belonged to
him (Num. 3:13). Thus, Israel's recollection of redemption must be
accompanied by expression of their separateness, their holiness, not
only through practical obedience in the moral and legal realm (cf.
Exod. 19:4-6) but also through the symbolism of the consecration of
the firstborn to Yahweh. As Brevard S. Childs notes, "The initial
point that God claims the first-born has been spiritualized. This claim
had been extended from the first-born to all Israel. God has a special
claim on his people: 'he belongs to me.' "[34] The rite was the symbolic
link, in other terms, between redemption and sanctification.

This link between the practices surrounding the firstborn and
Israel's relationship with God has been interestingly developed by
Arthur Mason Brown. Presenting the thesis that the sociological
and legal institution of inheritance was also used theologically as a
vehicle for expressing the continuity of that relationship throughout
the generations, he sees the firstborn as the "key-person" in the
theological concept as well as in the sociological institution. The
firstborn has a "central role in the relationship between Yahweh and
Israel. He is the one in each family whom Yahweh calls his own."[35]

It would be attractive to suggest a further dimension to this
association, in the designation of Israel as *Yahweh's firstborn* son
in Exod. 4:22. This idea does not occur explicitly in any of the
explanations of the rite of the firstborn, and although Israel's filial
status before Yahweh is found frequently elsewhere (cf. above, pp.

32. J. Philip Hyatt, *Exodus*. NCBC (Grand Rapids: Wm. B. Eerdmans and
London: Marshall, Morgan & Scott, 1980), p. 146.
33. Hyatt, "Ancient Historical Credo," p. 162.
34. *The Book of Exodus*, p. 204.
35. "The Concept of Inheritance," p. 297.

15-22), Exod. 4:22 is the only occasion where Israel is described as Yahweh's firstborn son (in the Pentateuch; cf. Jer. 31:9). Nevertheless, this unique occurrence in Exodus is surely therefore all the more significant in the context of the theological impact of these chapters, taken as a whole in their final shape.[36] There is a correspondence between the initial reference to "firstborn" in Exod. 4:22 and the prominent placing of the rite of the human firstborn immediately after the Exodus and closely intertwined with the Passover. At the outset, the demand is made of Pharaoh: "Release my firstborn, Israel, or I will slay your firstborn!" In the course of events the Egyptian firstborn are indeed slain, but the Israelite firstborn are delivered, and Israel, the firstborn of Yahweh, is released. Thereupon Israel is required immediately to express symbolically their status and relationship to Yahweh, namely, as his firstborn, by consecrating to him their own firstborn sons.

2. The consecration of the firstborn was also a declaration of the *continuity and permanence* of Israel's relationship with Yahweh. In laying special claim to the firstborn in each family, God was in effect laying claim to the succeeding generation as his own. Just as the birth of the first son ensured the all-important continuation of that family into the succeeding generation, so Yahweh's claim to that son, as symbolic of the next generation, ensured the continuation of Yahweh's relationship with Israel into that generation also. There was thus established a thread of historical continuity in the assertion and experience of the divine ownership of the nation. Israel belonged to Yahweh henceforth "from generation to generation."

Not only the rite itself, but also the explanatory material which surrounds it, emphasize this aspect of its significance. The explanation is couched in catechesis (Exod. 13:14), which in itself involves the continuing line of teaching handed on, from father to children, within the family. Furthermore, the hortatory address stresses that

36. The complex problems of the redaction of these chapters of Exodus and the date at which their present shape was achieved need not detain us here, because we have already seen that the primary concept under discussion, the sonship of Israel, was, from the evidence of other texts, very ancient. The redaction has given it a particular theological slant; but it was not responsible for the origination of the concept.

this rite, like the Passover (note the parallel between Exod. 13:16
and 13:9), is to serve as a constant memorial for future generations
of the great redemptive events of the Exodus.

> The setting of the address on the very day of the exodus (13.3) in
> the mouth of Moses, anchors the claim in the basic redemptive
> event of Israel's faith. The address follows the narrative of the
> deliverance and draws its implications for future generations ...
> in calling for an ongoing experiential appropriation from the heart
> in response to what God had done.[37]

It was, as we have now seen clearly, above all the *family* which
provided the major vehicle for this "ongoing experiential appro-
priation."

To sum up, then: the family was of pivotal importance in Israel's
relationship with God. This has been seen in the military and judicial
spheres (in both of which the household's ownership of land was
also found to be important), and even more so in the various aspects
of the family's part in maintaining and perpetuating the traditions of
Israel's faith. Hence, on this wide basis, the proposition advanced
earlier may be affirmed with clarity. The relationship between Israel
and Yahweh was vested, initially at any rate, in the socio-economic
fabric of household-plus-land units. On them lay a large measure of
responsibility for the fulfillment of the obligations of the relationship
and for the preservation of its historical traditions.

Furthermore, it was by belonging within a household, with its
portion of land as the proof of its share in the people of Yahweh,
that the individual Israelite shared in the privileges and protection
of this relationship.

> The covenant between Yahweh and his people was a covenant
> with each family, if not with each individual. Since protection was
> an important concern of all covenants, each Israelite family was
> thus placed under the direct protection of God, and could be
> attacked only at the risk of incurring God's enmity.[38]

37. Childs, p. 204.
38. George E. Mendenhall, "Ancient Oriental and Biblical Law," *BA* 17 (1954):

The household with its land provided the tangible link between theological concepts of national scope and the living experience of them by the individual. To illustrate this is the purpose of the second angle of our investigation in this chapter.

B. THE IMPORTANCE OF LANDOWNING HOUSEHOLDS FOR THE INDIVIDUAL'S STANDING IN THE COMMUNITY

In what ways was the individual's standing within the community of Yahweh's people affected by, or even dependent upon, his or her belonging within an Israelite household in the land? The best way to approach this question is by considering that broad class of individuals in Israelite society who can be called "dependent persons"—that is, women, children, slaves and resident aliens, and laborers. Some of these will be the object of closer scrutiny in Part III. The point at issue here is this: whatever their precise *legal* status (see Part III), were they included in the community of those who shared in the privileges and obligations of the nation's relationship with Yahweh, and if so, on what grounds?

The question has been framed in this manner because it is deceptively easy to *equate* legal standing with "covenant membership." This is what Anthony Phillips does at the outset of *Ancient Israel's Criminal Law*, and it affects much of his argument in the rest of the book as regards dependent persons. Thus, without argument or evidence he asserts:

> Initially only free adult males were subject to Israel's criminal law, for only they *could have* entered into the covenant relationship with Yahweh. It was to them that the covenant stipulations of the Sinai Decalogue were addressed. (p. 14, my italics)

39, repr. in *The Biblical Archaeologist Reader 3,* ed. Edward F. Campbell and David Noel Freedman (Garden City: Doubleday, 1970).

1. Women

In the case of women, this leads Phillips to the logical conclusion that since "they had no legal status, being the personal property first of their fathers and then of their husbands" (a common view which is strongly disputed below, Chapter 6), they "did not enter into the covenant relationship, and were therefore outside the scope of criminal law" (p. 15).

This view that women were not originally subject to the criminal law recurs frequently throughout the book (pp. 44, 57, 82, 110, 144, 152). It is Phillips' contention that women remained outside the covenant community until, in the seventh century, the Deuteronomist raised their status to include them in it and make them legally liable to covenant law for the first time. As a result of Deuteronomy's "revolutionary legislation," the Decalog came to be "understood to have been addressed to adult members of both sexes" (p. 16). This is a view which bristles with difficulties. It is not denied that aspects of Deuteronomic legislation affected women for the better, but it seems highly unlikely that women would have been excluded from the covenant community to the extent of having had no liability for criminal offenses before the seventh century. Some specific points may be made against Phillips' contention.

(a) Phillips' view simply assumes, without the slightest clue in the actual text to the effect, that the Exodus Decalog was understood to have been addressed to adult males only, whereas the Deuteronomy Decalog was addressed to both sexes (p. 70). In this way, Exod. 22:18, prescribing death for a sorceress (i.e., an apparent case of criminal liability in a woman), can be explained as "plugging a legal loop-hole"—the loophole being that since the Third Commandment, forbidding the use of the divine name for magical purposes, applied only to men, a man could have enlisted a woman to perform magic on his behalf with impunity for them both (p. 57). But in that case, a man could have used a woman for theft or murder with impunity. Where are the provisions to plug these "loop-holes"?

(b) In the case of the Fourth Commandment, the theory does not quite fit—at least not on the presuppositions of the literary critical dating of the documents to which Phillips adheres. For although the fact that the wife and her domestic work were not specifically mentioned in the Exodus Decalog agrees with the theory of that Decalog applying only to males, should not the Deuteronomy Decalog *ex hypothesi* have mentioned these things? But it does not. Inexplicably, the extension of the commandment to include women and their domestic work was not made until the P legislation (Exod. 16:23; 35:3; Num. 15:32ff.).

(c) In the case of the Sixth Commandment, Phillips admits that a murderess would undoubtedly have been executed—not as criminally liable, but rather with the kind of reduced liability of the goring ox (p. 91). It is hard to see what practical difference would have been involved—none, to be sure, from the condemned woman's point of view.

(d) As regards the Seventh Commandment, Phillips argues that the death penalty for adultery was not applicable to women prior to Deuteronomy, since the commandment in Exodus held men alone responsible for that crime. Divorce would have been the woman's fate. This involves taking Deut. 22:22 as new legislation, which is not explicit in the text, and also placing too heavy reliance on the figurative language of Hos. 2:2-3 and Jer. 3:8. In both these prophetic passages the possibility of a return and reconciliation of Israel to God is in the near context, so that capital execution would obviously have been an inappropriate figure to employ. It was, after all, open to a man who discovered or suspected that his wife was adulterous to divorce her privately rather than expose her publicly and demand her execution—even if the latter might be his proper legal duty (cf. Matt. 1:19).

(e) With regard to women's general obligations and liability under the covenant, it should be noted that in the eighth century two prophets denounced *women* for sins of oppression, pride, and vanity (Amos 4:1; Isa. 3:16-23; 24:2; 32:9ff.). The first of these is couched in language which suggests that Amos held women just as guilty as men for breach of the injunctions of the Book of the Covenant (e.g., Exod. 22:21ff.; 23:6ff.).

Phillips' restriction of the covenant relationship to the limits of legal status alone runs contrary to other evidence that women, and

particularly wives, did share in the privileges of the relationship.
There is, for example, the record of their presence at important
occasions of covenant renewal (Josh. 8:35; Deut. 29:11) as well as
at ordinary cultic events (1 Sam. 1:3ff.). There is also the prominent
fact that the mother, no less than the father, was to be held in esteem
and honor—and this under the sanction of the death penalty.[39] Her
position within the household had its clearest expression in this
respect, and is thrown into even sharper relief by the reversal of
circumstances caused by widowhood. The large number of injunctions to charitable care for widows underlines their perilous
economic position. But our contention that sharing in the privileges
of the relationship with Yahweh was to a large degree bound up with
belonging within a landowning household adds another dimension
to the widows' plight—namely, the loss of such privilege and
protection as that relationship afforded in the social sphere. Thus
they were particularly vulnerable to oppression and injustice, from
which—in spite of the exhortations of the charitable laws—their
only recourse was directly to Yahweh himself (Exod. 22:23-24).

The special cases of the priest's household are also an illustration
of the critical factor of being inside or outside the "boundaries" of the
household (cf., e.g., Lev. 22:10-13). The excluded categories of
women for a priest's wife (Lev. 21:14) may owe their exclusion partly
to the consequences of not belonging within a household and therefore lacking unambiguous inclusion in the religious community.

The "Loose Woman" in Proverbs

The view being put forward here also provides a fresh perspective
on the question of the "loose woman" (*'iššâ zārâ w^enokrîyâ*) in

---

39. This is clearly an embarrassment to Phillips' theory: "Since women were
not members of the covenant community, it may seem surprising that the mother
was given equal status with the father" (p. 82). Indeed! Phillips' explanation actually
explains nothing: "But . . . initially marriage would have been with another member
of the clan, and so with a daughter of a member of the covenant community" (p. 82).
But what difference does this make? According to Phillips' argument, she did not
belong to the covenant community because she was a woman, *qua* woman, no
matter who her father may have been.

Prov. 2:16ff., etc., and on the fate of the man who succumbs to her seduction. The significance of the words *zārâ* and *nokrîyâ* to describe the woman in these passages has been much discussed. Least convincing to me is the view that she was an ethnic foreigner, the adherent of a foreign god and/or a cultic prostitute.[40] On the other hand, the view that the words simply denote "otherness," in a weak sense, does not appear an adequate interpretation.[41] In agreement with L. A. Snijders,[42] it seems best that the terms should be given here a meaning which is well attested for both of them elsewhere: outside or beyond the bounds of the *family.*[43] The man is being warned against an affair with an "out-of-family" woman—not referring to a woman outside his family, but to a woman outside her own family. That is to say, here we have a woman who by her actions and designs has repudiated her own marriage relationship and thereby set herself "outside" her own household. Now this does not necessarily mean that she has been divorced and physically expelled, for Prov. 7 portrays her seduction as taking place within her husband's house during his absence. Rather, it means that by her rejection and betrayal of the bonds of her marriage she becomes—figuratively and spiritually, if not physically—*zārâ* and *nokrîyâ* to her own household.

This understanding of the identity of the woman is supported by Prov. 2:17, and indeed renders that verse more significant:

40. Gustav Boström, *Proverbiastudien: die Weisheit und das fremde Weib in Spr 1-9.* Lund Universitets Årsskrift 30/3 (1935), esp. pp. 103ff. Some recent works on women in the Old Testament, where they discuss this figure in Proverbs at all, simply call her "foreign" with no discussion: e.g., Athalya Brenner, *The Israelite Woman: Social Role and Literary Type in Biblical Narrative.* The Biblical Seminar 2 (Sheffield: JSOT Press, 1985), p. 111; James G. Williams, *Women Recounted: Narrative Thinking and the God of Israel.* Bible and Literature 6 (Sheffield: Almond, 1982), pp. 90ff.

41. Paul Humbert, "La 'femme étrangère' du Livre des Proverbes," *Revue des Études Semitiques* 2 (1937): 49-64.

42. "The meaning of זר in the Old Testament," *OTS* 10 (1954): 1-154.

43. E.g., Prov. 5:10; Gen. 31:15; Exod. 21:8; Lev. 22:10; Deut. 25:5. Claudia V. Camp, *Wisdom and the Feminine in the Book of Proverbs.* Bible and Literature 11 (Sheffield: Almond, 1985), interacts positively with the interpretation offered here.

Who forsakes the companion (*allûp)[44] of her youth
And forgets the covenant of her God.

Since a wife could not divorce her husband, the "forsaking" can
only be the kind of repudiation of the marriage relationship described above. In this context, therefore, the primary meaning of
the phrase *berît* *elōheyhā* is most naturally regarded as the covenant
of marriage, as sanctioned and witnessed by God (cf. Mal. 2:14 and
[figuratively] Ezek. 16:8). But our contention in this chapter regarding the significance of the household would also allow the phrase
the wider, secondary allusion to the covenant between God and
Israel. For as we have said, by betraying her marriage the woman
"looses" herself from the household and becomes *zārâ* *wenokrîyâ*
to it. But in so doing she also "looses" herself from that which
enabled her to belong within the wider "covenant community." She
thus indeed, as the verse says, turns her back on the "covenant of
her God" and becomes in a still deeper, spiritual sense *zārâ*
wenokrîyâ ("alien"), in the sense of one "outside" the community
of those eligible to claim and enjoy the relationship with Yahweh.

This in turn sheds some light on why this woman is everywhere
associated with death. She is beyond question a *femme fatale* (Prov.
2:18-19; 5:5; 6:26; 7:23-27; 9:18). One who has intimate entanglement with a woman who has thus cut herself off from the community's vital relationship with God is clearly himself heading for

---

44. Taking *allûp* as referring to the woman's husband. However, some ancient
versions read it as "teaching" or "teacher" (LXX *didaskalían*), as though from the
piel of *'lp*, "to teach." According to Berend Gemser (*Sprüche Salomos*, 2nd ed. HAT
16 [1963], p. 111) this was the opinion of Godfrey Rolles Driver, and it is translated
thus in the NEB, though Gemser himself in his translation (p. 24) does not adopt
this. McKane favors the view that it refers to her early education.

If this were the correct understanding, then, in view of what was said above
about the didactic role of the family, it would still indicate that the woman was
deliberately stepping "outside" the family—in this case rejecting the discipline and
teaching of her parental home. Taken thus the latter half of the verse would probably
have to refer to the covenant in the wider, national sense, as inculcated through the
family's teaching. However, bearing in mind the sexual coloring of the context and
the similarity to Mal. 2:14, it seems preferable that the verse is primarily referring
to the marriage relationship as that which is being "forsaken" and "forgotten,"
though wider allusions may well be present too (see text).

calamity. The threat does not consist simply in the practical consideration of the jealous husband's revenge (6:34), but much more seriously in the reduction of the man's *own household* to virtual extinction. This might come about through the squandering of his substance (6:26, 35), through the passing of family property into "alien" hands[45] because of debts thus incurred (5:9-10), through loss of status (6:33), through failure to build up his own progeny by dissipating his virility (5:15-17), or through a combination of all these factors. A man who "lost" his own house and substance in this way put in grave jeopardy his own standing within the community[46] and could indeed cut himself off from it altogether—which was undoubtedly a kind of "death."

In this light, the concluding verses of Prov. 2 take on a deeper intrinsic meaning and a more significant connection with their preceding context than their language (sounding much like cliches) at first sight suggests.

20 *So you will walk in the way of good men*
   and keep to the paths of the righteous.
21 *For the upright will inhabit the land,*
   and men of integrity will remain in it;
22 *but the wicked will be cut off from the land,*
   and the treacherous will be rooted out of it.

McKane and others rightly point out the links between these verses and Deuteronomic theology with its emphasis on possession of the land and the conditions for life in it. In this respect, comments McKane, these verses are "thoroughly Yahwistic."[47] But is there a reason why they would follow so closely on the warning of the fatal consequences of association with the "loose" woman? Surely it is that the "death" referred to in vv. 18-19 is being explicated in v. 22

45. The terms *zār* and *nokrî* are here used clearly in the sense of one outside the family. In Job 31:9 such an occurrence is regarded as a just punishment for social injustice; here it is the economic effect of an adulterous entanglement.
46. This is probably the implication of 5:14, "I was at the point of utter ruin in the assembled congregation."
47. P. 288.

in terms of being cut off and uprooted from the land. And this, as
we have seen, is the fate of one who loses his family and substance.
This could happen in a variety of ways: through oppression and
eviction (as denounced by the prophets; cf. Mic. 2), by sheer
misfortune (cf. the effects on Job), or, as here, by one's own culpable
stupidity. The disastrous course of events was clearly well known
and dreaded, as the graphic curses of Ps. 109 portray.

The thread of thought, then, which runs through Prov. 2:12-22
and the related passages, is this: one who, by attention to wisdom,
is saved from the "loose" woman and so maintains the integrity and
strength of his own household stays within the community of the
"righteous" (v. 20) and continues to enjoy its prime privilege—
possession of a share in the land (v. 21). But one who gets entangled
with such a woman, who has thrown off the obligations of her
family and marital relationship and has thus stepped "outside" both
her household and thereby also the spiritual relationship of the
nation to Yahweh (i.e., one who is zārâ wᵉnokrîyâ), is likely to end
up ruining his own family and substance. In so doing he will cut
himself off[48] from the privilege of sharing in the land with the rest
of God's people. Worst of all, he risks, through neglect of his family,
the complete extinction of extirpation.[49] In short, he "has no sense";
he "destroys himself" (6:32).

This understanding of the "loose" woman and the fate of the
man who allows himself to be seduced by her fits in well with the
general practical viewpoint of these chapters of Proverbs. The legal
and moral aspects of the matter are for others to deal with.[50] The
sage draws attention rather to the *social and economic* aspects,
especially as they concern the *households* of both parties, and
relates that side of the issue to the wider concern of the whole
community and its enjoyment of God's gift of the land in relationship with him. The fact that he does so indicates strongly that here,

48. The niphal *yikkārētû* could, in this text, have something of its reflexive
sense rather than a simple passive.

49. On the horror of extirpation and all it involved, cf. Herbert C. Brichto,
"Kin, Cult, Land and Afterlife," *HUCA* 44 (1973): 1-54.

50. The correspondence between this Wisdom treatment of adultery and the
legal aspects is discussed further below (pp. 206-7).

as in other areas of the Old Testament already observed, the household was seen to be of primary importance as the locus of the individual's experience of the privileges and obligations of national relationship with God and, to a large degree also, as the basis on which his membership of the privileged community was founded.

2. Children

The mistakenness of basing inclusion in the religious community upon legal status alone is even more apparent when we consider the position of children. Like women, their presence is recorded on great occasions of covenant renewal (Deut. 29:11; Josh. 8:35) and was required at the reading of the law (Deut. 31:12). Circumcision was regarded as a sign of the covenant (Gen. 17:10-11).[51] So was the sabbath (Exod. 31:13-17), and children are explicitly included in the privilege of rest. We have also discussed the significance of the firstborn son and may add here also the place of children in the Passover, including probably their liturgical participation. They formed part of the family in cultic worship (1 Sam. 1:4). Further illustration of the place of children within God's community lies in the fact that part of the motive for the polemic against sacrificing children to Molech[52] was that it meant giving to another deity what Yahweh claimed as exclusively his own, so much so that he speaks of children "borne to *me*," "*my* children" (Ezek. 16:20-21; 23:37). Finally, the wording of Deut. 5:2-3 regards those who had been children, or even unborn, at the time of the Sinai theophany as having been included in and bound by the covenant made there, just as surely as had been the adult parents of the Exodus generation.

There is, then, ample evidence that children belonged within the national relationship with Yahweh, quite regardless of technical legal status. It was possible, however, for a child or youth to *lose*

51. Though this passage is assigned to P, the association of circumcision with covenant is undoubtedly preexilic. This is clear from the figurative use of the concept to describe what should have been the proper response of Israel to God's word—especially in Deuteronomy and Jeremiah (Deut. 10:16; 30:6; Jer. 4:4; 6:10; 9:25-26).

52. On child sacrifice, see more fully below, Chapter 8.

this privilege. This could happen in two ways—both of which
involved the family. On the one hand, a youth could *place himself*
"outside" by deliberate and incorrigible disregard for the internal
authority of the head of the house (Deut. 21:18-21). On the other
hand, he could be *the victim* of adverse economic forces which, by
destroying or scattering his family, ejected him from the security of
a household and its stake in the land. This latter was a sufficiently
common occurrence by the eighth century to figure in the social
preaching of the prophets. Thus Mic. 2:9 not only describes clearly
what was happening, but points out the consequences—which were
more than merely economic.

> The women of my people you drive out from their pleasant
> houses;
> from their young children you take away my glory *(hᵃḏārî)*
> forever.

To eject children from the stable family environment was to take
away from them Yahweh's "glory."

What is the meaning here of *hāḏār*? And what does it mean to
be deprived of it? It is rendered "glory" in most translations. BDB
cites Mic. 2:9 with the comment: "[Yahweh]'s glory as the possession of his people, lost by exile & slavery."[53] The word can also
refer to ornamental, festal garments, and some early commentators
took it thus and referred it to garments taken in pledge (Exod.
22:26). But is it likely that creditors were taking *children's* clothes
as pledges? And why *festal* garments? Most commentators,
however, favor the view that the word refers to the glory of being
part of the people of God, which children were being deprived of
by being rendered homeless, or losing fathers into debt bondage, or
both.[54]

But now, if thus being rendered homeless through the breakup
of the family could be described as being deprived of the glory of
Yahweh, and if glory in this context means the privilege of belong-

---

53. P. 214a.
54. In addition to the majority of commentators, G. Warmuth also explains
hāḏār in Mic. 2:9 in this sense ("hāḏar [hādhār]," *TDOT* 3:360.

ing to the community of Yahweh's people, then this verse provides confirmation for our argument that that privilege was vested in landowning households. Children, therefore, as long as they belonged securely within such groups, were included in the religious community and shared the privileges of its relationship with Yahweh. The literary form of the Hebrew poetry of the verse allows us to include women in that statement too. For just as both women and children are being driven out from their homes, so the women as well as the children are being deprived of "my glory." The description of them as "women of *my people*" also strengthens the view that *hāḏār* here refers to belonging to the people of Yahweh.

The family, then, as the primary sphere of the individual's experience of and sharing in the relationship with Yahweh, needed to be protected on two "fronts": (1) from the disruption of its *internal* authority by flouting of parental discipline, and (2) from the diminution or total loss of its landed property by *external* forces. Confirmation that both of these represented threats, not only to the family but also potentially to the nation's standing before God (in virtue of their threat to the household), is found in the list of curses in Deut. 27:15ff. In the first place comes the curse on the fundamental sin of idolatry. This is then immediately followed by curses which relate to both the above-mentioned aspects of threat to the family:

(1) Internal—"Cursed be he who dishonors his father or his mother"

(2) External—"Cursed be he who removes his neighbor's landmark."

3. Dependent Labor: Slaves and "Resident Aliens"

Here we are dealing with what is rather the reverse of the situation of women and children. The latter, we have seen, were included within the community of God's people by the natural and normal circumstances of belonging within an Israelite family living on Israel's land; yet they could, by their own action or by misfortune, find themselves "outside" that community. Slaves and aliens, in contrast, stood outside this relationship by natural circumstances, but in certain ways they could be—and were—brought "in" to share in its privileges.

As the results of our study so far would lead us to expect, the primary requirement was inclusion within, or very close association with, an Israelite landowning household. In the case of *slaves,* this could be taken for granted, and provided they were circumcised (Gen. 17:12ff.; Exod. 12:44) slaves were included in practically every aspect of Israel's cultic life and enjoyed most of the privileges of belonging to the religious community. Thus they too were present at festivals (Deut. 16:11ff.), were included in sabbath rest (Exod. 20:10), could eat the Passover (Exod. 12:44), and were even entitled to eat the holy things if they belonged to a priest's household (Lev. 22:11). Indeed, it is ironical that, by their total absorption within a family, slaves were in a better position in some respects than the "resident aliens," who may have had a higher social and legal status (cf. below, pp.159-160).

At this point we have to take issue again with Anthony Phillips, who considers that slaves did not belong to the covenant community owing to their lack (or loss, if they had once been free) of legal status. Thus he regards the seventh year release of slaves in Deut. 15 as designed to enable them to be present as free men at the covenant reading festival held every seventh year (Deut. 31). As slaves, he contends, they would not have been able to be present.[55] But in view of the clear inclusion of slaves in the ceremonies and privileges mentioned above, it is impossible to maintain that social freedom was a necessary condition of religious. participation. Belonging to a household was clearly a far more important factor. This fact gives additional point to the reluctance of a Hebrew slave to take advantage of the opportunity of freedom after six years and his preference to remain within the security of his master's house— additional, that is, to the emotional and economic reasons given in Exod. 21:5-6 and Deut. 15:13-14.

The position of the "resident aliens" (the *gērîm weṭôšāḇîm*), like

---

55. *Ancient Israel's Criminal Law,* pp. 16-17, 76-77. This idea is derived in fact from Abram Menes, *Die vorexilischen Gesetze Israels.* BZAW 50(1928): 82.

their identity and composition, is somewhat ambiguous in the Old Testament.[56] The fact that they did not share in the ownership of the land put a question mark over their membership in the religious community, whose greatest privilege was possession of the land as a gift from Yahweh. On the other hand, their functions as resident labor with Israelite landowning households did give them a *de facto* degree of inclusion within the community which was recognized in various practical ways. Thus, they could participate in the major festivals of Weeks and Booths (Deut. 16:11, 14) and are recorded as present at the covenant renewals or readings of the law (Josh. 8:33; Deut. 29:11; 31:12). The rules governing participation in the Passover appear at first sight to exclude them, but closer examination of this text (Exod. 12:43-49) confirms that the crucial factor governing eligibility was indeed full inclusion within an Israelite family.

43 *This is the ordinance of the passover; no foreigner (ben-nēḵer) shall eat of it;*
44 *but every (male) slave that [has been] bought for money may eat of it after you have circumcised him.*
45 *No sojourner (tôšāḇ) or hired servant (śāḵîr) may eat of it. . . .*
48 *[But] when a stranger shall [reside] with you (wᵉḵî-yagûr 'ittᵉḵā gēr) and would keep the passover to the* LORD, *let all his males be circumcised, then he may come near and keep it. . . .*

The contrast between v. 45 and v. 48 cannot be explained in terms of a distinction of status between the *gēr* and the other two classes, since on wider Old Testament evidence it seems incorrect to differentiate the "stranger" *(gēr)* from the "alien" *(tôšāḇ)* and the "hired laborer" *(śāḵîr)* in terms either of social status or of essential

56. For a thorough sociological survey of this whole stratum in Israelite society, see Mayer Sulzberger, "The Status of Labor in Ancient Israel," *JQR* N.S. 13 (1922/1923): 245-302, 397-459, which also takes account of earlier works in the area, such as Alfred Bertholet, *Die Stellung der Israeliten und der Juden zu den Fremden* (Freiburg im Breisgau and Leipzig: Mohr, 1896). See also E. Marmorstein, "The Origins of Agricultural Feudalism in the Holy Land," *PEQ* 85 (1953): 111-17; and Bernhard Lang, "The Social Organization of Peasant Poverty in Biblical Israel," *JSOT* 24 (1982): 47-63.

function. Rather, the most acceptable view is that "stranger" was the general term, within which "alien" and "hired laborer" were subdivisions according to respective occupations and means of livelihood.[57] Rather, the best sense of the passage is obtained as follows: vv. 43-45 set out the *general rule* regarding eligibility— "slaves may eat; foreigners and non-Israelite laborers may not." Then v. 48 introduces a significant *exception* regarding the last group. The circumstance which gives rise to the exception lies in the words $w^e \underline{k}i$-$yag\hat{u}r$ *$itt^e \underline{k}\bar{a}$ $g\bar{e}r$*, namely, "a 'stranger' who is residing *with* you." I would suggest that *$itt^e \underline{k}\bar{a}$* should here be taken to imply "in your employment and as part of your household." Mayer Sulzberger also argues that *'$\bar{e}\underline{t}$* and *'im* can sometimes have the technical sense of "in the employment of" (e.g., Lev. 25:35, 40; Gen. 29:14; 1 Chr. 4:23; Judg. 17:7-13).[58]

Judg. 17:7-13 provides an excellent case of precisely the sort of "family-membership-as-a-resident-employee" pattern which we are suggesting is involved in Exod. 12:48. Judg. 17:8 gives the Levite's intention as *$l\bar{a}g\hat{u}r$ $ba^{*a}\check{s}er$ $yim\dot{s}\bar{a}^*$*. In the light of the context it would not be stretching the words to translate "to settle down wherever he could find (employment)." It is then described how he went and dwelt *"with"* Micah (v. 10 *'im*, v. 11 *'$\bar{e}\underline{t}$*), in his employment (v. 10), as part of his household ("like one of his sons," v. 11), and within his house (v. 12). It is this type of family, residential employee that Exod. 12:48 envisages and in whose interest it modifies the law. In such a situation, if the "stranger" wishes to enter the family feast of the Passover, then, provided he and his dependents are circumcised, he is to be regarded as part of the family and allowed to partake.

This then is an example of the practical difference it made for those in the broad class of the *gērîm*, who did not have land of their own, to be attached to and under the protection[59] of an Israelite

57. Bertholet, p. 159; Sulzberger agrees on this. The basic difference appears to be that the * śā\underline{k}îr* was a short-term hired laborer, whereas the *tôšā\underline{b}* was a more or less permanent residential laborer.

58. Pp. 287ff.

59. We have already noted the "household" use of *'ēt* and *'im* as "under the protection of" (above, p. 64); cf. Horst Dietrich Preuss, "ēt [ē th], 'im," *TDOT* 1 (1977): 450.

household which did. In the absence of such patronage, "strangers" were in the same perilous position as others who lacked family and/or land, such as widows, orphans, and Levites. Like them, therefore, they are frequently commended to the charity and impartial justice of the rest of Israel.[60]

60. Peter D. Miscall, "The Concept of the Poor in the Old Testament" (diss., Harvard, 1972), appears to be in general agreement with the above brief glance at the social situation of the broad class of dependent labor (cf. the abstract of his thesis in HTR 65 [1972]: 600). He emphasizes an essentially social, rather than spiritual, understanding of the poor as "the landless, the disinherited, and the outcast." For a recent survey of the status of the gērîm and their relation to the ʿapiru, see Frank Anthony Spina, "Israelites as gērîm."

Conclusion to Part One

A. SUMMARY

The position of the household within the pattern of relationships between Israel, Yahweh, and the land, which we have now examined from various angles, may be expressed diagrammatically, by way of summary[1] (see p. 105).

The outer triangle represents the three major relationships of Israel's theological self-understanding: the primary relationship between Yahweh and Israel (AB); Yahweh as the ultimate owner of the land (AC); the land as given to Israel as an inheritance (CB). As we have seen, the family is not only the basic unit of Israelite social and kinship structure (BD), but also the basic unit of Israel's system of land tenure and the prime beneficiary of the inalienability principle (CD). These family-plus-land units were then seen to be the basic fabric upon which Israel's relationship with God rested (AD). Social, economic, and theological realms were thus bound together inextricably, all three having the family as the basic focal point at which

1. This is in fact an elaboration, by the inclusion of the family, of a similar diagrammatic presentation of the concept by H. Eberhard von Waldow, "Israel and Her Land: Some Theological Considerations," p. 502 in *A Light unto My Path*. Festschrift Jacob M. Myers (Philadelphia: Temple University Press, 1974).

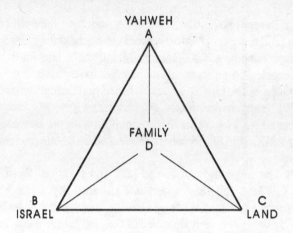

the conjunction of the three realms issued in ethical responsibilities and imperatives, to which we shall come in Part Two.

B. THE SOCIO-ECONOMIC FACTOR IN THE PROPHETS

To conclude this part of our study, I wish to recall and briefly amplify some remarks made above, concerning the light that this appreciation of the role of the landowning households sheds upon the motivation behind the social and economic emphasis of some prophetic preaching.

Much has been written on the economic history of the Monarchy period and the factors involved in the decline of the landowning peasantry.[2] Therefore, we need only summarize them. The seeds were sown during the reign of Solomon and included:

2. In addition to the general histories, see, e.g., Edward Neufeld, "Royal-Urban Society"; S. W. Baron, *A Social and Religious History*, 1:63-101; Alfred Bertholet, *A History of Hebrew Civilization* (London: G. G. Harrap and New York: Brentano's, 1926), pp. 235-253; Antonin Causse, "La Crise de la solidarité de famille et de clan dans l'ancien Israel," *RHPR* 10 (1930): 24-60; Theodore H. Robinson, "Some Economic and Social Factors in the History of Israel," *ExpTim* 45 (1933/1934): 264-69, 294-300; H. Eberhard von Waldow, "Social Responsibility and Social Structure in Early Israel," *CBQ* 32 (1970): 182-204; S. Herbert Bess, "Systems of Land Tenure in Ancient Israel," pp. 154-202; J. A. Dearman, *Property Rights*.

(1) The reorganization of the state, which, in the northern part at least (and there for political reasons), cut across the older kinship groupings in some cases.[3] By centralizing the bureaucratic control of economic and military affairs, it must have reduced the social importance of the kinship structure based on familial units.

(2) The acquisition of foreign territories where the concepts and practices of land tenure were incompatible with the Israelite rationale of inalienable family inheritance based on divine ownership of the land.[4]

(3) The imposition of forced levy and taxation. Even if and where this levy fell only upon the Canaanite population,[5] it still represented a substantial tax on Israelite landowners, inasmuch as they were being regularly deprived of their agricultural labor force.[6]

(4) The growth of a wealthy class, made possible by the vast influx of wealth from Solomon's empire. As well as hardship probably caused by the devaluation of money values (1 Kgs. 10:21), this wealth and the associated intrusion of royal grants and favors into land tenure[7] accelerated the accumulation of large estates at the expense of small farmers.

All these factors were detrimental to the social fabric of

3. Cf. T. N. D. Mettinger, *Solomonic State Officials*, pp. 111-127.

4. Mettinger, p. 127, regarding Solomon's policy of annexing Canaanite territories directly to the state rather than to existing tribes.

5. See Mettinger, pp. 134-39, for a detailed discussion of the problem of whether and how a distinction was made in this matter between Israelite and non-Israelite populations.

6. Cf. Mayer Sulzberger, "The Status of Labor in Ancient Israel," pp. 271-74. The burden of this taxation was a major factor in the revolt against Rehoboam. Abraham Malamat relates it to external political pressures and defense costs; "Origins of Statecraft in the Israelite Monarchy," *BA* 28 (1965): 61, repr. in *The Biblical Archaeologist Reader 3*, ed. Edward F. Campbell and David Noel Freedman; cf. also Donald J. Wiseman, "The Laws of Hammurabi Again," *JSS* 7 (1962): 168.

7. On this royal intrusion, see Bess, pp. 161-189; Mettinger, pp. 80-110; and Zafrira Ben Barak, "Meribaal and the System of Land Grants in Ancient Israel," *Bibl* 62 (1981): 73-91. Clues to this include 1 Sam. 22:7; 2 Sam. 13:23; 14:30; 24:24; 1 Kgs. 2:26; 16:24; 2 Chr. 26:10; 32:28. Some of the estates mentioned could not have belonged to their owners by tribal inheritance, so presumably they must have been obtained by royal grant.

landowning households. The process accelerated disastrously in the succeeding centuries and is well summarized by W. A. L. Elmslie:

> In the period of the two centuries 800-600 B.C. . . . the political and economic conditions in Palestine changed disastrously, and *the family ideal that had been the bond of society dissolved.* Battles with Syrian and Assyrian armies decimated the peasantry and ruined them economically. Authority and wealth rapidly concentrated in a few hands. New classes of men, lacking the old instinct of kinship-obligation, sprang up. The kings encouraged foreign trade; and now there were merchants pitilessly intent on gain (Amos 8:4-6), large landowners needing slaves and hirelings to work the fields which the impoverished peasants sold or forfeited for debt (Isa. 5:8); officials of the court ready to take bribes and deny justice to the landless, the widows, and the orphans now multiplied in both the kingdoms. The two royal cities . . . were shockingly corrupt. . . . So complete was the moral degeneracy that the temporary prosperity from 780 to 740 served only to increase the debauchery of the powerful, and make more poignant the sufferings of the poor.[8]

It is against this background that the prophets of the eighth century emerge with their condemnation of these evils.[9] In the past, the prominence of this socio-economic emphasis in these prophets has been accounted for in two ways.

(1) In early sociological studies the prophets stand out as social heroes, champions of the oppressed, indignant at injustice, proclaiming *new* ideals of equality and freedom.[10] The religious and ethical significance of their achievement was secondary to and

---

8. "Ethics," pp. 283-84 in *Record and Revelation,* ed. H. Wheeler Robinson (Oxford: Clarendon, 1938) (my italics). Cf. also the remarks of George E. Mendenhall, "Relation of the Individual," p. 103.

9. Amos 2:6-7; 3:10; 4:1; 5:7, 10ff.; 6:4-7; 8:4-6; Mic. 2:1-3, 8-9; 3:1-3, 9-11; 7:5-6; Hos. 5:10; 12:7-8; Isa. 1:15, 17, 23; 3:13-15; 5:8-10; 10:1-2; 33:15.

10. E.g., Antonin Causse, *Les Prophètes contre la Civilisation* (Paris: Alençon et Cahors, 1913), p. 15: "the first preachers of social justice"; Henry Schaeffer, *Social Legislation,* ch. 8; Louis Wallis, *God and the Social Process;* William Creighton Graham and Herbert G. May, *Culture and Conscience* (Chicago: University of Chicago Press, 1936), pp. 177ff.

derivative from this social struggle.[11] This viewpoint, however, was soon not only shown to be intrinsically inadequate,[12] but also externally challenged by new knowledge. The insight into the official cultic functions of some prophets had sociological implications, as pointed out by P. L. Berger.[13] They could no longer be seen as "social marginals" in total, implacable opposition to the "establishment" but rather as operating within the social structure though radically challenging it. Also it was seen that much of their social message was not *in itself* unique nor unprecedented. Both Erling Hammershaimb[14] and F. Charles Fensham[15] pointed out the Canaanite and Mesopotamian precedents and parallels for the basic social concern expressed by the prophets.

(2) A fresh theological appreciation of the prophets accompanied the upsurge of interest in the covenant, in the mid-1950s and 1960s. No longer regarded as innovators, the prophets were seen against a background of covenant and legal traditions already centuries old. Furthermore, they were seen as calling the people *back* to obedience to the known demands of the covenant relationship which were presupposed in their preaching.[16] Within this framework, the social and economic evils were regarded as symptomatic of the nation's rebellion, as evidence that they had "broken" the covenant.

11. Cf. Wallis' remark (*God and the Social Process,* pp. 14-15) on social evolution moving into "higher and higher ethical planes. . . . Thus the deeper concerns of religion were liberated from the secular process which gave rise to prophecy."

12. Herbert G. May ("A Sociological Approach to Hebrew Religion," p. 99) draws attention to the dangers and limitations of the attempt to "completely comprehend religion in terms of contemporary sociological factors." Cf. also Nahum N. Glatzer's review of Max Weber, *Ancient Judaism* (Glencoe, Ill.: Free Press, 1952), *Journal of Religion* 34 (1954): 133-35.

13. "Charisma and Religious Innovation: the Social Location of Israelite Prophecy," *American Sociological Review* 28 (1963): 940-950. See also Robert R. Wilson, *Prophecy and Society in Ancient Israel* (Philadelphia: Fortress, 1980).

14. "On the Ethics of the Old Testament Prophets," *VTS* 7 (1960): 75-101.

15. "Widow, Orphan and the Poor in Ancient Near Eastern Legal and Wisdom Literature," *JNES* 21 (1963): 129-139.

16. Ronald E. Clements, *Prophecy and Covenant,* is representative of this line of thought at that time. The complexity of the relationship between prophetic preaching and pentateuchal laws, with the added complication of royal statutes, is examined by Dearman, ch. 1.

Whereas, on the older sociological view, the prophets were primarily
concerned with socio-economic matters and in the process innovated
radically new religious and ethical concepts, this later theological
view saw the prophets as primarily concerned with the religious issue
of the threat to Israel's relationship with Yahweh, and in the process
pointing to socio-economic evils as evidence for their case.

Although it is the second of these approaches which undoubtedly
has the right perspective, it still does not seem to me to have brought
the socio-economic factor into true focus. The abuses in that sphere
were not merely a "symptom" of Israel's degeneracy. They constituted in themselves, in fact, a major "virus" which threatened the stability of society and *thereby also* the relationship with Yahweh. The
prophets denounced them so vehemently because they saw in them
an *intrinsic* threat to that relationship through the effect they were
having on the units of landowning households. This familial aspect
becomes explicit in such texts as Mic. 2:1-3, 8-9; 7:5-6;[17] and Isa.
5:8-10. If, as we have sought to establish in the preceding chapters,
the experience of the relationship with God was vested in the household units of Israel—just as possession of the land was vested in
inalienable family inheritances—then the socio-economic forces and
changes which were destroying these family land units would inevitably and "internally" destroy the nation's relationship with God as
well. The theological status of Israel was earthed and rooted in the
socio-economic fabric of their kinship structure and their land tenure,
and it was this fabric which was being dissolved by the acids of debt,
dispossession, and latifundism. The prophetic protest against these
evils, therefore, must be illumined by the fact that there was an
essential link between the social and economic facts of life and the
theological self-understanding of Israel. That link was the family.[18]

17. On this aspect, cf. Leslie C. Allen, "Micah's Social Concern," *Vox Evan-
gelica* 8 (1973): 22-32.
18. The essential structural link between the social structure of Israel and their
religious system is a major part of Norman K. Gottwald's study, *The Tribes of
Yahweh*, though he presents it from an ideological perspective very different from
my own theological and ethical position. Cf. my reflections on the subject in
Christopher J. H. Wright, "The Ethical Relevance of Israel as a Society," *Transformation* 1/4 (1984): 11-21.

C. FROM ISRAEL'S LAND TO CHRISTIAN FELLOWSHIP

We cannot, however, conclude this part of our study without noting that there developed in Israel an awareness that their relationship with God, while it was undoubtedly grounded in and experienced through the whole socio-economic realm of land and family, did transcend that realm and was not permanently or exclusively bound to it. We have already noted this feature inherent in Israel's sonship, and the reassertion of Israel's status as the people of Yahweh even after the total loss of the land, in both priestly and deuternomistic theology. Then there is the fact that Amos can describe as "righteous" those who had been deprived of precisely those things—land and family—upon which, externally, their "right" relationship with Yahweh depended, whereas those who now possessed these visible qualifications in abundance he denounced as violating the whole essence of that relationship.

Most significant, however, in my view, is the fact that in the developing eschatological emphasis in later Israelite prophecy there can be discerned a "loosening" of—almost a dispensing with—the ancient family land basis in the future "constitution" of the relationship between God and his people. This is entailed in the descriptions of its all-inclusiveness, which will bring into full and assured relationship with God categories of people whose position, on a family-land criterion, would have been ambiguous or insecure. Thus, for example, in Isa. 56:3-7 the doubts of the foreigner, who had no stake in the land, and of the eunuch, who could have no family or posterity, are alike allayed by the promise of permanent acceptance and inclusion in the new covenant. Likewise, in Isa. 54:1 the barren woman is called on to rejoice. Thus, too, Ezekiel's idealized picture of the future land tenure of Israel makes a point of explicitly including those who previously had to exist in a state of parlous dependence—the "aliens" *(gērîm)* (Ezek. 47:22). Their share in the inheritance of God's people will no longer depend on charity and fortune, but will be permanently secure.

It is this eschatological expectation which the New Testament sees as fulfilled in the inclusion of the Gentiles in the people of God through Christ by the work of the Holy Spirit. It was Paul's "boast" in Christ to have been the vehicle of this new dimension of the gospel, and the Old Testament background of this part of his message is very clear in the classic exposition of it in Eph. 2:11–3:6.[19]

Paul begins by summarizing the previous position of the Gentiles in terms equivalent to the position of those who had had no share in the land-kinship membership of Israel: "excluded from citizenship in Israel and foreigners to the covenants of the promise" (Eph. 2:12, NIV). Then, having described the work of Christ on the Cross as the breaking down of the barrier, making peace and providing access to God for believing Jew and Gentile alike, he returns to the Old Testament imagery to describe the new position of the Gentiles in Christ: "Consequently, you are no longer foreigners and aliens [words that correspond to *gērîm* and *tôšāḇîm*], but fellow citizens with God's people and members of God's household" (2:19, NIV)—language of permanence, security, and inclusion. And as the climax of this outline of "his gospel," Paul sums up the new position of the Gentiles in three words in 3:6, one of which he appears to have coined. They are "joint heirs" *(synklēronóma)*, a "joint body" *(sýnsōma)*, and "joint sharers" *(synmétocha)* with Israel in the promise in the Messiah—Jesus. The inheritance language, as we have seen, evokes the triangular pattern of relationships between God, Israel, and the land.

So then, by incorporation into the Messiah, all nations are enabled to enter upon the privileges and responsibilities of God's people. Christ himself takes over the significance and function of the land kinship qualification. "In Christ," answering to "in the land," denotes a status and a relationship, a position of inclusion and security, a privilege with attendant responsibilities. This is the *typological* understanding which was referred to briefly in the Introduction. But what then has become of the socio-economic dimension of the land which we found to have been of such importance in Old Testament Israel? Has it simply been transcended, as spiritualized and forgotten? By no means.

19. I have discussed this further in *An Eye for an Eye / Living As the People of God*, ch. 4.

The role of the Holy Spirit in the incorporation of Jew and Gentile together into God's new community in Christ is referred to twice in the passage we have just considered (Eph. 2:18, 22). We noted earlier (above, p. 22) how Paul even regards the gift of the Spirit itself as the fulfillment of the promise to Abraham in Gal. 3:14. In that context he also relates the *oneness* of believers in Christ to their status as seed and heirs of Abraham (Gal. 3:28-29). Now this oneness of believers in Christ and their shared experience of Christ is no mere abstract "spiritual" concept. On the contrary, it has far-reaching practical implications in the social *and* economic realms, both of which are included in the New Testament understanding and practice of "fellowship."

A study of the Greek root *koinōn-* in the New Testament reveals that a substantial number of the occurrences of words formed or compounded from it signify, or are in contexts which relate to, actual social and economic relationships between Christians—a far cry from that watery "togetherness" which is the common popular understanding of the term "fellowship." Some examples will make the point. The first consequence of the outpouring of the Spirit at Pentecost was a new community who, in "devoting themselves to . . . the fellowship" (*tē koinōnía*; author's translation), shared everything in common (Acts 2:42, 44) and ensured that nobody was in need (4:34). In Rom. 12:13 believers are urged to share hospitality with the saints *(koinōnoúntes)*. In 1 Tim. 6:18 the rich are to be commanded to be "generous" *(koinōnikoús);* the same duty is laid on all Christians in Heb. 13:16. Paul refers to this financial collection among the Greek churches for the aid of the Judaean Christians as "an act of fellowship" (*koinōnían tinà,* Rom. 15:26, author's translation), which he justified on the grounds that, if the Gentiles had shared *(ekoinṓnēsan)* spiritual blessings from the Jews, they owed it to them to share material blessings (v. 27). The same reciprocal principle applies in the relationship between the teacher and the taught in Gal. 6:6 *(koinōneítō).* Indeed, in commending the Corinthians for their eagerness to share in the financial *koinōnía* collection (2 Cor. 8:4; 9:13), Paul describes it as proof of their *obedience to the gospel,* implying that such concrete economic evidence of fellowship was of the essence of a genuine Christian profession. Is it then coincidental that when Paul's own gospel was accepted as authentic in Jerusalem by means of the "right hand of *koinōnía*," he was immediately asked to "remember the poor"—as if in proof (Gal. 2:9-10)? His collection for the Gentiles did indeed bear out his professed eagerness to honor that gospel fellowship. Likewise, when he thanks God for the Philippians' "partnership in the gospel" (Phil. 1:5), the rest of the letter makes it clear that he is thinking concretely, not just spiritually. They had been partners *(synkoinōnói)* with Paul (Phil. 1:7) in practical financial support (4:15ff.).

The extent of this kind of language in the New Testament understanding of fellowship leads me to the view that it has deep roots in the socio-economic ethics of the Old Testament. There are so many similarities which show that the experience of fellowship in its full, rich New Testament sense fulfills analogous theological functions for the Christian as the possession of land did for Old Testament Israelites. Both must be seen as part of the purpose and pattern of redemption—not just accidental or incidental to it. The explicit purpose of the Exodus was the enjoyment of the rich blessing of God in his "good land"; the goal of redemption through Christ is "for a sincere love of the brethren" (1 Pet. 1:22), with all its practical implications. Both are linked to the status of sonship and the related themes of inheritance and promise. Both thereby constitute a proof of an authentic relationship with God as part of his redeemed community. For fellowship, like the land, has limits, so that the person who departs permanently from it—or refuses to accept it—shows that he has no real part in God's people (cf. 1 John 2:19; Matt. 18:15-17).

Above all, both are *shared* experiences: the land, by the nature of the Israelite economic system as we have outlined it; fellowship, by very definition of the word *koinōnía*. This gives to both that deeply practical mutual responsibility which pervades both Old and New Testament ethics. There is the same concern for the poor and needy (cf. 1 John 3:17), the same ideal of equality among God's people, both economically (cf. 2 Cor. 8:13-15 with its Old Testament allusion) and socially (cf. Jas. 2:1-7). There is even the same prophetic indignation at those whose sin deprives or defrauds fellow members of God's people of their rightful share in what God has given for the enjoyment of all his people. Compare with the Old Testament prophets' condemnations of the unjust oppressors who drove fellow Israelites off their land Jesus' strictures on those who refuse to forgive a brother (Matt. 18:21-35), Paul's horror at the factionalism and lack of love at Corinth and the priority he gives in his various lists of sins to those which harm the fellowship (e.g., Eph. 4:25ff.; Phil. 2:1-4, 14; Col. 3:8ff., etc.), and John's refusal to accept as a child of God the one who hates his brother (1 John 2:9-11; 4:7ff., etc.).

So then, this is one way in which the socio-economic thrust of Old Testament ethics "feeds through" into the New Testament and is made available for Christian ethical reflection. Christianity *has* a social basis, which has transcended the land and kinship structure of Old Testament Israel—but not in such a way as to make that original structure irrelevant. In this, as in so many other ways, Christ and all that flows from Christ "fulfills" the Old Testament, taking it up and transforming it into something that can be the experience of everyman—everyman in Christ. There is thus great perception in a passing remark of the Jewish scholar Raphael Loewe: "the sociological basis on which Christianity rests is not the tie of kinship, as is the case of Judaism, but that of fellowship—fellowship in Christ."

Those who desire the spiritual renewal of the inner life of the Church—of its "fellowship" in the New Testament sense—would thus do well to take seriously its deep roots in the social and economic soil of the Old Testament. This, of course, is by no means to confine the relevance of Old Testament socio-economic ethics to this typological application. But, in view of the organic unity of the Israel of God in both testaments, it is certainly the proper place to start.

PART TWO | Land and Property Ethics

INTRODUCTION

Our aim in the next two chapters is to see how the socio-economic and theological pattern developed in Part One was expressed in practical detail. That is, we will examine the ethical principles relevant to family land and property, the rights and responsibilities of ownership, and their embodiment in laws and institutions. In order to set this part of our investigation also in its theological context, we shall first discuss briefly the basis on which property rights in the Old Testament may be said to rest.

The widest basis that the Old Testament provides for its property ethics is the creation belief. It includes two complementary concepts relevant to our purpose. On the one hand, God as Creator is LORD and ultimate owner of all created things. Therefore, any claim of ownership made by mankind is secondary and subordinate. Mankind is a steward of creation; they have no absolute ownership. On the other hand, God has given the earth to mankind as his trustee. Part of the implied purpose of making mankind in his own image was so that they should be given dominion over the rest of the created order. That seems a fair deduction from the close conjunction of the two ideas in Gen. 1:26-27. So within the context of that conferred dominion over a given earth, mankind's exercise of discretionary powers of ownership and use over the earth and its resources is morally and theologically legitimate. The Psalmists express this duality:

> The earth is the LORD'S, and everything in it. (Ps. 24:1, NIV)

but also:

> The earth he has given to man. (Ps. 115:16, NIV)

and also:

> You have made him ruler over the works of your hands. (Ps. 8:6, NIV)

If we look at each of these aspects more carefully, we also find that very soon they link up with other aspects of Old Testament theology.

A. DIVINE OWNERSHIP

We have already studied the belief in divine ownership of the land of Canaan as part of Israel's land theology. But, as has just been noted, the Old Testament also has a wider concept of God's ownership as extending over the whole earth and including every living and inanimate thing upon it.[1] Everything, therefore, which a person, family, or nation can possess comes as a gift from God. This includes the land itself, as well as wives and children,[2] all material prosperity,[3] and even the power to get it.[4] It is insufficient, however, to leave the concept in such abstract, "neutral" terms, for there is another significant dimension of Old Testament belief in God's universal ownership. That is the belief that God's sovereign right of disposal over creation as a whole is exercised particularly and specially on behalf of Israel, his own redeemed people. This is certainly the thrust of Deut. 10:14-15, for example:

1. Ps. 24:1; 89:11; 95:4-5; Jer. 27:4ff.; Hag. 2:8; 1 Chr. 29:11.
2. Ps. 127:3-5; Prov. 19:14; Job 1:21.
3. Hos. 2:8; Jer. 5:24-25; Ps. 65:9-13; 1 Chr. 29:14.
4. Deut. 8:18.

> To the LORD your God belong the heavens, even the highest
> heavens, the earth and everything in it. Yet the LORD set his
> affection on your forefathers and loved them, and he chose you,
> their descendants, above all the nations, as it is today. (NIV)

This shading off of the creation belief into the realm of Israel's
experience of election and redemption indicates yet again the
importance of the latter in determining Israel's property ethics.

B. DIVINE GIFT

Without getting involved in the argument over what precisely the
image of God *is*, it will be allowed that one of the functions of that
image is to enable mankind to exercise dominion over the earth,
which God has given into their care for their use (Gen. 1:26-29).
Certainly, this is an aspect of our humanity that the Old Testament
asserts elsewhere (cf. Ps. 8:6ff.). Mankind does, therefore, have "an
accredited discretionary power"[5] over the rest of creation, inasmuch
as God has given it to them. But insofar as this can be called
"ownership," it can only apply to the common ownership of the
material resources of the world. It is not possible to rest arguments
for the legitimacy of *individual,* private property on the "creation
ordinance" to "subdue the earth . . . and have dominion" alone.[6] The
earth is given to all mankind. The creation narrative can only justify
(indeed it requires) shared use of its resources. This implies that the
right of all people to have access to, and use of, the resources of the
earth is a prior right to the right of any person or group to claim
private ownership and use of some section of those resources—an
important ethical axiom for a biblical view of economics. This is
not to say that the Old Testament has no place for legitimate
personal wealth and property. Its emphasis, however, is that such

---

5. The phrase is borrowed from a definition of ownership suggested by the
sociologist Thorstein B. Veblen, "The Beginnings of Ownership," p. 358.

6. Nor on the Eighth Commandment alone, as Robert Gnuse has shown in *You
Shall Not Steal: Community and Property in the Biblical Tradition* (Maryknoll,
N.Y.: Orbis, 1985).

legitimate personal wealth derives not from mankind's supremacy over nature, but from the gift and bounty of God. (It recognizes, of course, that, given the effects of sin and the fall, personal wealth can often be illegitimate—the result of injustice, theft, oppression, greed, etc.). Thus, although Ps. 115 does express the idea of the earth belonging to mankind in a creation sense (v. 16: "the earth he has given to man" [NIV]), when it comes to praying for *individual* prosperity, it does so on the understanding that it will be as a blessing of *Yahweh* (vv. 14-15), a blessing characteristic of the historic love and covenant faithfulness of God to Israel (vv. 1, 12) rather than as a result of his creatorhood (v. 15b).

Both these aspects of the creation belief, divine ownership and divine gift, lead us inevitably to realize that for Israel the most significant and consequential basis for property ethics was the experience of historical redemption and the relationship with God that arose therefrom. This affected the matter of property ethics in two ways. On the one hand, it gave legitimacy and protection to a person's property, within a certain framework. Provided the phrase is carefully explained, this can be termed "property rights," and this is the subject of Chapter 4. On the other hand, it set clear limitations on a person's exercise of those rights, in the form of wide-ranging responsibilities to God, to his family, and to other people. These are examined in Chapter 5.

4 | *Property Owners' Rights*

Although the legitimacy of private individual property rights can hardly be grounded in creation beliefs, we have seen (above, pp. 117-18) that for an Israelite these rights did have a very strong basis in the concept of Yahweh's ownership of the land and the system of family land tenure which that concept sanctioned. The head of an Israelite family owned the land of his patrimony legitimately, not simply by the technical legality of his inheritance but ultimately because he and his family held it from Yahweh. This "divine right," as it were, was protected in two practical ways: by the inalienability of family land and by the security under the law of property in general. We shall examine these in turn.

A. INALIENABILITY OF FAMILY LAND: LAND REDEMPTION AND THE JUBILEE

We come now to examine the practical procedures which embodied the theological principle of Lev. 25:23 as they are laid down in the verses which follow, 25:24-28.

24 *Throughout the country that you hold as a possession, you must provide for the redemption of the land.*
25 *If one of your countrymen becomes poor and sells some of his*

> *property, his nearest relative is to come and redeem what his
> countryman has sold.*
> 26 *If, however, a man has no one to redeem it for him but he himself
> prospers and acquires sufficient means to redeem it,*
> 27 *he is to determine the value for the years since he sold it and
> refund the balance to the man to whom he sold it; he can then
> go back to his own property.*
> 28 *But if he does not acquire the means to repay him, what he sold
> will remain in the possession of the buyer until the Year of
> Jubilee. It will be returned in the Jubilee, and he can then go
> back to his property.*

Three possible situations are envisaged in these verses as
resulting from the sale of property by an impoverished Israelite: (1)
the recovery of the property by a kinsman redeemer, the *gōʾēl*, (2)
the recovery of the property by the seller himself if he later has the
means, and (3) the eventual return of the sold property to the seller
in the Year of Jubilee.

It is very probable that there is a combination in these verses
of general *redemption* laws with particular *Jubilee* provisions,
owing to certain common features, but this combination has caused
some confusion. One aspect of this confusion is the question
whether, in the first of the three cases, the "redeemer," having
bought the property, restored it to the impoverished brother or kept
it for himself. Some have argued for the former, particularly on the
grounds of consistency with the other two provisions, in which
clearly the brother recovers his property.[1] But "consistency" here

---

1. Martin Noth (*Leviticus.* OTL [1965], p. 189) takes the view that the
redeemer bought the land "not in order to retain it himself, but only to return it to
the original owner." The same view is expressed by Donald A. Leggett (*Levirate
and Goel*, p. 95), explicitly on the grounds of understanding "the texts as we have
them"—i.e., for the sake of consistency. The majority of scholars, however, prefer
the view that the redeemed property was retained by the *gōʾēl*. Cf. Johannes
Pedersen, *Israel: Its Life and Culture* 1:84; William McKane, "Ruth and Boaz,"
Transactions of the Glasgow University Oriental Society 19 (1961-1962): 35;
David Daube, *The New Testament and Rabbinic Judaism* (London: University of
London Press, 1956), pp. 272-73. Both Edward Neufeld, "Socio-economic Back-
ground of *Yōbēl* and *Semiṭṭâ*," *Rivista degli Studi Orientali* 33 (1958): 76; and

may be an unnecessary demand if, on the one hand, the juxtaposition of redemption and Jubilee provisions is purely literary and if, as we shall argue, in actual practice the redemption custom and the Jubilee institution had somewhat different aims and functions. These differences have been obscured by the "telescoped" literary form of Lev. 25, but can nevertheless be discerned. Basically, the difference was that redemption had the main aim of preserving the land of the "kin group," whereas the Jubilee was concerned with restoration of the land of individual *households*.[2] Let us see how this worked.

1. Redemption

It has been pointed out that Lev. 25:25, 35, 39, and 47 all begin with or contain the phrase "if one of your countrymen becomes poor (*yāmûk*)" and probably represent the original series of *redemption* regulations, unconnected, at first, with Jubilee regulations. The first three of the references may be regarded as the descending stages of poverty of an Israelite and the corresponding steps, required at each stage, of the kinsman with the will and the means to act as "redeemer."

a. First Stage

Initially (v. 25), the Israelite in difficulties offers a portion of his landed property for sale, and this is redeemed or preempted by the "redeemer."

It is debated whether v. 25 refers to redemption proper (i.e., buying back property already sold to a third party) or to preemption (i.e., buying property from a kinsman before it is put on the open market). Advocates of consistency with the other two provisions in vv. 26, 28 argue for redemption proper, since in those cases the land

---

Robert G. North, *Sociology of the Biblical Jubilee*, pp. 165ff., are noncommittal, however, on this question.

2. Cf. F. P. W. Buhl, "Social Institutions," p. 738 (with reservations on his relating the Jubilee to "personal possession of the individual").

clearly passes out of the poor brother's possession. However, of the only two clear cases of land redemption in actual operation in the Old Testament, one is obviously preemption (Jer. 32), while the other (Ruth 4) is probably a case of redemption of land which had previously been sold. It is impossible to be certain in this latter case, but I find myself persuaded by the view that *māk^erâ* in Ruth 4:3 should be translated by a full past tense, and taken to mean that Boaz is proposing the redemption from its present occupants of Elimelech's and Naomi's land which they *had sold*—in their poverty—*before* they emigrated to Moab. It would appear therefore that either redemption or preemption is possible as an interpretation of Lev. 25:25, and the law may intend to allow for both. What *is* clear is that it is the kinsman's duty to see that property stays within the kinship group—by whatever means.[3]

b. Second Stage

If the person still cannot stay solvent, presumably even after several such sales (v. 35), it is then the kinsman's duty to maintain him as a dependent laborer and with interest free loans (vv. 36ff.).

The fact that the poor brother was to be supported with *loans* (not plain gifts) gives added weight to the persuasion that in v. 25 the "redeemer" kept the property he had redeemed (until the Jubilee) rather than having restored it to the brother. This is especially so if it was a matter of preemption, for to buy some land from a kinsman and then return the land to him forthwith would have amounted, in effect, to nothing more than a simple gift of money.

c. Third Stage

As a last resort (v. 39), having no land left to sell or use as security for loans, the person is reduced to selling himself and his family entirely into the service of his kinsman, in which case he is not to

3. For a fully documented study of the complex problems of this verse, see Leggett, pp. 211-222. In addition to the literature cited by Leggett, see also Herbert C. Brichto, "Kin, Cult, Land and Afterlife," pp. 14-16; and Raymond Westbrook, "Redemption of Land," *ILR* 6 (1971): 372-73.

be treated like a slave, but again as a dependent laborer.[4] These were the stages in the exercise of redemption.

2. Jubilee

The *Jubilee* then functions as an "override" to all of this, in that it provides for the restoration to the impoverished Israelite of his freedom (if he had got as far as losing that) and of all his original land. This has the implication that the portion of land redeemed or preempted in v. 25 (assuming that it had been kept by the "redeemer") was also released and restored to the original owner (or more probably his descendants) in the Jubilee.

It would make nonsense of the law if land redeemed as provided for in v. 25 were not to be returned to the original seller in the Jubilee, as provided for in v. 28. For if land sold to an "outsider" could be recovered in the Jubilee but land redeemed or preempted by a kinsman could not, there would be a strong preference to sell outside the kinship group, which is precisely what the law was designed to prevent.

This argument is supported by v. 33 in the MT, which concerns the redemption of houses in the cities of the Levites:

> *Whoever redeems from the Levites, then shall go forth* (be released) *the sale of the house in a city of their possession* (reading *bêt 'îr* as in *BH³*, following the LXX), *in the Jubilee. (author's translation)*

It was probably the misunderstanding that what was redeemed did not need to be released in the Jubilee, perhaps because it was thought to be restored to the original seller by the act of redemption, that led Jerome to insert a negative before the first verb: "whoever does *not* redeem (from the Levites)." *BHS* adopts this insertion, and it is followed by the RSV and NEB. Robert G. North is also puzzled by this verse, for the reason just given: "if it has already been redeemed, it need not be restored in the jubilee."[5] But this is not the case. If, in

---

4. The matter of the release of such persons and the comparison with other slave release legislation is dealt with in Chapter 8.

5. P. 169, n. 2.

order to maintain the property within the kinship group, a kinsman redeems a house from a Levite *and keeps it*, then the operation of the Jubilee is to restore the house to its original owner and seller.

It can be seen, therefore, that the redemption procedures were designed to keep land within the wider "kinship group"—specifically, the *mišpāḥâ*[6]—whereas the Jubilee was intended to restore the tenure of land to the smaller household units within the "kinship group." It was a necessary "override" inasmuch as the regular operation of redemption over a period could result in the whole territory of a clan coming into the hands of comparatively few families with the rest of the families in a kind of dependent serfdom. The Jubilee was an attempt to prevent this and to preserve the social fabric of multiple family landholdings by a restoration twice a century—that is, every few generations.

This fact—that, whereas redemption could be practiced at any time, the Jubilee only occurred twice a century—shows that the right of inalienability was for the benefit of the family and not a private, individual right, except insofar as the individual head of the household represented the whole family (past, present, and future). It was *not* provided that an Israelite who, for whatever reason, failed to maintain his property should automatically and immediately have it restored to him, but that a person's descendants should not have to suffer in perpetuity the consequence of the economic collapse of his generation. The specific mention of children in Lev. 25:41, 54 points to the fact that more often than not the Jubilee would benefit the posterity of the impoverished Israelite rather than the impoverished person himself.

The Jubilee, therefore, has to be seen as an attempt to preserve, or periodically to restore, the economic viability and independence of the smaller family-plus-land units. In the light of the importance of these units as the basis of Israel's national relationship with Yahweh, this amounts to far more than an idealistic measure of

---

6. This is clear from the list of potential redeemers, given in v. 49, for one who has entered debt bondage to a "stranger." It concludes with "one from the flesh of his 'kinship group.'" The redemption provisions were thus concerned to preserve both the territory and the persons of the "kinship group"—a further confirmation of our estimate of its importance in Chapter 2.

social justice, but rather is a serious attempt to maintain the integrity of the socio-economic ground of the nation's theological identity. This is underlined three times in the reminders of the deliverance from Egypt and the nature of the relationship thereby established between God and Israel (vv. 38, 42, 55), as well as being involved in the assertions of v. 23 (see above, pp. 63-65).

It is this concern for the economic viability of the *family* as the central point of the Jubilee which explains the exceptions made regarding city houses in vv. 29-30. No doubt these distinctions regarding walled cities (village property was counted as part of the rural land) reflect the urbanized system of pre-Israelite, Canaanite tenure and the necessary concessions which were made to it. But it is also true, as S. Herbert Bess points out, that "Israel was less concerned about redemption of city property for the reason that *it was not the means of economic support for a family* in the same way as rural property."[7] Nor did the buying and selling of city houses have any effect on the overall territory of the "kinship group," and so did not need to be controlled by any permanent right of redemption either.

3. Was the Jubilee Practicable?

Sooner or later, of course, in any discussion of Lev. 25, one must face the question: were the Jubilee regulations "real" legislation— that is, practicable and effective—or were they academic and utopian? Supporters of the first alternative regard the law as belonging to Israel's early, premonarchic period, whereas those who take the latter view attribute the formulation of the law to the same period as they attribute the compilation of the chapter—the exilic era.[8]

7. "Systems of Land Tenure in Ancient Israel," p. 82 (my italics).
8. Confining ourselves to those scholars who have written on the subject in this century, we find that the majority argue for an early date for the origin of the Jubilee institution: e.g., Henry Schaeffer, *Hebrew Tribal Economy and the Jubilee,* p. 1; Anton Jirku, "Die israelitische Jobeljahr," p. 178 in *Reinhold-Seeberg-Festschrift,* 2, ed. Wilhelm Koepp (Leipzig: D. W. Scholl, 1929); J. P. M. van der Ploeg, "Studies in Hebrew Law," *CBQ* 13 (1951): 171; S. Stein, "The Laws on Interest in the Old Testament," *JTS* N.S. 4 (1953): 164; North, p. 212; Hans Wildberger, "Israel und sein Land"; Neufeld.
Those who place it in the late, exilic period include: E. Ginzberg, "Studies in

Actually, the validity of our arguments hitherto does not wholly
depend on a decisive answer to the literary-historical question—
even if it were possible to give one, which for lack of evidence it is
not. For we have been concerned to elucidate the ethical principles
which motivated the framing of such a law, and in a sense they are
unaffected by whether the law was an early attempt to control what
should happen or a later reflection on what should have happened
and might yet be introduced.

Nevertheless, granted that the aim of the Jubilee was, as
outlined above, to maintain or restore the socio-economic basis
of the nation's relationship with God, the likelihood of its being
an exilic or postexilic invention is reduced and the case for placing
its origins in Israel's early history is correspondingly strengthened. This follows from the evidence referred to above (p. 110)
of an awareness in the later period that Israel's theological identity
and national relationship with God could no longer be so closely
tied to a socio-economic system, and that land ownership and
family membership could no longer have such critical weight in
the matter of one's standing within the religious community. If
this were so, it is hard to see what purpose would have been served
by framing new legislation designed to preserve these very things.
It seems to make much better sense to find the roots of the Jubilee
in the early period, in agreement with a majority of scholars at
present. The silence of the preexilic texts,[9] of course, makes it
impossible to prove this view, but does not thereby prove its

---

the Economics of the Bible," p. 368; Roland de Vaux, *Ancient Israel*, p. 177;
Arthur M. Brown, "The Concept of Inheritance in the Old Testament," pp. 216-17;
R. Westbrook, "Jubilee Laws," *ILR* 6 (1971): 211ff.; Rudolf Kilian, *Literarkritische
und formgeschichtliche Untersuchung des Heiligkeitsgezetses*, pp. 130ff.

My inclination to agree with the former group is based not only on their majority,
but more on the fact that they include those who appear to have done the most detailed
and substantial work on the subject and also those who have brought to bear the
additional light of comparable ancient Near Eastern practices (see below, n. 10).

9. The silence is perhaps not total, if one finds an allusion to a Jubilee Year in
Isa. 37:30. The verse appears to refer to a double year of fallow, which would have
been a particularly disastrous time to have to endure a military invasion as well.
But there can be no certainty, and it is perhaps more likely that Isaiah is referring
to the inevitable consequences for agriculture of a foreign invasion—i.e., an
enforced fallow.

opposite—namely, that it was either nonexistent or never put into effective operation. Likewise, it is inadmissible to deny that the Jubilee *could* ever have been put into practice on the grounds that it would have been too severe an economic upheaval, since similar customs are known to have been actually practiced in Mesopotamia from very early times.[10]

In conclusion, we may say that this right enjoyed by the Israelite landowner, that his land should remain inalienably in his family, was based, not on a vague belief in the rights of property nor merely on the tribal system of land ownership, but (1) on the specific theological belief in God's prior ownership of the land (as discussed in Chapter 2) and (2) on the importance of preserving the

10. On the Mesopotamian antecedents and parallels to the biblical Jubilee and related institutions cf. Cyrus H. Gordon, "Parallèles nouziens aux lois et coutumes de l'Ancien Testament," *RB* 44 (1935): 38ff.; Jacob J. Finkelstein, "Ammiṣaduqa's Edict and the Babylonian 'Law Codes,'" *Journal of Cuneiform Studies* 15 (1961): 104, n. 19 (recording the fact of *mišarum* debt releases as early as the third millennium B.C.); Hildegard and Julius Lewy, "The Origin of the Week and the Oldest West Asiatic Calendar," *HUCA* 17 (1942/1943): 1-152c (comparing the seven- and fifty-year cycles of the Old Testament *šᵉmiṭṭâ* and Jubilee with the Assyro-Amorite calendar of the second millennium, they observe: "In view of the fact that the Jubilee cycle can be traced in the Assyrian sources of the early second millennium, the opinion . . . that this cycle represents a late, even post-exilic, institution, is, of course to be abandoned" [p. 97, n. 391]); Cyrus H. Gordon, "Sabbatical Cycle or Seasonal Pattern," *Orientalia* N.S. 22 (1953): 79-81 (comparing Ugaritic parallels, he says: "The view that the Sabbatical and Jubilee cycles are late and artificial legislation can no longer be maintained" [p. 81]); Julius Lewy, "The Biblical Institution of *Dᵉrôr* in the Light of Akkadian Documents," *Eretz-Israel* 5 (1958): 21*-31* (on the basis of the Amorite influence he links Lev. 25 with Israel's premonarchic period [p. 29]); Jacob J. Finkelstein, "Some New *Mišarum* Material and its Implications," *Studies in Honor of B. Landsberger*. Assyriological Studies 16 (Chicago, 1965): 233-246.

"In the light of the *mišarum* material discovered and published in recent years," argues Moshe Weinfeld (*Deuteronomy and the Deuteronomic School*, p. 153, n. 1), ". . . the whole problem of shemitta and Jôbel (sic) in ancient Israel has to be reconsidered. The laws in Lev. 25 cannot be seen anymore as post-exilic but, on the contrary, as reflecting very ancient tribal reality." This evidence is, however, unknown to or ignored by Westbrook, "Jubilee Laws," who regards the fifty-year cycle as precisely that which is "academic and theoretical" about the Jubilee provision. The only explanation he offers for it is that it is as good a round number as any and, as such, typical of P—hardly a judgment to inspire confidence!

socio-economic viability of the household and, therewith, the stability of the nation's relationship with God.

B. SECURITY AND PROPERTY

Another common property right which in Israel was placed in the context of their distinctive theological beliefs was the protection by law of the security of one's property. In this section we shall consider the prohibitions on the removal of landmarks and the Eighth and Tenth Commandments. Lesser civil regulations on damages, compensation, and so forth are listed at the end of Chapter 5.

1. The Prohibition on the Removal of Landmarks

Reference has already been made to Deut. 27:17, in which a curse is laid on one who removes his neighbor's landmark (above, p. 99). It was seen to occupy a prominent place alongside the curse on one who dishonors his parents, both of them aiming to protect the stability of the family—externally from loss of its land and internally from loss of domestic authority. The importance of the external protection is apparent from the number of other references to the crime of boundary encroachment.

a. Deut. 19:14.

> Do not move your neighbor's boundary stone set up by your predecessors in the inheritance you receive in the land the LORD your God is giving you to possess. (NIV)

Deuteronomy places this law directly after the regulations concerning cities of asylum for homicide. Calum M. Carmichael has suggested a reason for this.[11] The asylum law (Deut. 19:1-13) presupposes the historical material of Deut. 4:41-43 (the asylum cities east

11. "Deuteronomic Laws, Wisdom, and Historical Traditions," *JSS* 12 (1967): 198-200.

of Jordan) and 3:12-17 (the division of territory there). The land-mark law, which immediately follows and uses similar terms ($g^e\underline{b}\hat{u}l$ and $nah^a l\hat{a}$), has been recalled and recorded at this point because it too is connected with land division and boundaries. This is therefore an example of Deuteronomy's characteristic use of Israel's past history as a didactic aid and as a justification for retaining an ancient law of a very common kind.[12] The double use of *nhl*, coupled with the distinctive phraseology of the land given and divided up by Yahweh to his people, makes boundary encroachment a crime against Yahweh himself—not solely against the neighbor.[13] Furthermore, the term *ri'šōnîm* shows the familial and ancestral dimension of the law.[14] The word refers to the "forefathers," which in this setting means the generation to whom the land was initially divided up.[15] Boundary encroachment was potentially destructive, not just of a single individual and his immediate household but of his whole ancestral line.[16]

a. Hos. 5:10

> Judah's leaders are like those
> who move boundary stones . . . (NIV)

In the light of this double seriousness of the crime, it is under-standable that it should become a byword for the kind of behavior which deserved the severest judgment of God. Thus Hosea uses it

12. For other examples, cf. Samuel Rolles Driver, *A Critical and Exegetical Commentary on Deuteronomy*. ICC (Edinburgh: T. & T. Clark and New York: Charles Scribners, 1895), pp. 234-35.

13. This point is emphasized by John Alexander Thompson, *Deuteronomy*. Tyndale Old Testament Commentaries (London and Downers Grove: InterVarsity, 1974), p. 217.

14. As does Prov. 22:28, where the term *'a\underline{b}ô\underline{t}eykā* is used in the same grammatical position, ". . . boundary stone set up by your forefathers."

15. The meaning is determined by the context. In Lev. 26:45 the same term also refers to Israel's ancestors, but in that context to the generation of the Exodus.

16. On the link between the preservation of ancestral land and the survival of the family line, cf. Brichto.

as a conveniently brief way to damn the princes of Judah. This is the only prophetic text to mention the removal of landmarks explicitly, but it was certainly involved in the land-grabbing denounced by Isaiah (Isa. 5:8) and Micah (Mic. 2:2).

c. Prov. 23:10-11

> Do not move an ancient boundary stone
> or encroach on the fields of the fatherless,
> for their Defender is strong;
> he will take up their case against you. (NIV)

The reference in the first half of this verse to the "fatherless" indicates again the familial perspective, since those without the natural protection of a family stood in greatest need of the protection of the law. The reference in the second half to God as their redeemer[17] immediately brings in also the other aspect of the crime— its offensiveness to Yahweh himself.

d. Job 24:2-4

> Men move boundary stones;
> they pasture flocks they have stolen.
> They drive away the orphan's donkey
> and take the widow's ox in pledge.
> They thrust the needy from the path
> and force all the poor of the land into hiding. (NIV)

Although the above text from Proverbs envisages Yahweh acting on behalf of the victim, Job is more pessimistic, in view of the fact that blatant suffering of this kind of economic oppression so often

---

17. Assuming here, in the light of such passages as Ps. 10:14, 18; 68:5; 140:12; 146:7-9 that the verse refers to *Yahweh*, though he is not actually named and $g\bar{o}^{\,a}l\bar{a}m$ grammatically could mean a human redeemer. Cf. William McKane, *Proverbs*, pp. 379ff.

goes unremedied and unrequited. Job, in these verses, sees precisely the same evils as are denounced by Isaiah, Amos, and Micah, but without the prophetic vision of impending judgment on those who perpetrated them.

2. The Prohibition of Theft and Coveting

Laws and curses to protect boundaries, it has been noted, were very common in the ancient world, yet in Israel the sacredness of the boundaries of family land had a special character in connection with Israel's theology of the land and their historico-redemptive traditions. Can the same thing be seen regarding the even more common prohibition on theft?

This leads us to the Eighth and Tenth Commandments, and thereby to the confused scene of Decalog study. The precise question before us here, however, is: What significance may be attached to the fact that two[18] of the prohibitions in the Decalog are apparently concerned with property? This cannot be answered without some prior judgment on the nature and significance of the Decalog itself in Israel's faith, and this is an issue which bristles with theories from every critical discipline. Unfortunately, literary-critical, form-critical, and traditio-historical researches on the Decalog have not yet reached a conclusive consensus, linked as they are to the wider questions of Israelite law as a whole.[19] Nevertheless, while awaiting further enlightenment in these areas, it is still possible to recognize the importance of the Decalog within the Old Testament and that it had a special position in Israel's relationship with Yahweh—whatever may be our final view of its origin and development.

The evidence that it was assigned a unique place of importance by the Old Testament itself, and not just by subsequent Jewish and

18. Two, that is, following the more common numeration of the Decalog which regards Exod. 20:17 as a single commandment. For the varieties of enumeration, see Eduard Nielson, *The Ten Commandments in New Perspective*. SBT, 2nd ser. 7 (1968).

19. For surveys of literature in all these areas, see J. J. Stamm and M. E. Andrews, *The Ten Commandments in Recent Research*. SBT, 2nd ser. 2 (1967); and also Brevard S. Childs, *The Book of Exodus*, pp. 385-401.

Christian interpreters, is manifold. The commandments have a special name, the "ten words" . . . (cf. also Ex. 31.18; Deut. 4.13; 9.9, etc.). Again, they are repeated in Deuteronomy as providing the foundation for the new promulgation of the covenant. The narrative framework of Exodus, but particularly of Deuteronomy, stressed the finality of the commandments: "These words Yahweh spoke . . . and added no more" (Deut. 5.22). Finally, the reflection of the commandments in the prophets (Hos. 4.1ff., Jer. 7.9ff.), and in the Psalms (50 and 81) testify to their influence upon Israel's faith.[20]

The strength of this influence is reflected in the association of the Decalog with Sinai, which indicates that it was felt to be essential as the revelation of what in practice was required of those who there had become God's people.

Whatever one thinks about the authorship, the fact that the Decalogue early held a central position in Israelite life remains as the most important result of recent research. . . [it] stood in association with the review of the Sinai events as the binding charter expressing the will of the divine Lord of the Covenant.[21]

A recent attempt to account for and define this distinctive character and importance of the Decalog has been made by Anthony Phillips in *Ancient Israel's Criminal Law,* and his work gives us a useful point of departure for our discussion here. Phillips argues that the Decalog was Israel's "criminal law-code"—defining "crime," in this context, as offenses against the whole community inasmuch as they were offenses against the relationship with Yahweh upon which the community was founded and depended— the covenant. In support of this, Phillips regards it as highly significant that, although penalties are not specified in the Decalog itself, all offenses for which there was a judicial *death* penalty in the Old Testament were either direct breaches of the commandments or were closely related to them.

20. Childs, p. 397.
21. Stamm-Andrews, p. 39.

Aspects of Phillips' thesis have been criticized already above (e.g., pp. 89-91, 100), and some feel that his whole attempt to define the Decalog as a criminal law code is erroneous.[22] Nevertheless, in my opinion Phillips has a valid insight in drawing a distinction between laws prohibiting the kinds of behavior which would threaten the basic relationship between God and Israel (what he calls "crimes") and those dealing either with lesser offenses of a civil nature or with questions of interpretation, applicability, and punishment arising from the first category. He is also right to emphasize that the difference is one of content, not solely of form,[23] and that the criterion of form alone is an unreliable guide.

Difficulty arises, however, with Phillips' insistence on making the judicial death penalty the essential defining criterion of his category of criminal law, namely, the Decalog. Neither the Eighth nor the Tenth Commandments, as traditionally understood in their present form, could carry a death penalty.[24] The Tenth, indeed, could hardly be related to any judicial penalty in a human court. Now this produces the dilemma that if one is to maintain that the death penalty was the essential factor in distinguishing "crimes" against the national relationship with God, then either one must abandon the view of the Decalog as entirely and exclusively the summary of "crime" in that sense or else one must find a way of reinterpreting the Eighth and Tenth Commandments so as to make them capital offenses. Phillips chooses the second course, and is fairly criticized for doing so in the *a priori* interests of his theory.

22. E.g., Bernard S. Jackson, "Reflections on Biblical Criminal Law," *JJS* 24 (1973): 29-37, repr. in *Essays.*

23. *Ancient Israel's Criminal Law,* p. 13.

24. Various arguments that have been advanced for the existence of a legal death penalty for ordinary theft in Israel have been thoroughly examined and convincingly refuted by Bernard S. Jackson, *Theft in Early Jewish Law* (Oxford: Oxford University Press, 1972), pp. 144-154.

a. The Eighth Commandment

> You shall not steal. (Exod. 20:15)

With plenty of scholarly support, Phillips takes the Eighth Commandment as referring originally to kidnapping,[25] which was a
capital offense (Exod. 21:16). This particular hypothesis is linked
with (rather, was partly the result of) an interpretation of the Tenth
Commandment as referring to actual misappropriation and not
merely to mental coveting.[26] But even this view (which he in any
case rejects) would be inadequate for Phillips' theory, for it would
still leave the Tenth Commandment as a property offense, and
therefore noncapital. So, in the weakest link in his chain of argument, Phillips proposes a crime of "depriving an elder of his status"
(and thereby of his judicial qualifications) through dispossession.[27]
The original verb which stood for this crime of dispossession was
replaced by ḥāmaḏ, "covet," when the original commandment had
become obsolete after Jehoshaphat's judicial reform had allegedly
removed the judicial function of local elders.[28]

Apart from the inherent weakness of this last hypothesis, the
critical reinterpretation of both commandments which underlies it
has recently been examined and found wanting by Bernard S.
Jackson.[29] He demonstrates convincingly that there are no adequate
grounds—exegetically, historically, or theologically—for rejecting the traditional sense of the Tenth Commandment. It thus be-

25. This is a view which, as Jackson points out, goes back to rabbinic
interpreters (*Theft in Early Jewish Law*, p. 148, n. 5), and in modern times has been
advocated by Albrecht Alt, "Das Verbot des Diebstahls im Dekalog," *Kleine
Schriften* 1:333-340.
26. This theory was proposed by Johannes Herrmann, "Das zehnte Gebot,"
pp. 69-82 in *Sellin-Festschrift*, ed. Anton Jirku (Leipzig: Deichert, 1927). A
bibliography of the scholarly debate on the subject is provided by Bernard S.
Jackson, "Liability for Mere Intention in Early Jewish Law," *HUCA* 42 (1971): 198,
repr. in *Essays*.
27. *Ancient Israel's Criminal Law*, pp. 149ff.
28. See above, p. 79 for my disagreement with Phillips over this view of
Jehoshaphat's reform.
29. "Liability for Mere Intention."

comes correspondingly unnecessary to reinterpret the Eighth Commandment to refer to kidnapping.

What then becomes of the dilemma posed above? If the death penalty is the criterion of offenses against the "covenant relationship," then the Decalog apparently contains prohibitions which do not fit into such a category. But is this criterion of death (or any) penalty appropriate? Jackson seems closer to the truth:

> The proper conclusions to be drawn are rather, in my view, that there was no single punishment (in a human court . . .) for breach of the Decalogue, and that the nature of . . . particularly the tenth commandment shows that human justiciability of the Decalogue was not intended.[30]

So the special nature of the Decalog in itself cannot be expounded by equalizing the penalties for breaking it, especially since the Decalog itself is not concerned to specify penalties. One must look to some intrinsic coherence, not to secondary judicial penalties. Here again one agrees with Jackson who, in pointing out that legal penalties are in any case no sure guide to social values, comments: "surely the inclusion of the prohibition of theft alongside that of murder in the Decalogue tells us something of Biblical values."[31] The question is, however: since it does *not* mean that theft, like murder, was punishable by death, what *does* it tell us?

The answer can only be that theft in general and the coveting of one's neighbor's household or land were considered sufficiently serious to be included among specific kinds of activity which were fundamentally incompatible with personal loyalty to Yahweh and membership of the community of his people. As to why this should have been so, we are again driven to the vital link, established and defined in Chapters 2 and 3, between a person's ownership of land and household and his membership of that community and share in its privileges. An Israelite's land and property were the tangible symbol of his personal share in the inheritance of Israel, as well as the vital means of economic support for his household (and there-

30. "Reflections on Biblical Criminal Law," p. 37.
31. "Reflections on Biblical Criminal Law," p. 16.

fore also essential for *their* share in the inheritance and membership of the religious community). Accordingly, theft meant at least the diminution of a person's practical enjoyment of the blessings and tangible privilege of belonging to the people to whom God had given the land; at worst, if it involved his whole substance, it meant the loss of his very standing within the community and dire consequences for his family. Theft, therefore, was not solely an attack on property, but indirectly on the fellow Israelite's person and on the stability and viability of his family. The prohibition of theft, therefore, did not imply the "sanctity of property" *per se,* but rather *the sanctity of the relationship between the Israelite household and Yahweh.* It was this relationship which could be impaired or destroyed in its material aspects by theft. In such a threat at the domestic level lay, as we have seen, a potential, intrinsic threat to the national relationship with God.

A distinction is necessary at this point between this absolute prohibition on theft in general and the particular regulations in cases of actual theft.[32] The latter could obviously vary from petty pilfering to person-stealing (kidnapping), and the penalties varied accordingly. But the strength of the absolute prohibition counteracts the temptation to conclude that, because Israel's case law does not treat theft as capital, the Old Testament attitude toward property offenses was therefore one of leniency. This is an impression one gets in some studies which compare Old Testament law with other ancient Near Eastern legal corpora.[33] Against such an impression we need Jackson's reminder that the presence of the prohibition of theft in the Decalog is a measure of the seriousness with which it was regarded in principle. And we need further to take account of the

32. The comprehensive scope of Jackson's work *(Theft in Early Jewish Law)* makes it unnecessary to go into detail on the particular casuistic legislation on theft in the Old Testament. See also Robert Gnuse, *You Shall Not Steal.*

33. E.g., P. Rémy, "Le Vol le droit du propriété," *Mélanges de science religieuse* 19 (1962): 5-29; Moshe Greenberg, "Some Postulates of Biblical Criminal Law"; Shalom M. Paul, *Studies in the Book of the Covenant in the Light of Cuneiform and Biblical Law.* VTS 18 (1970). Some criticisms of the assumptions and methods behind these studies—particularly of a too facile drawing of contrasts between biblical and cuneiform laws—are registered by Jackson, "Reflections on Biblical Criminal Law."

nonlegal texts where theft is denounced, in far from "lenient"
language, as utterly abhorrent to God and quite incompatible with
obedience to his will. As one might expect, it is one of the sins
condemned by the prophets (Hos. 4:2; 7:1; Isa. 1:23; Jer. 7:9-10).
Ps. 50:16-18 ranks it with adultery as an offense which is irreconcilable with professed loyalty to the covenant. Prov. 30:9 regards it
as a profanation of the very name of Yahweh. Lev. 6:1-7 prescribes—in addition to material restitution—a guilt offering for a
person guilty of various kinds of property offense. Prov. 29:24
speaks of the curse falling on those who withhold witness to a theft,
because they are implicated or share in it *post factum*.[34] But the most
strongly-worded pronouncement of a curse upon the thief is undoubtedly Zech. 5:3-4.

The range of these texts and the depth of feeling they show
against theft are a much more telling commentary on the Eighth
Commandment than is at all possible if its application be limited to
the more remote offense of kidnapping. They illustrate the distinction referred to between the Decalog prohibition and the case laws
concerning theft. It is not a matter of two kinds of equally justiciable
legislation—criminal and civil (as in Phillips' theory). Rather, civil
legislation consists of regulations governing evidenciary tests,
degrees of punishment and compensation, self-help, and so forth,
from the perspective of *human* judicial procedure. By contrast,
criminal legislation is an expression of the absolute moral demand
on Israel by Yahweh, from whose *divine* perspective, as revealed in
the above texts, theft is an abomination, accursed, a profanation of
his name, a mockery of worship and a denial of the covenant. This
kind of language can be used against it because the thief robs his
fellow Israelite, not merely of some of his economic property, but
of part of what is his as a blessing and gift from God (as a person)
and of part of his share in the inheritance of the people of Yahweh
(as an Israelite). So although the material aspects of the offense
might be treated with *comparative* leniency, it is this spiritual and

---

34. Cf. also Lev. 5:1 and, on the question of the curse in judicial practice,
Herbert C. Brichto, *The Problem of "Curse" in the Hebrew Bible*. JBL Monograph
13 (Philadelphia: SBL, 1963), esp. (on these verses) pp. 42-44.

theological significance which makes the offense so serious and has dictated its inclusion in the Decalog.

b. The Tenth Commandment

You shall not covet your neighbor's house; you shall not covet your neighbor's wife, or his manservant, or his maidservant, or his ox, or his ass, or anything that is your neighbor's. (Exod. 20:17)

As regards the Tenth Commandment, the distinction between the Decalog prohibition and human judicial procedure is even greater, for no legal penalties existed at all in any human court of the Old Testament period for coveting—or mere evil *intention* of any sort. This is not to deny that evil intention, including coveting, was regarded as sin. It undoubtedly was, and as such was liable to divine judgment.[35] The point here is that the Tenth Commandment prohibits as being incompatible with loyalty to Yahweh something which could not by its very nature be sanctioned by actual legal penalties. This very fact underlines the importance of this prohibition, since in this respect it is unique among the commandments. The full significance of the Tenth Commandment, however, lies deeper yet, as shown by two further considerations.

(1) In addition to prohibiting something not liable to legal penalty, it prohibited something which could also be "realized" in practical deed without necessarily breaking the law. It was (and remains) possible to fulfill a covetous desire without doing anything technically illegal. The Tenth Commandment, therefore, provides that radical thrust to the Decalog which distinguishes it from mere legislation, for it indicates that, while having done nothing illegal by human standards, a person can nevertheless be morally guilty before God.[36]

35. Cf. the craving in the wilderness (Num. 11:4-34), the evil of mankind's heart as the reason for the Flood (Gen. 6:5), and God's scrutiny of the heart (1 Sam. 16:7). On this subject, see Jackson, "Liability for Mere Intention."

36. A fine illustration of this is found in Jesus' encounter with the rich young man (Mark 10:17-31). There is no suggestion in the story that his wealth had in any

(2) The *content* of the commandment is significant for our purpose in that it specifies the neighbor's household and (in the Deuteronomic version) his land. It thus prohibits at source the desires that led to land-grabbing "latifundism." Now it is probable that some of the methods used by the wealthy to acquire land at the expense of smallholders were not technically illegal—such as foreclosure of mortgages, debt bondage (which, even if a Jubilee were in operation twice a century, would still have been devastating on many households), and even the redemption of land from impoverished kinsmen. Nevertheless, though legal, such methods when ruthlessly pursued became fundamental violations of the moral requirements of the relationship between Yahweh and Israel, and stemmed from ambitions that contradicted the Tenth Commandment. For that reason it is *prophets* who in the name of God pronounce *divine* judgment on offenses about which *human* courts were unable or, through corruption by the offenders themselves, disinclined to do anything. Mic. 2:2 shows this awareness of what the real sin was that lay behind the external acts of acquisition— covetousness.

There is therefore a certain irony in the fact that, although Phillips' chapter on the Tenth Commandment contains his weakest conjecture in his attempt to "upgrade" it into a precise criminal law, it nevertheless perceives very clearly the kind of social calamity for an Israelite and his household that was entailed if the commandment were disregarded and he became dispossessed (cf. above, pp. 80-81). It is perhaps also ironic that to interpret it as a precise criminal law actually deprives the commandment of the kind of radical ethical thrust suggested above. This must then be "restored" to it by dint of an alleged "spiritualizing" of the original law after Jehoshaphat's reform.

It has not been the intention of this section on the Eighth and Tenth Commandments in any way to limit whatever relevance and importance they, with the rest of the Decalog, may be accorded as

---

way been acquired illegally—or even, like Zacchaeus, by legalized extortion. Yet Jesus' questioning reveals that his claim to be entirely observant of the Law foundered on the radical thrust of precisely the Tenth Commandment.

general or universal moral requirements in a scheme of biblical ethics.[37] Like several other requirements of the Decalog, they were by no means unique to Israel, nor unknown to Israel and their ancestors before Sinai. But the question is *not*: How are we to explain and express the uniqueness of the *Decalog* (since parts of it are not at all unique)? Rather, it is: How are we to understand the meaning of the Decalog within the historical context of the uniqueness of *Israel* and their self-understanding in relationship to Yahweh? Theft and coveting would have been morally wrong in Israel even had they not been the people of Yahweh. But granted that they did understand themselves to be so, through their historical experiences of redemption and revelation, and granted further that the possession of the land was regarded as the proof of their relationship with God—their inheritance from him as his sons, so that the relationship was vested in the socio-economic structure of landowning households—then there emerges a dimension to these particular commandments which surely transcends the common human disapproval of stealing and greed. It is this additional dimension, *the result of the fusion of Israel's theological self-understanding with their socio-economic circumstances*, that this section has sought to bring into sharper relief.

CONCLUSION

When we speak of "property rights" in the Old Testament, it is clear from the foregoing that we are not concerned with an abstract, impersonal principle, nor with an *inherent* sacrosanctity of property *per se*.[38] A person's right to the security and integrity of his ancestral land and other property was based (1) on his relationship to Yahweh, as a member of the community of his people, of which relationship

37. See, e.g., Walter C. Kaiser, Jr., *Toward Old Testament Ethics, in loc.*
38. Cf. the comments of Walther Zimmerli on the Eighth Commandment: "This command, however, envisages something quite different from the sacredness of private property—an interpretation which has often been given it in modern capitalistic society" (*The Old Testament and the World* [London: SPCK and Atlanta: John Knox, 1976], p. 79). Cf. also similar arguments in Gnuse.

and status his land was the symbol and guarantee and (2) on the fact that his land and property were essential to the economic viability of his household, with all its social and religious significance for the individuals within it and for the national well-being before God.

On the basis of the Old Testament, therefore, we cannot speak of property itself being "sacred" or of the "sanctity of property." It is the *relationships,* Godward and humanward, of which property is a function and indicator, which are alone sacred.

5 | *Property Owners' Responsibilities*

The limitations and responsibilities imposed upon the ownership of property in the Old Testament may be analyzed into three categories: the primary responsibility to God, the closely related responsibility to one's whole family line, and various responsibilities to others.

A. RESPONSIBILITY TO GOD

We have already emphasized that all wealth was considered a gift from God, the ultimate owner of all, and that the divine gift of the land must be kept in closest union with Israel's relationship with Yahweh and the obligations which that entailed. The ramifications of these obligations to Yahweh in the realm of personal wealth were enormous, however, and it is possible here only to concentrate on one major institution as representative—namely, the Sabbatical Year on the land. This necessary selection means that we shall not discuss the whole range of cultic offerings required of pious Israelites, save to say that there were demands on livestock and on produce of the land, as well as freewill offerings of various sorts. The extent of these is impressive, and throughout much of it theological and social considerations were present alongside the cultic element. Norman K. Gottwald *(The Tribes of Yahweh)* has pointed out that Israel's egalitarianism and liberating economic ideals are reflected also in their cult. It did not consume a heavy proportion of the national agricultural produce; it did not support a privileged and powerful clergy elite; it did not cast Yahweh in the role of protector and benefactor of an elite landowning minority.

THE SABBATICAL YEAR AND Šᵉmiṭṭâ

Two preliminary points need to be made before entering on a detailed comparison of the passages connected with the seventh year on the land. (1) In the interests of clarity, it is best to deal separately with the questions of land fallow and slave release. It seems to me that several recent studies on these topics suffer from unnecessary confusion and difficulty by conflating the two.[1] (2) It must be borne in mind that the concept and practice of a sabbatical cycle of years was pre-Israelite and already had definite religious and cultic associations long before it became an Israelite institution, as has been shown by Cyrus H. Gordon.[2] This means that, although the earliest text concerning the fallow year (Exod. 23:10-11) mentions only a humanitarian motive, we cannot assume that deeper religious considerations were unknown when the law was framed thus in an Israelite context. It also means that when the religious significance of the institution is spelled out clearly in Lev. 25:2-7 it need not be assumed that this represents a late, cultic reinterpretation of the law. These points will be developed in the discussion of the texts which follows.

1. This is true, e.g., of Anthony Phillips, *Ancient Israel's Criminal Law,* pp. 73-79; and also of Niels P. Lemche, "The Manumission of Slaves—The Fallow Year—The Sabbatical Year—The Jobel Year," *VT* 26 (1976): 38-59. For this reason, our discussion of slave release is postponed until Chapter 8.

2. "Sabbatical Cycle or Seasonal Pattern." Gordon cites mainly, though not exclusively, Ugaritic material in demonstrating the existence of seven-year cycles of nature, including a fallow year, of which the purpose was to ensure agricultural prosperity in the ensuing seven-year period. The effects of the victory of Ba'al over Mot was not seasonal or annual, but lasted for seven years. Cf. Gordon, *Ugaritic Literature.* Scripta Pontificii Instituti Biblici 98 (1949), pp. 5, 57-62, and texts 49:V:8-9 (p. 47), 75:II:46 (p. 55), and I Aqht 42ff. (p. 94).

1. Exod. 23:10-11: The Fallow Year

10 *For six years you are to sow your fields and harvest the crops,*
11 *but during the seventh year let the land lie unplowed and*
   unused. Then the poor among your people may get food from
   it, and the wild animals may eat what they leave. Do the same
   with your vineyard and your olive grove. (NIV)

This law is the earliest of our texts and reflects very ancient practice.
It will probably remain impossible to define precisely the original
significance of the seventh year fallow—whether it was primarily
religious, or a kind of primitive agrarian science, or a restoration
for the land by giving it rest.[3] The first two can hardly be separated
anyway, because agricultural practice and religious belief were so
closely bound together in the ancient world.

> . . . Even though the practical importance of the fallow year for
> the soil is not explicitly mentioned in Ex. xxiii.10-11, this may
> well be implicitly understood according to the reasoning of the
> time. The cultivation of the soil and the harvesting of its products
> have always been subjected to religious conceptions.[4]

In the context of the Book of the Covenant, the fallow year, like the
rest of the requirements of the Book, was implicitly an obligation
to Yahweh, so that a religious emphasis cannot have been lacking.

3. This last is Martin Noth's view (*Leviticus*, pp. 183ff.). The theory that the
seventh year fallow was connected with a redistribution of tribal lands has already
been rejected (see Appendix to Chapter 2).
4. Lemche, "The Manumission of Slaves," p. 42, n. 14. Lemche continues:
"and it is wrong, based on modern farming and its particular working morale, to
draw any conclusions regarding farming conditions of the past." Curiously,
however, Lemche himself does something of the sort when, in order to justify his
view that *l^{e}karm^{e}kā* "to your vineyard" is a secondary addition to the text in Exod.
23:11 (which has been retained in Lev. 25:3b), he comments: "There is no economic
reason to include the vineyards. . . . It is rather useless to a winegrower to let his
vineyard lie fallow every seventh year. To-day it is normal that a vine has an
uninterrupted production time of thirty years . . ." (p. 48 and n. 34). But if "religious
conceptions" are the controlling factor, then this "economic" observation, by
Lemche's own principle, is irrelevant and the text need not be suspected on these
grounds.

The humanitarian motivation, however, gives the law an additional dimension and blends it in with the preceding series of humanitarian injunctions.

The form of the humanitarian motive clause also affects the question of whether the fallow year was a fixed year over the whole land or something to be observed individually by farmers on their own land. Though it is not made explicit in the text, it must surely have been the latter. The poor of the people and the wild beasts[5] would derive little sustenance from a single fallow every seven years, but the continuous presence of some land lying fallow in every locality would obviously provide some relief.

2. Lev. 25:2-7: The Sabbatical Year

2 *Say to the people of Israel, When you come into the land which I [am going to] give you, the land [itself] shall keep a sabbath to the* LORD.

3 *Six years you shall sow your field, and six years you shall prune your vineyard, and gather in its fruits;*

4 *but in the seventh year there shall be a sabbath of solemn rest for the land, a sabbath to the* LORD; *you shall not sow your field or prune your vineyard.*

5 *What grows of itself in your harvest you shall not reap, and the grapes of your undressed vine you shall not gather; it shall be a year of solemn rest for the land.*

6 *The sabbath of the land shall provide food for you, for yourself and for your male and female slaves and for your hired servant and the sojourner who lives with you;*

7 *for your cattle also and for the beasts that are in your land all its yield shall be for food.*

A literary comparison of the verbal parallels between this passage and Exod. 23:10-11 quickly demonstrates that it is dependent on

---

5. Phillips rightly observes: "The poor would have been those without land. Slaves and domestic animals would have been cared for by their owners" (*Ancient Israel's Criminal Law,* p. 75, n. 49).

the Exodus passage and an expansion of it. Three developments have been effected by the expansion.

(1) It is almost certain that the seventh year fallow has become a single year for the whole land. The injunctions are still in the second person singular, but the change from 'arṣeḵā, "your land" (Exod. 23:10), to the repeated hā'āreṣ, "the land" (Lev. 25:4, 5, 6), points to this.

(2) The religious dimension of the institution is emphasized, in that it is called a Sabbatical Year to Yahweh in the phrases šabbaṭ šabbāṭôn and šabbāṭ laYHWH, which do not appear in Exod. 23. However, in the light of our introductory comments, it is not necessary to regard this as an innovating addition to replace the original humanitarian motive. It is just as likely that this is giving clearer expression to a religious significance which was always present, and which had in fact itself been supplemented by a humanitarian element in the Book of the Covenant.[6] For this reason also it is not necessary that the Leviticus form of the law, though clearly secondary, should be considered late. In fact, there is very little cultic elaboration present.

(3) The humanitarian aspects have almost all been removed. But they have not been lost altogether, for other laws have been framed to take over their purpose—namely, the laws concerning harvesting, gleaning, and vintage in Lev. 19:9-10 and 23:22. None of these laws occurs in the Book of the Covenant, where their humanitarian function was already adequately served by the continuous presence of some fallow land in different farms in each locality. But the introduction of a universal fallow in the seventh year alone would necessitate this kind of annual charitable behavior.

In describing the seventh year as a "sabbath to the LORD" for the land, Leviticus appears to be linking the original text in Exod. 23:10-11 to the immediately following verse (Exod. 23:12) on the sabbath day and interpreting it in that light—that is, the land too is

6. Noth sees this possibility: "This sacramental reason (cf. especially the apparently set form 'sabbath for Yahweh' in Lev. 25:2bβ, 4bβ) might well be the more original one . . . in point of content" (Leviticus, p. 186). Cf. also Gerhard von Rad: "The practice of leaving the land fallow . . . was a definitely sacral arrangement" (Deuteronomy. OTL [1966], p. 105).

to enjoy a sabbatical rest as an expression of its relationship to Yahweh. This fits in with the theological conception of the land expressed in Lev. 25:23.

> It rests on the understanding that Yahweh is the true owner of the land . . . and that the directness of this relationship ought to be restored every seventh year, without the land having its "rest" disturbed by the intervention of men to whom it has passed and who use it for their own purposes.[7]

3. Deut. 15:1-3: The Šᵉmiṭṭâ

> At the end of every seven years, you shall make a release (šᵉmiṭṭâ). . . . Every holder of a pledge shall release what has been pledged to him for debt by his neighbor. He shall not press his neighbor or his brother for payment, for Yahweh's release has been pro-claimed. . . . (author's translation)

It is appropriate to deal with the law of release at this point, since it is best interpreted as an extension of the agrarian principles of the fallow year for the *land* rather than a *slave* release law, linked in some way to the Hebrew slave release laws of Exod. 21:1-11 and Deut. 15:12-18. The šᵉmiṭṭâ text does not mention slaves at all, and it is here that the confusion and difficulties of those who identify too closely all the seventh year "happenings" become most acute. The text of Deut. 15:1-3, especially the first two verses, presents several exegetical difficulties, which are discussed in detail in the Appendix at the end of the chapter.

Our understanding of the verses, as argued in the Appendix, can be outlined in summary as follows:

1. That the Deuteronomic version is the latest of the three sabbatical laws and thus presupposes both the agrarian fallow of Exodus and the sacral Sabbatical Year of Leviticus;

2. That Deuteronomy has extended the principle of "release" to include human beings as well as land;

3. That the "release" applied to pledges taken for debts, which

---

7. Noth, *Leviticus,* p. 186.

would have consisted mainly of mortgaged land, but could also have included dependent persons whose labor was "pledged" to pay off debts;

4. That "release" probably meant a year's suspension of the repayment, rather than a total cancellation of the debt. There is, however, a continuing scholarly debate on this last point, and it is impossible to be certain which was intended.

Thus the dominant feature of the law itself, whatever its precise meaning, as well as of the "preaching" which surrounds it is the *humanitarian concern for the impoverished*—extended now not only to the landless poor, as in the case of the original fallow year, but also to those landowners under increasingly heavy burdens of debt. Just as Leviticus extended the Exodus law in terms of the following verse (Exod. 23:12) on the sabbath, so Deuteronomy has extended it in the light of the preceding verses that prohibit injustice and oppression. And both Leviticus and Deuteronomy very clearly understood the institution and its extensions— and the material sacrifices entailed—as *an obligation and responsibility to God himself,* to be expressed through one's land and one's relationship with impoverished fellow Israelites. Both the sabbath for the land and the release for the debtor are "to (or 'for') the LORD" (Lev. 25:4; Deut. 15:2). We are thus presented in this particular economic sphere with an ethical pattern familiar elsewhere in biblical thought—the fulfillment of one's obligations to God by means of the discharge of one's responsibilities for one's fellows.

4. Observance and Failure

Turning to the question of the *observance* of the Sabbatical Year, we again find a lack of evidence, though not so severe as was the case with the Jubilee. Two historical events appear to stand in some relationship to the sabbatical institutions: the manumission of slaves under Zedekiah in Jer. 34 and the agreement of creditors to release pledges of land and persons in Neh. 5. But the relationship is by no means clear-cut. Both events occur as *ad hoc* reactions to emergencies and cannot therefore be expected to exemplify the typical operation of any of the sabbatical laws.[8]

Of much greater interest is the fact that there was an awareness of the *lack of observance* of the sabbatical institutions, and that the Exile was interpreted partly as a punishment on Israel for failure in this respect and partly as "compensation" to the *land* for its loss of sabbath years. In Lev. 26 this is doubly emphasized, in vv. 34 and 43. The Chronicler echoes the point and links it with a prophecy of Jeremiah (2 Chr. 36:21; Jer. 25:11-12; 29:10). The emphasis in Lev. 26 can be seen in that (1) v. 34 follows immediately upon the climax of the series of threats for disobedience, culminating in v. 33 with the threat of exile and devastation of the land, and that (2) v. 43 stands "sandwiched" between God's two acts of "remembering"— his covenant with the patriarchs (specifically including the land, v. 42) and his covenant with the "forefathers" of the Exodus generation (v. 45). How are we to interpret this emphasis?

Looking at the present redactional form of the Holiness Code, there are grounds for regarding Lev. 25 and 26 as intentionally juxtaposed in order to form the climax of the Code:

(1) There is the unique insertion of the rubric: "The LORD said to Moses *on Mount Sinai*" in 25:1 (the reference to Sinai being hitherto unparalleled in the Code[9]), which is then echoed at the

8. On the release of slaves during the siege of Jerusalem decreed by Zedekiah, see Martin David, "The Manumission of Slaves under Zedekiah," *OTS* 5 (1948): 63-79; and Nahum M. Sarna, "Zedekiah's Emancipation of Slaves and the Sabbatical Year," pp. 143-49 in *Orient and Occident.* Festschrift Cyrus H. Gordon, ed. Harry A. Hoffner, Jr. Alter Orient und Alten Testament 22 (Neukirchen-Vluyn: Neukirchener Verlag, 1973). On the basis of the very close correspondences between Jer. 34 and Deut. 15, Sarna argues that Zedekiah's release occurred in an actual Sabbatical Year and was modelled on the Deuteronomic law (in historical fact as well as in literary record). He is opposed in this by Lemche, "The Manumission of Slaves," pp. 51-53 and 59. See Lemche, pp. 53ff. and literature cited there on the subject of Nehemiah's reform. Also see below, pp. 259-260, for my own comments on Jer. 34 and its relationship to the *šeᵉmiṭṭâ*, Jubilee, and Hebrew slave release laws.

9. ". . . The naming of the mountain of Sinai is unusual and remarkable, and indicates the fundamental quality of the following ordinances" (Noth, *Leviticus*, p. 185).

conclusion of ch. 26, in the redactional conclusion—probably for the whole Code—of 26:46.

(2) Ch. 26 is itself unique in not being prefaced by "The LORD said to Moses," as are all the other chapters of the Code. This has the effect that ch. 26 "runs on" from ch. 25 without any clear break.

(3) There is also the recurrent recollection of the deliverance from Egypt, which appears like a refrain through both chapters (25:38, 42, 55; 26:13, 45), but is very infrequent elsewhere in the Code (19:36; 23:43).

Now if the two chapters are so closely related, then we must interpret the word "sabbaths" in 26:34-35 and 43 in the light of the whole of ch. 25—that is, as referring both to Sabbatical Years (in the seven-year cycle) and to the Jubilee, which was undoubtedly regarded as a special Sabbatical Year. Now the overall impact of ch. 25 is clearly socio-economic and, as we have seen, is concerned with the intended security of tenure of Israelite families on the land, the alleviation of poverty and periodic restoration of individuals and families to freedom and repossession of ancestral property—all as part of Israel's responsibility to Yahweh. When, therefore, Lev. 26 speaks of neglect of the "sabbaths" and of sin against the *land,* the conception is not primarily cultic but *moral and socio-economic.* The focus of attention is not the land *per se,* but the land as the "middle term" between Yahweh and Israel, the land as the tangible symbol and ground of his blessing and claim on them and their relationship and obligation to him. This point emerged clearly from our study of Lev. 25:23, and it is reinforced by the way in which in ch. 26 the land is very much the "stage" on which God's blessing or curse will be enacted (vv. 3-33). It is also supported by the interesting arrangement of 26:42-45, in which the land and the moral relationship of the people to it stand prominently—like a fulcrum—in between the mention of the covenant with the patriarchs, to which Israel owed their existence as a people, and mention of the covenant at Sinai, to which they owed their status as the people of God (cf. v. 45b, "that I might be their God"). For it was "through" the land that the promise of God to the patriarchs became a historical reality for Israel, and likewise "through" the land that the reciprocal discharge of their responsibility to him became, or should have become, a practical reality in the socio-economic realm. For this reason, *neglect* of sabbatical institutions, specifically concerned with the land, both involved the moral evil that accompanied neglect of social justice and charity, as urged in ch. 25, and also symbolized the *wider* rejection of the obligations of Israel's relationship to Yahweh. Thus, 26:43 links the desolation of the land with the general judgment that Israel had spurned God's ordinances and abhorrred his statutes.

In the light of these reflections, one can discern a considerable community of interest between the ideology and interpretation of the Exile found here in Leviticus and that with which we are familiar from the prophets. One is reminded of Samuel Rolles Driver's remark that the redactor of the Holiness Code was "at once a priest and a prophet."[10]

B. RESPONSIBILITY TO THE FAMILY

In view of the pivotal role of the household in the nexus of theological and socio-economic interrelationships, it is not surprising to find, as we do, that the Israelite landowner and subordinate members of his household should be conscious of a moral and, in some cases, legal responsibility towards the family as a whole in respect of the family land—a responsibility parallel and related to their primary responsibility to God himself.

The words "as a whole" are deliberate, for a person's responsibility to his family and its property was not limited to his immediate circle of living kin, but extended into the past and the future.

> The family was attached to the soil. . . . Laws of primogeniture, succession and inheritance rights, indivisibility and inalienability of real estate, the sacrilegious nature of the crime of moving a landmark all derive from this concept of the family and its real

10. *Introduction to the Literature of the Old Testament,* 9th ed. (Magnolia, Mass.: Peter Smith, 1972), p. 151.

holdings as a unit in any given generation (. . . its horizontal modality) and as a unit extending from its first ancestors to all future progeny (its vertical modality).[11]

It is responsibility to this "unit" in both its dimensions that concerns us in this section.

Clearly, the *Fifth Commandment* again becomes relevant at this point. We have already noted its significance in connection with the preservation of the internal authority of the family and the relation of this to Israel's security on the land. As regards our present context, the question is: How far are we to extend the range of the commandment to honor one's parents? Is it limited to one's biological progenitors? Or is it possible to see in this commandment the duty of honoring the ancestors of one's whole family line? If the latter be admitted, is it merely commemorative piety that is entailed, or are the ancestors thought to benefit in some real way by its exercise?

These questions are focused in the *Naboth* incident.[12]

The LORD forbid that I should give you the inheritance of my fathers. (1 Kgs. 21:3)

Naboth's reply to Ahab epitomizes the sense of responsibility to one's ancestors that shaped an Israelite's use of his land. He was not the sole owner; it belonged to the whole family line. The same rationale underlay the prohibition on removal of landmarks, as the references to "predecessors" and "forefathers" show (Deut. 19:14, NIV; Prov. 22:28). To repeat and amplify our question: Was this responsibility to ancestors simply the emotional bond of kinship stretched back metaphorically into the past in order to hallow the practice of inalienable tenure of land? Or were the ancestors reck-

---

11. Herbert C. Brichto, "Kin, Cult, Land and Afterlife," p. 5.
12. The legal aspects of the Naboth trial and execution, though interesting, are not germane to our purpose at this point, though they have aroused considerable scholarly debate. Of recent literature, see, e.g., Francis I. Andersen, "The Socio-Juridical Background of the Naboth Incident," *JBL* 85 (1966): 46-57; Jacob Weingreen, "The Case of the Daughters of Zelophchad," *VT* 16 (1966): 521-22; Horst Seebass, "Der Fall Naboth im I Reg. xxi," *VT* 24 (1974): 474-488.

oned to have a continuing real existence in some kind of afterlife, the quality or felicity of which was in some way dependent on the continuance of a living family line on the ancestral land? Under the first alternative, *preservation of the patrimonial estate* would be the *primary end,* towards which a sense of loyalty to ancestors was a powerful, but auxiliary, means. Under the second, *the welfare of the ancestors* would be the *primary end,* and the preservation of their land a necessary means. Naboth's reply therefore could be interpreted, respectively, either as an appeal to filial piety in order to cling on to the threatened portion of land[13] or, reading his reply with the stress on "my fathers," as a refusal to part with his land for the sake of *their* (and later, his own) undiminished felicity.

The second of these views is propounded with detailed and vigorous argument by Herbert C. Brichto.[14] Space precludes a full account of this lengthy article, but his summary of his conclusions is worth quoting in full:

We believe that the evidence deduced from earliest Israelite sources through texts as late as the exilic prophets testifies overwhelmingly to a belief on the part of biblical Israel in an afterlife, an afterlife in which the dead, though apparently deprived of material substance, retain such personality characteristics as form, memory, consciousness and even knowledge of what happens to their descendants in the land of the living. They remain very much concerned about the fortunes of their descendants, for they are dependent on them, on their continued existence on the family land, on their performance of memorial rites, for a felicitous

13. If so, however, we must allow that it was a genuine appeal, and not, as Phillips says, "to get out of an awkward situation"—Ahab's request being "in no sense improper" (*Ancient Israel's Criminal Law,* p. 151, n. 11). He justifies this by reference to the Tenth Commandment, which he thinks may have given rise to the "Israelite conception of the ownership of reality in perpetuity. But since the commandment only applied to houses it could not properly be used in connection with land." But against this: (1) the Tenth Commandment did not produce Israel's belief in inalienability, as we have seen; it rather presupposes it. (2) "House" in Exod. 20:17 can probably be taken to mean a person's whole estate, not just his dwelling house, so that the distinction Phillips makes between house and land here is hardly tenable.

14. "Kin, Cult, Land and Afterlife."

condition in the after life. Such a belief is not to be confused with "immortality only in their posterity" . . . ; nor with a vague hope that the dead continue as individuals or names in the memory of later generations. Nor is it to carry in its train such conceptual baggage as Paradise, Elysian Fields, Resurrection, etc. This belief on the part of biblical Israel is not repudiated, nor are the basic practices attendant to it proscribed by the authoritative spokesmen of normative biblical religion. (pp. 48-49)

It is in the course of the arguments that lead Brichto to this conclusion, and partly in the light of them, that he advances his particular interpretation of the *Fifth Commandment*. Although rites on behalf of the dead are nowhere explicitly prescribed in the Old Testament, they are forbidden only in connection with foreign families and deities (Exod. 34:11-16; Num. 25:1ff.; cf. Ps. 106:28; Deut. 7:1-4), a fact which Brichto takes to imply that they were at least tolerated in Israelite families. He goes further, however, and suggests that such practical expressions of filial piety to deceased ancestors are in fact implicit in the frequent exhortations to respect for one's parents. And so the controversial suggestion is made that the Fifth Commandment itself refers primarily "to the respect to be shown for parents *after their death*" (p. 31, his italics); for it is *then*, being dependent in their afterlife on their descendants, that they stand in greatest need of protection from disloyalty or impiety. In support of this, Brichto (pp. 33ff.) points to what he calls "photographic negatives" of the Fifth Commandment in which one who fails to show respect to his parents will himself suffer extinction in the afterlife, by being deprived of burial (Prov. 20:20; 30:11, 17).

In this treatment of the Fifth Commandment, however, it seems to me that Brichto has overstated his case—which is a pity, for much in the rest of his argument carries conviction. It seems unlikely that the commandment could have signified piety to *deceased* ancestors without much clearer indication. The comment that "during their lifetime, parents in possession of the land . . . would know how to enforce respect" (p. 31), though true, in no way evacuates the accepted sense of the commandment of its force and validity. More

important still is the fact that Brichto's introducing the Fifth Commandment into his argument is at variance with his claim earlier in
the article that he would be presenting material that belongs only to
"certain areas of belief and practice, deriving from ancient mores
and folk-beliefs, to which normative Scriptural religion gives the
sanction of passive toleration but withholds positive prescription or
assent" (p. 4). But the Fifth Commandment, with its galaxy of
supporting laws and exhortations, stands squarely and prominently
in the mainstream of Old Testament "prescriptive" ethics, and this
would be quite inexplicable if it were primarily concerned with rites
and practices which enjoyed no clear sanction from Yahwism. One
must reject, therefore, this extension of the Fifth Commandment to
include deceased ancestors. Nevertheless, the rest of Brichto's article
does make some positive contributions to our purpose.

(1) Brichto's discussion of the socio-religious "cloth" on which
the Fifth Commandment is "woven" does usefully highlight those
aspects of its significance that we sought to emphasize in Chapter 3.

> Addressed to collective Israel (family, clan, tribe, people), it
> makes tenancy and tenure of the sacred soil contingent upon
> proper behavior towards one's progenitors. Once again the asso-
> ciation of parents, posterity and property! (p. 30)

Whereas, however, Brichto "unpacks" the significance of this association primarily in terms of the individual's happiness in the
afterlife (based on the twin pillars of his piety to his ancestors and
his inculcation of a like piety in his children towards himself), our
interpretation linked it rather to the concern for the maintenance of
the relationship between the *people* and God and the dependence
of that relationship upon the stability and security of the household
units. That is, we are concerned to bring out the theological significance of the commandment to Israel's historical faith, *beyond*
whatever social background or folk-religious roots and associations
it undoubtedly had. This is analogous to our interpretation of the
Eighth Commandment (above, pp. 139-140). There is no reason to
doubt that respect and piety towards parents and ancestors would
have been part of Israel's conventional social morality as an ancient

people, even had they made no claim to be the people of God or to have received special instruction for the purpose of maintaining and expressing that status. But since that status and its attendant obligations *were* believed to exist, and since, as we have seen, the household with its land was crucial in this *national* concern, then assuredly the Fifth Commandment is concerned with something much more than the personal felicity of parents in their afterlife. Its very presence in the Decalog indicates this decisively.

(2) Brichto has also performed a service in reminding us of the large bulk of practices and beliefs that must have existed in ancient Israel without finding clear mention in the canonical Scripture, either by way of prohibition or prescription. Within this realm, he has drawn our attention to the existence of a strong family cultus in which kinship (past, present, and future), land, and religion blended into a continuum. Chapters 2 and 3 showed from different perspectives the importance of precisely this socio-economic and religious infrastructure as the very basis on which, humanly speaking, the national relationship with Yahweh was grounded. It can now be seen that this represents a major example of the habit of Israelite Yahwistic religion of taking over established culture patterns and then transforming them into vehicles of its own distinctive theology and ethics. In this case, however, the particular social phenomenon is not utilized simply as an analogical model which can conveniently give expression to certain aspects of Israel's relationship with God—as, say, the father-son or king-subject models. Rather, it is utilized *functionally*. That is, the kinship land units, with their existing religious and cultic rationale and practices, were infused with a new meaning and given an actual, practical role in Israelite religion through becoming the essential link between the theological self-understanding of the nation in its relationship with Yahweh and the tangible, personal experience of that relationship in the "real" world, in the various practical ways explored in Chapters 2 and 3.

The fact that the kin-cult-land complex (to use Brichto's terminology) was employed in this way would explain why there is little or no apparent condemnation of certain cultic accoutrements of family religion, such as food offerings to the deceased and the mysterious *t^erāpîm*.[15] If they served the crucial end of sustaining the strength of the family-land bond and the inner cohesion of the family, then, *provided there was no question of the involvement of other gods than Yahweh*,[16] no necessity was apparently felt to jettison such practices as incompatible with the aniconic worship of Yahweh alone.[17] As Brichto says, "the presence of *t^eraphim* in Israelite homes need not reflect either idolatry in its literal sense nor ancestor worship in any sense. Veneration is not worship and iconoplasm is not idolatry any more than iconclasm is monotheism" (p. 47).

(3) The result of this adaptation and utilization was to harness the natural energies of filial piety and loyalty to kin and land and to identify them with loyalty to Yahweh and the preservation of

---

15. Cf. "Kin, Cult, Land and Afterlife," pp. 28-20 and 46-47, for the relevant texts and a discussion of them. See also Phillips, *Ancient Israel's Criminal Law*, pp. 60ff., specifically on the *t^erāpîm*.

16. As there was, for example, at Peor, where sacrifices offered to the dead were linked with apostasy to Ba'al (Num. 25; Ps. 106:28).

17. We would not agree, therefore, with the view of Antonin Causse that it was primarily such household-clan cults that the prophets were condemning. In "Les Prophètes et la crise sociologique de la religion d'Israël," *RHPR* 12 (1932): 97-140, Causse puts forward the interesting paradox that although the prophets wanted to restore the ancient family solidarity (with which we agree, but for the reasons given above, pp. 105-9, and not, as Causse suggests, out of a reactionary "peasant ideal"), their polemic against idolatry actually tended to weaken it still further because the family cults (which Causse equates with idolatry) were an essential bond of the primitive social organism. However, it seems very improbable that the idolatry condemned by the prophets was simple ancestor worship, and Causse presents no clear evidence for such a view. Rather, it was apostate and syncretistic worship of other gods with which they were concerned.

Elsewhere Causse also discussed the relationship of the family to the land and the possibility of a cult of the dead in this connection (see "La Crise de la solidarité"). Causse, however, was very much in the grip of the then dominant view of Israel's sociological and psychological development as an evolutionary progress from the "primitive, mystical, and *collective* mentality to ethical, rational, and *individualistic* conceptions" (p. 26, my italics). For criticisms of this view, see below, p. 224.

Brichto does not mention these studies of Causse, although they do bear directly on his topic, nor yet the earlier work by Louis-Germain Lévy, *La Famille dans l'antiquité Israëlite* (Paris: F. Alcan, 1905), which also discusses the issue of the cult of the dead and the family-land link (pp. 33-43) but does not regard it a fundamental part of early Israelite religion.

Israel's relationship to him. This is precisely what the Fifth Commandment achieved. What would have been a natural instinct was amplified and transformed into a major ethical imperative. This imperative was then grounded not only on personal and familial prudence, but on the theological consideration of the national interest and, like the rest of the Decalog, on the historical events of Israel's redemptive faith.

This appears clearly in the case of the rebellious son in Deut. 21:18-21. We have already noted (above, p. 78) that this law illustrates how the good of the whole household was held in higher esteem than the life of one of its members, should that member present a threat to its stability or even survival. The family would not long survive if its land and assets fell under the control of one so obviously unfit to protect them. That the Fifth Commandment had an economic thrust as well as an ethical side is apparent here; the two are bound together. Brichto also discusses this case, explaining the punishment for the son's disobedience, selfishness, and ingratitude in line with his general theme: "if a son in his parents' lifetime shows himself a faithless ingrate, what is the prognosis for the future when in death they are dependent upon him" (p. 32)? The *family's* interest in the matter (whether it was seen in precisely these terms or not) is obvious, but the wider significance of the affair is seen in the fact that the case is tried by local *elders*, the punishment is inflicted by the whole *community*, and the lesson intended for *all Israel*. The interests of the whole community of God's people are thus inextricably bound up with the stability and survival of individual households.

Hence, an Israelite's responsibility to his family and its land (whether as landowner or in a dependent status) can be seen as a reflex of his primary responsibility to God himself. To fulfill the first was to go a long way towards fulfilling the second. Significantly therefore, Naboth's reply to Ahab, to return to our point of departure, incorporates both these dimensions of his obligations.

> *YHWH Himself* keep far from me (the thought even) to let you
> have the estate of my ancestors! (pp. 31-32; Brichto's translation,
> my italics)

Naboth's refusal to part with a portion of his ancestral patrimony was as much a duty to God (sanctioned in his mind by a self-curse) as to his ancestors. Correspondingly, the crime of Ahab and Jezebel of fraudulently robbing Naboth of the whole of his land went far beyond mere social injustice to Naboth and his family and resulted in the direct involvement of God, in prophetic condemnation (1 Kgs. 21:17ff.), and equivalent retributive punishment on them both—the punishments of having no posterity and being deprived of burial (1 Kgs. 21:21, 23-24; 2 Kgs. 9:30-37; 10:1-11).

C. RESPONSIBILITY TO OTHERS

In this final section of the chapter, we come to the lowest and widest stratum of the pyramid of responsibility—a person's general duties in respect of his land and property towards third parties who stand in varying degrees of relationship to him. The nature of the material gives this section something of the form of a catalogue, because many of the relevant texts need little discussion beyond their inclusion and because such exegetical questions as exist are mostly well covered in the commentaries. As a method of organizing the material, I have taken the stance of the Israelite landowner and worked outwards through widening circles of responsibility—beginning with those who work on one's land, then moving to others who happen to be on one's land, and then to the property of one's neighbor.

1. Workers on the Land

a. Slaves (See Chapter 8).
b. Other laborers (gērîm, tôšābîm, śᵉkîrîm) (See above, pp. 99-103).

The only specific law concerning the welfare of this group required that hired laborers be paid regularly and promptly (Lev. 19:13; Deut. 24:14-15). Legally, in fact, wage-earning laborers seem to have had less explicit statutory protection than slaves. S. W. Baron emphasizes this and comments that landowners may well have preferred hired laborers as being cheaper, expendable, and involving less legal responsibility: "If judged by purely economic standards, therefore, the position of the free laborer was not necessarily superior to that of a slave. In fact his rights were much more vague and ill-defined."[18] On the other hand, injunctions of a general charitable nature for the social and economic protection of this whole class are very numerous.[19] Again it is noticeable that the typical language of these latter injunctions indicates that the moral obligations of Israelite landowners to this landless, laboring class were but the practical outworking of their moral obligation to Yahweh.

c. Animals.

The concern for wild animals (Exod. 23:11) and for birds (Deut. 22:6) is complemented, for domestic working animals, by the injunction of Deut. 25:4, which forbids the muzzling of an ox that is threshing grain. This may be just a typical example of a wider kind of customary law that would have regulated the treatment of animals on the land. To this may be added Exod. 23:4-5 and Deut. 22:4, prescribing care for the beasts of burden belonging to a neighbor.

For all these three categories there was also the benefit of a prescribed sabbath rest. In fact, the Book of the Covenant specifies this as part of the purpose of the seventh day of rest (Exod. 23:12).

2. Others While On One's Land

a. The Goring Ox (Exod. 21:28-32).

28 "When an ox gores a man or a woman to death, the ox shall be stoned, and its flesh shall not be eaten; but the owner of the ox shall be clear.

29 But if the ox has been accustomed to gore in the past, and its owner has been warned but has not kept it in, and it kills a man

18. *A Social and Religious History of the Jews*, 1:71.

19. For an account of the conditions of this class and of the biblical material, see Roland de Vaux, *Ancient Israel*, pp. 74ff.

> *or a woman, the ox shall be stoned, and its owner shall also be put to death.*
>
> 30 *If a ransom is laid on him, then he shall give for the redemption of his life whatever is laid upon him.*
>
> 31 *If it gores a man's son or daughter, he shall be dealt with according to this same rule.*
>
> 32 *If the ox gores a slave, male or female, the owner shall give to their master thirty shekels of silver, and the ox shall be stoned."*

Few domestic animals can claim to have attracted more scholarly attention, outside the field of veterinary science, than the oxen of Exod. 21:28ff., ever since the discovery of similar statutes in Mesopotamian law codes.[20] The law becomes relevant for our purpose here at v. 29, at the point when the owner, having failed to take heed of the warning after a previous goring, becomes criminally and capitally liable for any subsequent fatal goring.

There is some difficulty in deciding what action the owner was expected to take as a result of this warning. The MT reads $w^e l\bar{o}$' $yi\check{s}m^e renn\hat{u}$, "but he does not 'keep' it." Was the beast to be "kept in"—that is, shut in or tied up? But that would render it useless to its owner for ploughing—its prime *raison d'être*. Was it to be "watched," or "guarded"? But how could that be done effectively by one person on an unpredictable and vicious animal? The law makes no provision for the confusing legal situation that would arise if the owner had taken such precautions, but the ox subsequently wrought its havoc notwithstanding. Could he still be held guilty and executed? The problem would be solved (for us and the ox owner)

20. The relevant comparative texts are CH 250, 251, LE 54, 55 (cf. Exod. 21:28-29), CH 252 (cf. v. 32), LE 53 (cf. vv. 35-36). More important recent work, taking into account the discovery of the Laws of Eshnunna, includes Adrianus van Selms, "The Goring Ox in Babylonian and Biblical Law," *Archiv orientálni* 18 (1950): 321-330, who emphasizes the differences between the codes; Reuven Yaron, "The Goring Ox in Near Eastern Laws," *ILR* 1 (1966): 396-406, who takes an opposite viewpoint and tries to account for the similarities; Bernard S. Jackson, "The Goring Ox Again," *Journal of Juristic Papyrology* 18 (1972): 55-93, repr. in *Essays*, who also rejects van Selms' argument for complete independence in favor of some degree of "influence" (pp. 77ff.); Jacob J. Finkelstein, "The Goring Ox," *Temple Law Quarterly* 46 (1973): 169-290.

if the LXX has preserved the true wording of the law. It reads *kaí mề aphanísēi autón,* on the basis of which the slight emendation to *yašmîḏennû* has been suggested (see *BH³*). This makes the warning and the law itself much more clear-cut. By *destroying* an ox with a history of ill temper, a person would at least have the price of its carcass and would be relieved of the risk of execution if a future incident should prove fatal. By *not* doing so after a warning he was showing utter disregard for the welfare of the whole community, and his negligence was patent and criminal.[21]

The penalty if such a fatal goring took place after a warning was twofold: the ox was to be stoned (as also in the case of unprecedented goring), and the owner was to be executed, unless a ransom is accepted for his life—presumably by the kin of the victim. Each of these is unusual and deserves attention.

(1) The stoning of the ox has no parallel in the Mesopotamian codes, a fact which has been variously explained. Some have seen it as a purely legal phenomenon, characteristic of the more primitive nature of Israelite law.[22] Others have explained it as essentially a religious difference, inspired by Israel's higher concept of the sanctity of life, as crystallized in Gen. 9:5.[23] Bernard S. Jackson disagrees with both views.[24] On the one hand, he argues, the stoning is not presented as a formal judicial death penalty, nor is stoning the legally prescribed penalty for homicide in the Book of the Covenant. On the other hand, he goes on, the motive is not so much religious as utilitarian, for the sake of community protection—a kind of "lynching." However, Jackson is not entirely successful in altogether discounting a religious rationale for the stoning; for elsewhere, as he himself points out, stoning does have very strong religious connotations (e.g., in Exod. 19:12-13, which includes the stoning of beasts, and 8:26). Although he excludes religious con-

21. This view is adopted by Jackson, "The Goring Ox Again," p. 71.

22. E.g., G. R. Driver and John C. Miles, *The Babylonian Laws* (Oxford: Oxford University Press, 1952), 1:444.

23. E.g., Moshe Greenberg, "Some Postulates of Biblical Criminal Law," pp. 15ff.; Shalom M. Paul, *Studies in the Book of the Covenant,* pp. 81ff.; and van Selms, p. 327ff.

24. "The Goring Ox Again," pp. 58ff.

ceptions as a *motive* for the stoning of the ox, Jackson nevertheless allows that the *reverse* may have happened, namely, that the law may have given rise to the religious conception:

> It thus seems likely that the law of the goring ox, in origin an utilitarian measure designed to protect the community, was instrumental in the creation within the biblical period, both of the idea of the divine accountability of animals, and then of their punishment at human hands. (p. 65)

But I am not convinced that this order of development should be considered any more likely than the other. It seems to me just as natural that the stoning of the ox, while obviously serving a utilitarian purpose, should have been the *result* of a religious concept as that it should have been the *cause* of one. It shows how seriously the sanctity of life was held that even animals were held accountable to God for human life shed, as Gen. 9:5 prescribed.

(2) The execution of the owner is also a unique feature of the biblical law which, again, some commentators have been quick to explain in terms of the operation of religious concepts on Israel's laws. And again, Jackson has been as quick to reject the same (pp. 71ff.). But, while rejecting it, he admits that he can offer in exchange no adequate reason for the fact, though he does make two suggestions in partial explanation:

(a) "The greater proximity of the *Mishpatim* to semi-nomadic conditions may account for the greater severity" (p. 73). Apart from being too nebulous to have much weight, this appears to resurrect the older belief that more primitive was necessarily more severe— a view of legal evolution exploded by Arthur S. Diamond[25] and certainly not espoused by Jackson elsewhere.[26]

(b) It was a "mirror" punishment for his failure to kill the ox. Death would be inflicted on the owner for neglect to inflict death on his

---

25. "An Eye for an Eye," *Iraq* 19 (1957): 151-55; *Primitive Law, Past and Present* (London: Longmans, Green, 1935), pp. 304ff.; *The Evolution of Law and Order* (London: Watts and New York: Greenwood, 1951), pp. 288-300.

26. As regards talion, cf. Jackson, "A Note on Exodus, 21:22-25 (MT)," *JJS* 27 (1976): 298; and as regards property offenses, *Theft in Early Jewish Law*, p. 153.

ox (assuming, as Jackson does, the validity of the reading
yašmiḏennû). But could this alone have justified the death penalty?
Does it not rather distract attention from the obvious, namely, that
the owner's execution is not for "omission" (i.e., because he had
omitted to kill the ox) but for "commission" (namely, of indirect
but nevertheless culpable homicide)? In "The Goring Ox Again,"
Jackson is following out the approach of his earlier article, "Reflections on Biblical Criminal Law," in which he criticized the method
of Moshe Greenberg, Shalom M. Paul, *et al.,* and cautioned against
a wholesale use of religious principles or values in explaining legal
phenomena (cf. above, p. xvi). But one feels that in this case he has
swung the pendulum too far in the opposite direction, in trying to
exclude altogether a religious rationale from any law—even where
it appears to be natural and unexceptionable and where no other
reason can adequately account for the peculiarity in question.

Then, in Exod. 21:31-32, the law is extended to include children
and slaves. The fatal goring of a son or a daughter is to be dealt with
according to the same principle as for adults;[27] that of a slave is to
be remedied by compensation.

This law, then, illustrates the extent of a property owner's
liability for his property, where damages result from his negligence.
Whether the law was paradigmatic (i.e., that comparable cases
would have been dealt with along similar lines) is difficult to
ascertain. It may be a selected example of a class of laws which
would have included measures similar to the cases of biting dogs[28]
and collapsing walls[29] in Mesopotamian law.

b. Parapets on Housetops (Deut. 22:8).

*"When you build a new house, you shall make a parapet for
your roof, that you may not bring the guilt of blood upon your
house, if any one fall from it."*

27. The significance of this, regarding children, is discussed below, p. 226.
28. Cf. LE 56, 57.
29. Cf. LE 58.

This is a precautionary measure arising from the frequent use of the flat rooftops for various purposes. Although the law does present clearly what the houseowner's duty is, it does not specify what, if any, legal penalties existed for failure to observe it. Could a person be punished for not having a parapet on his roof (a kind of contravention of building regulations)? Or would he have been punished only if and when an accident occurred? If a *fatal* accident did occur, was the owner guilty of homicide and liable to execution like the owner of the goring ox who had failed to take precautions? The text speaks of bringing blood upon the house. Anthony Phillips argues that "this must mean that the owner will be held liable for constructive murder."[30] David Daube, on the contrary, regards it as "highly unlikely that, if a man fell from your roof, whether before or after this law, vengeance would be legitimate or a court would sentence you."[31] It seems impossible to make a certain judgment here. The breadth of use of the phrase "blood upon . . . ," from highly figurative to strictly judicial, makes the "must" in Phillips' assertion somewhat overconfident. On the other hand, Daube's doubts could equally have applied to the case of the goring ox. It might well have been thought "highly unlikely" that if a person was gored by another person's ox when the owner had failed to take prescribed precautions the owner could have been put to death, were it not for the fact that the law in that case actually says so.

c. Sharing of Produce.

Apart from the fallow year, when all produce would be common, see also Lev. 19:9-10; 23:22; and Deut. 24:19-22 on the legal right of gleaning,[32] and Deut. 23:24-25 on the right to satisfy one's hunger in a neighbor's vineyard or grain field.

30. *Ancient Israel's Criminal Law*, p. 94.

31. "Direct and Indirect Causation in Biblical Law," *VT* 11 (1961): 251.

32. Many commentators point out how Leviticus and Deuteronomy have transformed into a humanitarian custom what was probably in origin an element in agricultural fertility cults—leaving gleanings for the spirit of the soil. E. A. Speiser has also suggested a connection between the $p^{e^{,}}at\ \acute{s}\bar{a}d^{e}k\bar{a}$ in Lev. 19:9 (the "fringe" of the field, to be left for the poor) and a similar custom involved in land deals at

3. A Neighbor's Property

This category contains a variety of civil laws concerning compensation in which the principle is fairly clear that where a person is in some measure responsible for damage to another's property—even if indirectly—he must make restitution. Where responsibility is denied or unprovable, religious expedients such as oaths are resorted to.

a. Loss of livestock (Exod. 21:33-34, 35-36;[33] and Lev. 24:18, 21).
b. Loss of crops (by burning and/or trampling) (Exod. 22:5-6).[34]
c. Damage or loss of goods deposited or borrowed (Exod. 22:7-15).[35]

Nuzi; "New Kirkuk Documents Relation to Security Transactions," *JAOS* 52 (1932): 350-367, esp. p. 365.

33. Cf. LE 53, which is almost identical; and for detailed comment the literature cited above, n. 20. The best examination of the *practical* legal implications of this law is by Jackson, "The Goring Ox Again," p. 74ff.

34. The meaning of v. 4 is disputed, as to whether *bāʿar* and its derivatives refer to burning or to grazing over. See Samuel Rolles Driver, *The Book of Exodus*. Cambridge Bible for Schools and Colleges (Cambridge: Cambridge University Press, 1911), p. 225 (and cf. the NEB); J. J. Rabinowitz, "Exodus XXII 4 and the Septuagint Version Thereof," *VT* 9 (1959): 40-46; Daube, "Direct and Indirect Causation," pp. 258-260; Brevard S. Childs, *The Book of Exodus*, pp. 449, 474-75; and, most recently, Jackson, "A Note on Exodus 22:4 (MT)" and the additional literature there cited.

35. Many laws comparable with this group exist in Mesopotamian law. Cf. CH 125; LE 36-37 (cf. Exod. 22:6-7); CH 124, 126 (cf. v. 8); CH 263-67 (cf. vv. 9-12); CH 245-49; LE 3, 10 (cf. vv. 13-14).

Anthony Phillips provides a useful analysis of, and bibliography to, the different cases and the judicial procedures involved, including the different kinds of oaths and the role of *hāʿelōhîm*, in *Ancient Israel's Criminal Law*, pp. 60ff., and 135ff.

APPENDIX   *Exegesis of Deut. 15:1-2*

a. *miqqēṣ šeḇaʿ-šānîm*

S. R. Driver points out that this can perfectly well mean "at the end of every period of seven years," in the sense of "in the seventh year," as it plainly does in Jer. 34:14.[36] But the words can retain their natural sense when agrarian conditions are borne in mind. Loans would normally be of seed for sowing in spring, and repayment would therefore normally begin after the harvest at the *end* of the year. The law is therefore prescribing that at the *end* of the seventh year there is to be a "dropping" of such loans (in what sense, we shall presently discuss).

b. *taʿᵃśeh šᵉmiṭṭâ*

These words undoubtedly pick up the phrasing of the Exodus fallow year law in Exod. 23:11 (*tišmᵉṭennâ*, literally, "you shall release it [the land]"), and are thus *prima facie* grounds for our contention that this passage is concerned with the land and not (initially at least) slaves.

The Deuteronomic law therefore presupposes the existence of the fallow year in its Exodus form. It probably also presupposes the Sabbatical Year formulation of Leviticus.

The question of the literary and chronological relationship of the three texts is very difficult, but it is my conviction that the Deuteronomic form, not that of Leviticus, is the latest.[37] From a

---

36. *Deuteronomy*, p. 174.
37. The common critical view, of course, places both H and P, to which Lev. 25 is generally assigned, later than Deuteronomy. However, it is also commonly agreed that the date of origin of particular laws in all three works may be quite unrelated to the date of their compilation, so that the documentary classification of the texts cannot really provide a decisive answer to the question of historical precedence. There is, furthermore, the case made by Moshe Weinfeld for seeing the divergences between Deuteronomic and Priestly material as arising from different social and ideological backgrounds, rather than from two distinct historical periods. He argues that many of the laws of P and the theological principles behind them

literary viewpoint, the form of the law in Lev. 25 is much closer
to the Book of the Covenant than that in Deuteronomy, in terms
of verbal parallels. This of itself would not prove much, but it
combines with another consideration of greater weight. It is
difficult to see why Lev. 25 omitted reference to the šᵉmiṭṭâ if it
was *already* an established institution of the seventh year, with
the same *sacral* overtones (*laYHWH*, Deut. 15:2) as the Sabbatical Year. Moshe Weinfeld remarks: "Leviticus 25 is very much
concerned with the commercial and financial implications of the
Sabbatical Year and the Jubilee, and if the P author had presupposed remission of debts, he certainly would have included it in
his law."[38] Anthony Phillips' reason, that P rejected the Mosaic
covenant concept and therefore abolished the year of release
because it was associated with the seventh year covenant festival,
is unlikely in itself (in view of the references to the Sinai covenant
in Lev. 26), and also based on a muddled fusion of the šᵉmiṭṭâ
with the release of Hebrew slaves and a groundless severance of
it from the agrarian fallow year.[39]

On the other hand, there is *no* difficulty in supposing that the
Deuteronomic law has taken for granted the existence of the fallow
year (including the fact that it has become a fixed year, as prescribed in Leviticus). Indeed, Deut. 15:1 has been regarded by
some scholars as an ancient formula prescribing precisely the
fallow year on the land—which Deuteronomy has then expanded
in v. 2.[40] But this expansion need not be taken to imply the
Deuteronomist's abolition or ignorance of the original agrarian
meaning of the formula. What v. 2 does is to extend the scope and
significance of the primary verb of the original law, *šāmaṭ*, so that
the seventh year becomes not only (though still) the year when land

---

appear to be much older in fact than those of D (*Deuteronomy and the Deuteronomic
School,* pp. 180ff.). Weinfeld actually cites the Sabbatical Year and the šᵉmiṭṭâ
among examples of this viewpoint (p. 223).

38. P. 223, n. 3.

39. *Ancient Israel's Criminal Law,* pp. 77-78.

40. Friedrich Horst, *Das Privilegrecht Jahves.* FRLANT 28(45) (Göttingen:
Vandenhoeck und Ruprecht, 1930), p. 57, repr. in *Gottes Recht*; von Rad, *Deuteronomy,* p. 105.

is not cultivated (the previous law being still in force), but also the year when the repayment of *human* debts is not to be demanded (in precisely what sense, see below). Certainly, I find this a more satisfactory view of the relationship between the three texts than that Exod. 23:10-11 had simply "lapsed" (Phillips), or that the Deuteronomist just ignored it (Weinfeld), or that it is simply inexplicably absent.[41] It is at any rate greatly preferable to Niels P. Lemche's confused handling of Deut. 15:1-18 as though it were intended to be all one single law, so that he is left bemoaning what the Deuteronomists have allegedly misunderstood, forgotten, and failed to harmonize.[42]

In presupposing both earlier laws, Deuteronomy now adds a further element by extending the principle of "release" from land to include human beings also. Thus Deuteronomy recaptures and intensifies in a characteristic and original way the humanitarian aspect of the law which had been removed to other legislation in Leviticus (Lev. 19:9-10; 23:22). Yet this is done without losing the sacral emphasis of the latter formulation.[43] The precise form of this extension is given in the exceptionally difficult first part of Deut. 15:2. The exegetical notes in the following paragraphs lie behind the translation offered above in this chapter.

c. *šāmôṭ kol-baʿal maššēh yāḏô ʾᵃšer yaššeh bᵉrēʿēhû*

The exegetical problem here revolves elliptically around two syntactical points: first, regarding the *subject* of the verb *šāmôṭ*, is the question whether *kol-baʿal* is construct to both the following words, or only to *maššēh*, or to neither; second, therefore, is the question

41. Cf. Rudolf Kilian's somewhat blunt comment: "This aspect (namely, the fallow) is missing in Deuteronomy" (*Literarkritische und formgeschichtliche Untersuchung des Heiligkeitsgezetses*, p. 131).

42. "The Manumission of Slaves," p. 45.

43. Cf. Deut. 15:2bβ: it is "the LORD'S release" which has been "proclaimed." Also, it is in the year of the *šᵉmiṭṭâ* that the ceremony of the reading of the covenant law is to be held (Deut. 31:10). Weinfeld is therefore rather short of the truth when he states: "The sabbatical year in Deuteronomy has only a social significance" (*Deuteronomy and the Deuteronomic School*, p. 223).

as to precisely which word or words constitute the direct *object* of
šāmôṭ. Several possibilities exist.[44]

(1) The most natural reading of the pointed MT is to take all
four words after *šāmôṭ* as its subject, and the relative clause at the
end as its object. Thus: "Every owner of a loan(?) of his hand shall
release that which he has loaned(?) to his neighbor."

(2) It is possible to regard *yāḏô* as the direct object, and change
the pointing of the preceding word to *maššeh*. Thus: "Every owner
of a loan(?) shall release his hand, (with respect to that) which he
has loaned(?) his neighbor." *Šāmaṭ* with *yaḏ* (probably; cf. *BH*[3]) as
object is found in Jer. 17:4; but in the nearer context of Deut. 15:3,
yaḏ is the *subject* of *tašmēṭ*, which makes this interpretation less
likely.

(3) Another suggestion is to regard *baʿal* alone as the subject
and sufficient in itself, in relation to its context, to signify "creditor."
Maššēh then becomes the direct object of the verb and is regarded
as a hiphil participle, masculine, singular, construct, meaning *"the
one who* has secured a loan by his own hand (= 'handshake')." Thus:
"Every creditor shall release him who took a loan(?) by handshake
(in respect of that) which he loaned(?) to his neighbor."[45] Apart from
the doubtfulness of whether *baʿal* on its own could mean "creditor,"
this interpretation *restricts* the law to the release of persons from
debt slavery, which does not seem to me to be textually or sociologically justified (see below). It also appears to make the last clause
of the line somewhat tautologous.

The first of these possibilities, therefore, seems to be the best
interpretation. But this still leaves the question of how we are to
understand *maššēh yāḏô* and *šāmôṭ*.

d. maššēh yāḏô

The most convincing translation of *maššēh*, in my view, is that it
refers not to the loan itself but to the pledge given in security for

44. Extensive bibliographical details on the syntactical debate over this
sentence are conveniently provided by Robert G. North, "*Yāḏ* in the Shemitta-Law,"
VT 4 (1954): 196-99.

45. This is the suggestion of Horst, *Das Privilegrecht Jahves*, pp. 59-60.

it.[46] *Ba'al* then has its natural meaning of "owner"—the creditor being one who has in his possession a pledge belonging to his debtor. Robert G. North's proposal to understand *yad* as "power," "disposition," or "control," in this text, also makes good sense. Thus he translates: *"every holder of a pledge at his disposition (yādô) shall release what he has received-by-pledge-loan-contract with his brother."* *Yad* thus signifies the "temporary dominion or control exercised by the holder of a pledge."[47]

Both Friedrich Horst and H.-M. Weil held that the pledge was a *person*. An important difference, however, is that Horst believed that the person was the debtor himself, taken into bondage by his creditor, whereas Weil distinguished carefully (and correctly, in my view) between bondage for the debtor himself and a person given as a pledge *(maššeh)*. The latter, he pointed out, was always (in the texts he cites) a dependent of the debtor and not the debtor himself.[48] Undoubtedly Weil is more accurate as regards the precise sociological sense of the *šᵉmiṭṭâ* law, but it seems even he lays too great emphasis on the pledging of *persons*. For Lev. 25:35ff. and Neh. 5:3-5 make it clear that the pledging of persons for debt was the *last* extremity, and was preceded by several stages in which *land,* vineyards, and so forth were mortgaged first. It is reasonable to suppose, therefore, that in any period of seven years there would be more people who had mortgaged part or all of their land than had yet begun to hand over children, slaves, and the like as pledges for their debts. What then happened to such pledges of land? The most

46. This is the view of both Horst, *Das Privilegrecht Jahves,* p. 61; and H.-M. Weil, "Gage et cautionnement dans la Bible," *Archives d'histoire du droit oriental* 2 (1938): 171-241. Weil translates the verse: "Let every master release the pledge in his power on which he has loaned to his neighbor" (p. 186).

47. *"Yâd* in the Shemitta-Law," p. 199.

48. Weil regards the pledge as "a method of repayment for the creditor . . . an 'antichretic' pledge." The creditor recovered his debt "by the work of the *maššâ,* which consisted of a child or a slave of the debtor" (p. 171, my translation). Later he points out that there was "a very clear distinction between the restoration of a debtor enslaved for debts himself and the release of a *maššâ*" (p. 192). "The *maššâ* was a pledge consisting of a person at one's disposal (child, slave), never the person of the debtor himself nor that of his wife (Neh. 5:5, 8, 10, 11; Deut. 15:1-3; 1 Sam. 22:2; 2 Kgs. 4:7; Isa. 50:1)" (p. 236).

convincing view is that the land was used by the creditor as an "antichretic" pledge—that is, the usufruct of the land was taken over by the creditor and went towards the repayment of the debt.

e. šāmôṭ

Thus the meaning of the initial verb šāmôṭ must be interpreted in this light. Was it a complete cancellation of the debt and renunciation of the pledge? Or was it a one-year suspension of repayment?[49] The latter view has been favored by those who translate maššēh simply as the loan itself. Thus S. R. Driver, though admitting uncertainty, feels that a total cancellation of all debts as frequently as every seven years would have been self-defeating in that few would have been prepared to lend—notwithstanding the exhortation of Deut. 15:7-10.[50] Carl F. Keil comes to the same conclusion on the analogy of the use of šāmaṭ in Exod. 23:11: "As it is not used there to denote the entire renunciation of a field or possession, so here it cannot mean the entire renunciation of what had been lent, but simply leaving it, *i.e.* not pressing for it during the seventh year."[51]

If, on the other hand, maššēh is rightly regarded as an antichretic pledge, then this view (that it was a suspension, not a total cancellation) becomes even more probable. On this view, what is being prescribed is that in the seventh year the pledged land should be released and its usufruct revert to its true owner—the debtor. This, then, would be a year in which all the produce of the whole of his land would be his own—even though it would be reduced in quantity, because it was also the fallow year. To one who was deeply in debt, with a large part of his land mortgaged to creditors, such a year would have been a very considerable relief. By the same token, it would have been a not inconsiderable surrender on the part of the

---

49. Bibliographical details of the scholarly debate on this question in the last century and early part of this are summarized in Abram Menes, *Die vorexilischen Gesetze Israels,* p. 79; and S. R. Driver, *Deuteronomy,* p. 179.

50. *Deuteronomy,* p. 179.

51. Carl F. Keil and Franz Delitzsch, *Commentary on the Old Testament,* 1: *The Pentateuch* III (Grand Rapids: Wm. B. Eerdmans, 1973), p. 369.

creditor—though this is usually minimized by those who argue that the š^emiṭṭâ must have meant the total cancellation of debts, on the grounds that otherwise Deut. 15:7ff. would have been unnecessary.[52] But, relating the whole matter again to agrarian conditions,[53] a loan of grain made, for example, in the spring of the sixth year and after perhaps a partial repayment at the end of that year, could not begin to be recovered until the autumn of the eighth year—in modern terms, an extended credit, with little or no repayment, of two and a half years. With such an economic prospect, the warning of v. 9 against an unwillingness to lend at the approach of the Sabbatical Year and the exhortation to lend adequately even in such circumstances become quite intelligible and necessary. However, one cannot finally be dogmatic on this question, and total cancellation of the debt and release of the pledge may not have been impossible.

52. Cf. Phillips, *Ancient Israel's Criminal Law*, p. 78.

53. Contra Lemche, who makes a strange distinction between "an agrarian ordinance" and "remission of debt" ("The Manumission of Slaves," p. 45), whereas it was precisely agrarian debt that the law is concerned about. That commercial debt was not involved is shown by the exclusion of the foreigner from the law (Deut. 15:3)—probably meaning foreign commercial traders.

Conclusion to Part Two

We may briefly conclude this section by noting that our analysis of the rights and responsibilities of property ownership does in fact reflect the pattern of relationships among God, Israel, and the land, centered on the household, that was developed in Part One.

We have seen that the ultimate basis of an Israelite's property right lay in God's ownership of the land and the historical traditions of his having given it to Israel. But this right was "channeled" at the individual, tangible level through the family by means of prohibitions designed to protect its economic viability. Then too, we have seen that a person's primary responsibility for his property was to God, its ultimate owner and giver, but that this too was "channeled" through his responsibility to the family and its ancestral heritage and also through the wider realm of social responsibility and charity in the whole community.

Before leaving this section, however, let us recall the theological framework of all this as outlined in the Introduction to Part Two—namely, the twin concepts of divine ownership and divine gift in creation. Now it is very clear how these two concepts with regard to the whole earth in respect of mankind in the *creation* context correspond to the same pair of concepts as regards the land of Israel and the people of Israel in the *redemption* context. This is by no means an accidental correspondence. The creation of the nation of Israel was God's answer to the fall of mankind.

174

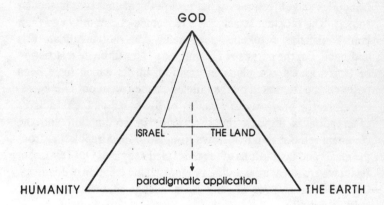

This is apparent in the opening of the redemption history with the call of Abraham in Gen. 12, coming immediately after the "global" effects of mankind's sin and arrogance, as typified in the story of Babel with which the "primal history" closes. Abraham's seed will be the nation among the nations for the nations, the vehicle of God's redemptive purpose, the "prototype" of God's redeemed mankind. As God had once dealt with mankind in the earth, so he would again, when mankind would be redeemed and the earth released from its curse. In the meantime, God would dwell with his people in the land which was both his and theirs. So, just as Israel represents mankind, their land represents the earth, and when all nations acknowledge the God of Israel, then likewise the whole earth will be filled with the knowledge of the God who, meanwhile, "makes his name dwell" in the land of Israel where he is worshipped.

This is the theological key which unlocks the ethical relevance of the Old Testament to the wider world of nations and the global mission of the Church. It is, in fact, the *paradigmatic* application referred to in the Introduction.[1] What God did with Israel in their land functions for us as a model or paradigm from which we draw

---

1. This paradigmatic approach to Old Testament laws and institutions is explored more fully in *An Eye for an Eye / Living As the People of God.*

principles and objectives for our socio-ethical endeavor in secular society. The fact that Israel was a redeemed community and their land a gift that betokened that status does not invalidate this approach. For the purpose of redemption is the ultimate restoration of God's ideals and plans in creation, ideals which have been polluted and frustrated by the fall. Given the fact of our fallenness, therefore, the only way to a quality of life based on the principles of creation is through the experience of redemption and the covenant relationship that flows from it. So in extrapolating from the ideals and institutions of the redeemed people of Old Testament Israel we are not at all denying or ignoring the creation ordinances. On the contrary, we thereby acknowledge and establish their abiding validity.

In order to illustrate the approach being suggested here, let us take *the Jubilee,* an institution we have examined in its Old Testament context in some depth in Chapters 2 and 4. Taking the Jubilee as a paradigm enables us to avoid two errors of interpretation. On the one hand, we must avoid any attempt to work out a literal application of the strict provisions of Lev. 25. Like other commandments of Old Testament law, they cannot simply be lifted out of their socio-economic context in ancient Israel and transplanted into the industrial twentieth century. On the other hand, it is a mistake to assume that, just because the Jubilee is undoubtedly used in a spiritual and eschatological sense both in Isa. 61 and by Jesus in Luke 4, it therefore has no further social relevance at all. At least four areas of contemporary relevance may be suggested as socio-ethical derivatives from the Jubilee.

(1) *The Jubilee existed to protect a certain kind of land tenure.* We have seen that Israel's system was multiple ownership of the land based on a relatively equitable division over the whole kinship structure, with the household as the basic unit of ownership. The word "relatively" is important. Obviously geographical differences, different sizes of families, and numbers of families within a "clan" must have resulted in greater potential and actual prosperity for some. The important principle was not strictly quantitative equality, but that the land should be enjoyed by all in

some measure; not that all should have exactly the *same,* but that every family should have *enough* to be economically viable and self-sufficient.

We have also seen that the theological reason behind this, namely, that the land was God's redemption gift to his people and meant to be enjoyed by all his people, is itself a reflection of God's wider original creation purpose for mankind on the earth. That all people should have access to some of the resources of the earth that is God's gift is a basic human right which takes priority over the unchecked accumulation of private ownership. Israel, as God's redeemed, "model" community, were given an institution designed to protect this principle in their own stewardship of their land. So we may justifiably take it as a moral paradigm and apply its force as a "lever" in Christian-based arguments for land reform. We may well need other means and methods in other given economic situations, but the principle seems clear, that ownership of the land should be as widely and equitably spread as possible.

(2) *The Jubilee existed to counter the tendency for land to accumulate in the hands of a few.* We have also seen that God's desire that the land should be given to his entire people would not have been satisfied if it had been owned by, for example, a king or a small group of tribal chiefs, with the rest of the population in a serf status, enjoying the fruit of the land but not sharing in its ownership. That was more or less the Canaanite system of land tenure which Israel deliberately replaced. It was a reversion to such a system that Samuel feared when he warned the people of the economic dangers of monarchy (1 Sam. 8:10-17). Samuel's fears were fully borne out by the land-accumulating activity of kings from Solomon onwards.[2] But at a humbler level, it was also possible for a wealthy kinsman to use the perfectly legal, and indeed apparently "charitable," procedure of land redemption to

2. The relevance of Samuel's warning and its relation to historical conditions in Canaan and the transition of Israel to monarchy is helpfully elucidated by Baruch Halpern, "The Uneasy Compromise: Israel between League and Monarchy," pp. 59-96 in *Traditions in Transformation,* ed. Halpern and Jon D. Levenson (Winona Lake: Eisenbrauns, 1981).

acquire the land of poverty-stricken families. The Jubilee checks such expansionism in its concern that the smallest economic units of society—an individual and his household—should enjoy meaningful ownership of some of the land. The Jubilee stands therefore as a critique both of massive private accumulation of landed wealth and also of large-scale forms of collectivism which destroy any meaningful sense of personal ownership, where the individual is as much a slave of the system as the serf is the slave of his landlord.

(3) *The Jubilee existed to support the family.* We have seen that this is the heart of the Jubilee, just as the Jubilee is at the heart of a whole Old Testament ethos which, culturally and theologically, was very supportive of the family. The family was the focal point of social, economic, and religious life. Now we need to bear in mind this wider framework within which the Israelite family functioned if we are concerned to "support the family" in our own contemporary culture. The Old Testament should disillusion us if we imagine that we can promote *morally* "healthy" family life while neglecting the other areas of family "health" which it considers important—not least the economic dimension. The Jubilee encourages us, in any community, to work towards the objective that families should have social value and freedom, economic independence, and the opportunity and freedom of spiritual nourishment. This is not to say that the Jubilee sanctions any one exclusive pattern of family life (if it did, it would not be the Western, isolationist, nuclear family). Rather, it does establish the principle that any social or economic policies we advocate should consult the interest of the *smaller* kinship units within which individual human beings find their primary status and sense of identity.

(4) *The Jubilee existed as a safety valve to release the pressure of economic forces on the poor.* What it meant, in effect, was that the insolvency of one generation in a family, for whatever reason, should not mean debt slavery for their descendants forever. The effect of one person's economic collapse should be limited, roughly, to the next generation only. The Jubilee was an attempt

periodically to halt the relentless economic forces in society whereby the rich get richer and the poor get poorer. However, for all that this is an incentive to strive for economic measures to the same end in our own society, we must note that the Jubilee law was under no illusion that this could be achieved just by goodwill and sympathy. The provisions of the Jubilee go far beyond mere compassion and call for a costly waiving of self-interest in favor of the poorer kinsman. This is seen in the requirements both that the poor one should be financially supported, by interest-free loans and direct maintenance if necessary, *until* the Jubilee, and that his debts should then be canceled and he be restored to his land and freedom. Undoubtedly this would have been financially sacrificial. It is therefore no wonder that Lev. 25 emphasizes that motivation comes from the experience of redemption. For no other motive is adequate.

If in our day the rich—individuals or nations—cannot be *persuaded* to make the sacrifices necessary to enable a more equitable deal for the poor, we face the moral and political question of whether they should be *compelled* to do so, whether by radical revolutionary means or by the more gentle process of redistributive taxation. Again, I would argue that the paradigmatic application of the Jubilee furnishes us with a principle and an objective, but it cannot be claimed as a sanction for any one political means to that end. It is sometimes loosely described as a "redistribution of capital" by those who favor some kind of compulsory equalization of wealth by redistribution. But it was not in fact a redistribution; it was a *restoration.* And the restoration was to an earlier *status quo* which, as we have seen, may not necessarily have been strictly egalitarian. If a person had been a struggling farmer in the hills, the Jubilee would not mean that he got a "redistributed" slice of fertile acres from some wealthier farmer in the plain of Jezreel. So we must take care that our application of the Jubilee, as of any other Old Testament economic custom, is based on accurate analysis and understanding of the original institution. Once we have acquired that understanding, then an awareness of this paradigmatic approach to contemporary application is a fruitful means of opening up the ethical relevance of what would otherwise remain merely interesting antiquarian specimens of ancient oriental economics.[3]

---

3. As a commendable example of this paradigmatic approach, I would mention the work of John Mason. As a professional economist, Mason attempts both to understand the dynamics and mechanics of Old Testament economic legislation for the relief of poverty, in its own context, and also to relate it paradigmatically to the critique and reform of modern American assistance programs. See Mason, "Biblical Teaching and Assisting the Poor," *Transformation* 4/2 (1987):1-14.

On a broader scale, Walter Brueggemann's stimulating study, *The Land*, surveys the historical themes of land promise, land gift, land loss, and land recovery throughout the Old Testament period. As he proceeds, Brueggemann not only engages in the kind of typological and Christocentric reflection which was the focus, but also the terminus, of W. D. Davies' *The Gospel and the Land*. He also explores the paradigmatic links between these biblical themes and contemporary issues related to human possession, use, loss, and gaining of "turf" (as he calls it). Brueggemann's subtitle shows that his purpose is not merely the exegesis of a biblical theme in its own theological context but to see how it speaks to modern humanity: *Place as Gift, Promise, and Challenge in Biblical Faith*.

Such paradigmatic application will always require serious wrestling with the text itself, as well as intelligent understanding of the contemporary world. That is nothing less than the task of responsible hermeneutics. I do not pretend that it is simple or will always lead to agreed results, even among those with a strong commitment to biblical authority and relevance. Willard M. Swartley, *Slavery, Sabbath, War and Women* (Scottdale, Pa.: Herald, 1983), discusses precisely some of the matters which are central to this present work, with a view to showing the great variety of ways in which the biblical material has been held to be relevant and applicable. Out of these *Case Issues in Biblical Interpretation* (his subtitle), he seeks to model helpful and valid principles for handling such biblical material. Elmer A. Martens also adopts this kind of paradigmatic approach when he interprets the land theology of the Old Testament in terms of "life-style"—which obviously lends itself to transcultural application (*God's Design/Plot and Purpose in the Old Testament*).

PART THREE

Dependent Persons as Property

INTRODUCTION

Hitherto we have been studying the relationships between the family and its property and between both together and God. We now turn to the relationship between the head of the household and the rest of the family considered as part of his property, and to the status and rights of this "property in persons."

At the beginning of Part Two we emphasized the significance of God's ultimate ownership of all creation, including persons. The awareness of God's ownership of persons shows itself most clearly at the national level in texts where Israel confesses their belonging to Yahweh, or where Yahweh affirms the same reciprocally.[1] But it was also operative in the realm of private relationships and behavior. Thus, for example, God's peculiar claim of ownership upon the firstborn in each family had cultic and theological implications which we have already considered. In Lev. 25:42, 55 the admonition not to treat impoverished and indebted fellow Israelites harshly as slaves is based on the fact that they are already slaves belonging to

---

1. Cf. Ps. 100:3; Exod. 15:16; also the use of $s^e gull\hat{a}$ to describe Israel as Yahweh's special property, Deut. 14:2; Exod. 19:5.

Yahweh, owing to his having brought them forth from Egypt—an act already regarded as a kind of purchase.[2]

God's ownership has a similar effect on human property relations as we have seen it to have in the nonpersonal realm. It gives *legitimacy* to certain kinds of ownership between persons so that, for example, possession of a large household of dependents was as much a symbol of divine blessing as other forms of wealth (e.g., Gen. 26:12ff.). On the other hand, the divine ownership of persons also circumscribed with major *limitations* the extent to which a person might exercise rights over another person as his property. The varieties of these limitations will become apparent in the course of these last three chapters.

These preliminary reflections mean that generalizations about the "property status of all dependent persons" are bound to be misleading and inadequate. Too often, as we shall see, treatments of the subject have suffered, on the one hand, from ignoring altogether the theological dimension and, on the other, from subordinating social and legal evidence to *a priori* anthropological or sociological theories. What is needed is a careful analysis of the different aspects of dependents' legal, social, and personal status. The most important question concerns the position of wives— being the most commonly treated and the most commonly misunderstood. Our conclusion, to anticipate, is that in none of these aspects were wives regarded as chattel property. As regards children, it is clear that they did have a certain economic, property value, but there were clearly limited circumstances in which this fact was allowed any *legitimate* practical effect. Finally, we shall examine the position of slaves. Their status as property is clearest of all, but the rights accorded to them as persons in the Old Testament are often overlooked. In particular, we shall discuss the problematic relationship between the various laws of slave release.

2. Lev. 25:55 is particularly emphatic in its repetition of this point. Cf. also Isa. 43:1 and Ps. 74:2, the latter containing a similar parallel between *qnh* and *g'l*.

6 | Wives

A. THE SOCIAL CONDITION OF WIVES

1. Survey of Literature

A considerable number of studies exist on the position of women in the Old Testament. One can see an interesting change of attitude from the earlier works to the later. In the earlier studies, one finds frequent assertions that wives were simply property in the absolute sense—chattels of their husbands, with a few exceptions due to wealth or status. In later works a more moderate position is reached, partly through greater emphasis being given to the Old Testament respect for the rights of women as persons, and partly through a more astute perception of the different types and degrees of possession, particularly the distinction between ownership and authority. Nevertheless, the older view reappears with regrettable frequency in modern works, in spite of all the scholarship that has been expended in rendering it scarcely tenable.

The view that wives were simply purchased property in Israel goes back a long way. It was asserted before the end of the eighteenth century by John David Michaelis: "Among the Hebrews, wives were commonly bought . . . *A bondservant and a wife were*

of much the same value.... Bought wives can scarcely be ... much
better than a superior sort of slaves."[1] Of much more seminal
influence on works in this century, however, was the widely read
and much quoted work of W. Robertson Smith. "Marital rights are
rights of property,"[2] he wrote, with reference to the marriage of Ruth
and Boaz, and the wealth of corroborative material from ancient
Arabian society was generally regarded as applicable also to Israel.
Following this line in the early 1900s, the various editions of the
Hastings Dictionary of the Bible, under "Family" and "Marriage,"
have such typical statements as "[A man's] wives were his property
and absolutely subject to his authority" and "The wife was purchased like a slave."[3]

Robertson Smith exercised wide influence on Continental
scholarship also, and is quoted by most writers on the subject of
women, family, and so forth. Thaddaeus Engert was the most
extreme exponent of the wife's chattel status. Writing in 1905,[4] he
asserted that the wife was bought by the husband like a cow for his
herd and was entirely subject to his whim and despotism—treated
like goods and chattels.

A reaction to these extreme views soon followed in Germany,
in the work of Max Löhr (1908),[5] Andreas Eberharter (1914),[6] and
Heinrich Holzinger (also in 1914).[7] These scholars all pointed out

1. *Commentaries on the Laws of Moses* (London: F. C. and J. Rivington,
1814), 1: 450-53 (his italics).

2. *Kinship and Marriage in Early Arabia* (Cambridge: Cambridge University
Press, 1885), p. 87.

3. W. H. Bennet, "Family," in *A Dictionary of the Bible,* ed. James Hastings
(Edinburgh: T. & T. Clark and New York: Charles Scribner's, 1900), 1:847, 849.
Cf. also W. P. Patterson, "Marriage," 3:265; and E. G. Romanes, "Family," p. 259
in *A Dictionary of the Bible,* ed. Hastings (Edinburgh: T. & T. Clark and New York:
Charles Scribner's, 1909), for similar views.

4. *Ehe und Familienrecht der Hebräer.* Studien zur alttestamentlichen Ein-
leitung und Geschichte 3 (Münster: J. J. Lentner, 1905).

5. *Die Stellung des Weibes zu Jahwe-Religion und Jahwe-Kult.* Beiträge zur
Wissenschaft vom Alten Testament 1/4 (Leipzig: J. C. Hinrichs, 1908).

6. *Das Ehe- und Familienrecht der Hebräer.* Alttestamentliche Abhandlungen
V/1-2 (Münster: Aschendorffsche Verlagsbuchhandlung, 1914).

7. "Ehe und Frau im vordeuteronomischen Israel," pp. 229-241 in *Festschrift
Julius Wellhausen.* BZAW 27 (Giessen: Alfred Töpelmann, 1914).

that the wife's lot in actual life was much more favorable than her legal status suggested.

In America there appeared several studies around this time. Caroline M. Breyfogle produced two articles on women in the Old Testament,[8] the first of which was mainly devoted to illustrating the legal property status of the wife. One gets the impression, however, that her thinking is determined more by the anthropological *a priori* in the introduction that "in early society, woman was always in a state of dependence"[9] than by a careful study of the Old Testament material. In fact, Breyfogle's use of Old Testament references is careless and superficial.[10] The prevailing anthropological view also pervades M. J. Lauré's monograph of 1915,[11] in which he not only regards women as property but discusses them in a chapter headed "Slavery." It is no surprise, therefore, to read that "the wife and the children were as completely a property of the husband and father . . . as were the hapless captives of war" (p. 18). And since "the right of acquisition of female property was limited only by the cost of purchase and maintenance" (p. 32), Lauré advocates "caution in speaking of limitations to the property right in women" (p. 33). In the same year, Henry Schaeffer, also relying on Robertson Smith

8. "The Social Status of Woman in the Old Testament," *Biblical World* 35 (1910): 106-116; and "The Religious Status of Women in the Old Testament," *Biblical World* 35 (1910): 405-419.

9. "Social Status of Woman," p. 107. This view accords with then current sociological theory, as summed up by Thorstein B. Veblen: "All the women in the group will share in the class repression and depreciation that belongs to them as women. . . . Marriage is, by derivation, a ritual of initiation into servitude" ("The Barbarian Status of Women," *AJS* 4 [1899]: 507, 510).

For a critique of that era of sociological speculation in this particular area, cf. E. E. Evans-Pritchard, "The Position of Women in Primitive Societies and in Our Own," pp. 37-58 in *The Position of Women in Primitive Societies and Other Essays in Social Anthropology* (London: Faber and Faber and New York: Free Press, 1965).

10. Most of the references Breyfogle gives to support the property status of wives ("Social Status of Woman," p. 110) turn out to be concerned with concubines or daughters. The stories of Judg. 19 and of Abraham's treatment of Sarah (Gen. 20) are hardly typical, and it is misleading to describe the latter as intended to "serve the commercial advantage of her owner." Neither Exod. 21:22 nor Deut. 22:19 can properly be used to support the argument for a wife's legal property status. Both of these are dealt with in Section B below.

11. *The Property Concepts of the Early Hebrews.*

as his authority, could write, "With patriarchy on the ascendant and with the practice of marriage by purchase, the legal status of women is reduced to an extremely low level. It is important to bear in mind that wives are in a chattel relation to their husbands."[12]

A very different approach was made by C. Ryder Smith in 1923.[13] His method was to divide the Old Testament into three historical periods—before, during, and after the Monarchy—and to discuss the changing position of women from child-bearing chattels to the recognized status of persons. This he calls "the waning of a lower concept" and the "dawn of a higher," interrupted by a period of "stagnation and decay" under the Monarchy, owing to "the curse of the harem."[14] Where Smith departs most noticeably from previous writers is in his belief that there did emerge *within* the Old Testament period a time when "common thought treated her rather as a person than as an item of property" (p. 59).

In 1931 Elizabeth M. MacDonald produced a comparative study of the position of women in Babylon, Assyria, and Israel.[15] Her conclusions are that, while Hebrew women had not the same degree of social and economic independence as the others, "a more exalted idea of womanhood had developed among the Hebrew and her virtue and faithfulness were valued for their own sake" (p. 69). She considers that Hebrew marriage was not actual purchase marriage, accords no significance to the inclusion of the wife in the Tenth Commandment, and notes that the Deuteronomic writers "were interested in raising woman's status" (p. 56). Following Löhr, she stresses the need to distinguish between strict legal status and actual social position: "Admittedly her legal status was below her husband's, but . . . from her position as a mother, and from the fact that she was not excluded from participation in the religious life, we may conclude that as a wife she could not have held a greatly inferior position" (p. 57).

12. *The Social Legislation of the Primitive Semites,* p. 21.
13. *The Biblical Doctrine of Womanhood in its Historical Evolution* (London: Epworth, 1924), p. 59.
14. Cf. Johannes Pedersen, *Israel: Its Life and Culture,* I, p. 70.
15. *The Position of Women as Reflected in Semitic Codes of Law.* University of Toronto Studies. Oriental Series 1 (1931).

A more extensive comparative study on the single question of whether or not the basis of Israelite marriage was purchase was produced in 1938 by Millar Burrows.[16] He examines all the arguments for and against and concludes that the evidence is best accounted for, not by straightforward purchase, but by what he terms the "compensation-gift." The function of the gift lay in

> . . . creating an obligation, sealing a contract, and establishing a family alliance. Other gifts were exchanged and feasts were partaken to strengthen and confirm this alliance. Economic development eventually caused some formal approximation to the system of sale and purchase, but the nature of the transaction remained essentially the same. (p. 15)

Discussing the terms indicative of ownership in a husband's relation to his wife, Burrows points out that "it is possible to maintain that the power in question was authority rather than ownership" (p. 27), and that the "position of women in marriage was very close to the dividing line" (p. 28). So even if it were right to speak of ownership, it was so hedged with limitations as to be far from absolute.

The effect of this important distinction is felt in Edward Neufeld's comprehensive book on Hebrew marriage published in 1944.[17] For although he does maintain, as against Burrows, that the wife was bought and as such was the legal property of the husband, Neufeld is nevertheless at pains to stress that this ownership was not absolute,[18] and that her actual position was quite favorable (p. 235). Like Ryder Smith, Neufeld sees a historical development in the course of which "the wife . . . attained the advanced status of a person" (p. 235), though he does not make clear whether he believes that this took place within the Old Testament period or later.

---

16. *The Basis of Israelite Marriage.* American Oriental Series 15 (New Haven: American Oriental Society, 1938).

17. *Ancient Hebrew Marriage Laws* (London: Longmans, Green, 1944).

18. Neufeld rightly rejects, however, the argument that the limitations placed on the husband's power prove that it was not ownership (a point already conceded by Burrows): "A transaction does not cease to be a purchase because restrictions are placed on the purchaser" (p. 234).

In 1953 David R. Mace took a view which was consciously the reverse of Ryder Smith's and Neufeld's evolutionary view of the woman's development.[19] Mace finds it "hard to see how a complete evolution in thought about womanhood . . . can be substantiated by the facts" (p. 185). He weighs two possibilities: that the woman was generally regarded as a chattel but in exceptional circumstances was given the status of a person, or that she was really regarded as a person but was on occasions in practice debased to the level of a chattel. He prefers the latter and suggests that "her degradation to a lower level was due to a confusion of thought in two spheres— first, in the distinction between a wife on the one hand and a concubine or slave on the other; second, in the difference between authority and possession" (p. 186). In the second of these Mace accepts Burrows' explanation of the *mōhar* as a compensation gift. He then goes on to develop the idea suggested by G. R. Driver and John C. Miles,[20] and by Johannes Pedersen,[21] that what a husband possessed was his wife's sexuality, not her very person. That is, she "belonged" to him (in the ownership sense) only for the purposes which marriage exists to serve, and not just as an object among his possessions.

The extent to which Mace has moved from the position at the beginning of the century can best be seen by quoting a paragraph from the conclusion of his book, about the status of the Hebrew wife.

The idea seems to be almost universally and very tenaciously held that she was little better than a chattel belonging to her husband. This conception, I hold, is gravely inaccurate and mischievous. It is true that the Hebrew wife did not fulfill public and social functions, and was therefore confined largely, so far as power and influence were concerned, to the limits of the home. But to read into this state of affairs all that it would imply in our modern society is to make a fundamental error of judg-

19. *Hebrew Marriage: A Sociological Study* (London: Epworth and New York: Philosophical Library, 1953).
20. *The Assyrian Laws* (Oxford: Oxford University Press, 1935), p. 159.
21. 1:70.

ment. In the highly urbanized community life of today, a woman confined exclusively to the sphere of the home would certainly be deprived of many rights and opportunities. *But in the society the Old Testament describes, the home was virtually the center of the community life, and few events which took place could be considered as falling outside the sphere of the family.* The Hebrew wife therefore, as the proper mistress of the home, far from being a slave in her own world, was something decidedly more like a queen in it.[22]

It can be seen how this judgment, particularly the sentence in italics, is fully borne out by our own study of the importance of the household and the woman's place within it (in Chapters 2 and 3).

The influence of this newer point of view can be seen in such recent statements as these by Otto J. Baab: "This transaction [the *mōhar*], however, was not a transfer of chattel property. Rather it was the surrender of authority over a woman by one man to another. She remained a person. . . ."[23] "Too many difficulties stand in the way of the idea of purchase marriage to justify its unqualified acceptance."[24] Unfortunately, however, one still finds the older view cropping up in its starker forms, with little regard for all the evidence to the contrary which has been amassed for over half a century. Four recent examples may be given.

Anthony Phillips simply asserts: "They had no legal status, being the personal property first of their fathers, *and then of their husbands*";[25] "*Like a wife* or daughter a slave was treated as part of his master's personal property."[26] P. A. H. de Boer finds the Tenth Commandment sufficient evidence upon which to rest the wife's property status: "In the Decalogue the wife is placed in the same category as house, male and female slaves, ox, ass and everything belonging to the husband."[27] Paul K. Jewett, in his brief survey of

22. P. 263 (my italics).
23. "Woman," *IDB*, 4:865.
24. "Marriage," *IDB*, 3:284.
25. *Ancient Israel's Criminal Law*, p. 15 (italics mine).
26. "Some Aspects of Family Law in Pre-exilic Israel," p. 356 (italics mine).
27. *Fatherhood and Motherhood in Israelite and Judean Piety,* p. 6. Against this, see below, pp. 196-97.

"Women in the Old Testament and in Judaism," repeats all the evidence for her alleged social inferiority and property status, and little to the contrary.[28] Ruth 4:5, 10 are not only quoted to support the marriage-by-purchase theory, but "buying" and "bought" are italicized, when a glance at the Hebrew would show that the verb used, *qānâ,* need not involve purchase at all (see below, p. 193). One feels that Jewett presents this slant with a view to highlighting his very positive exposition of the New Testament material on womanhood. But it is sad that in a book which is both a work of serious scholarship and also apparently aimed at a wide readership there should be such misleading inaccuracies, perpetuating a view of womanhood in the Old Testament which many scholars have long since acknowledged to be false. The same could be said concerning Leonard Swidler's work, *Biblical Affirmations of Woman.*[29] Intended for the nonspecialist and apparently very comprehensive, it attempts a balance of positive and negative features of woman's place in successive biblical eras. But in places it is shallow and unaware of the scholarship surveyed above. The ideas that the wife was simply property (on the basis of the Tenth Commandment) and that adultery was a property offense (pp. 139ff.) reappear as though self-evident.

John H. Otwell[30] and Mary J. Evans[31] have produced works similarly intended for nonspecialist audiences, but offering a more positive evaluation.

In the 1970s and 1980s, interest in women in the Old Testament has taken two noticeable directions. One is the interest in feminist theology, for which the place of women in biblical society and religion is significant, from a historical—if not nor-

28. *Man as Male and Female* (Grand Rapids: Wm. B. Eerdmans, 1975), pp. 86-90. Cf. also James B. Hurley, *Man and Woman in Biblical Perspective* (Leicester: Inter-Varsity and Grand Rapids: Zondervan, 1981); and Stephen B. Clark, *Man and Woman in Christ* (Ann Arbor: Servant, 1980 and Edinburgh: T. & T. Clark, 1981).

29. Philadelphia: Westminster, 1979.

30. *And Sarah Laughed: The Status of Women in the Old Testament* (Philadelphia: Westminster, 1977).

31. *Woman in the Bible* (Downers Grove: InterVarsity, 1984).

mative—perspective.[32] The other is the interest in the feminine as a theme in Old Testament literature, in the mode of newer literary criticism.[33]

2. Arguments for the Wife's Status as Property

a. The mōhar

Clearly, if one interprets the word *mōhar* as simply the "purchase price" which a man pays to the father of his prospective bride, then the wife is as much her husband's property as anything else he buys for money. This interpretation had the weight of W. Robertson Smith's authority behind it: "Marriage by purchase is found throughout the Semitic races wherever the husband is the wife's *baʿal* or lord. The Arabic *mahr* is the same word with the Hebrew *móhar* . . . the etymological sense is simply 'price.'"[34] But the etymology is not so simple, as Edward Neufeld pointed out,[35] and the philological parallels are inconclusive.[36] Some Continental scholars therefore were not content with such common renderings as *Kaufpreis, Brautgeld,* or *prix d'achat.* Eberharter, for example, considers all the arguments for such translations inadequate and is certain that the *mōhar* was just a price paid for the person of the girl

32. One could include the work of Phyllis Trible, *God and the Rhetoric of Sexuality.* Overtures to Biblical Theology 2 (Philadelphia: Fortress, 1978); *Texts of Terror: Literary-Feminist Readings of Biblical Narrative.* Overtures to Biblical Theology 13 (Philadelphia: Fortress, 1984); Phyllis A. Bird, "Images of Women in the Old Testament," pp. 14-88 in *Religion and Sexism,* ed. Rosemary Radford Reuther (New York: Simon & Schuster, 1974); Carol L. Meyers, "The Roots of Restriction: Women in Early Israel," *BA* 41 (1978): 91-103; and Athalya Brenner, *The Israelite Woman.* Grace I. Emmerson provides a survey with broadly positive conclusions similar to those advocated in this chapter and a helpful bibliography; "Women in Ancient Israel," pp. 371-394 in Ronald E. Clements, ed., *The World of Ancient Israel.*

33. This includes Claudia V. Camp, *Wisdom and the Feminine in the Book of Proverbs*; James G. Williams, *Women Recounted*; and, in some respects, Brenner.

34. *Kinship and Marriage in Early Arabia,* p. 79.

35. *Ancient Hebrew Marriage Laws,* p. 94, n. 1: "The origin of the word *mhr* is very obscure, and it is one of those very ancient words of which the etymology is almost lost." Cf. Burrows, pp. 17ff.

36. Cf. Driver and Miles, *The Assyrian Laws,* p. 158.

herself.[37] René Dussaud was even more emphatic: "This term constituted one element in a system of reciprocal compensation which, by the union of a couple, sealed the alliance of two families. The nature of the term excluded, even in its origin, any idea of purchase price."[38] Included in the evidence adduced by Dussaud is the fact that when a man sells his daughter as a slave in Exod. 21:7, she becomes a "concubine" ('āmâ), not a "wife" ('iššâ), and there is no mention of the price being called a mōhar. More must have been involved, therefore, in the payment of a mōhar than the acquiring of a piece of female chattel property.

On the other hand, some scholars have maintained the meaning of "purchase price" for mōhar, but insisting that this did not entail a servile position in actual life. Neufeld's view on this has already been mentioned. Louis M. Epstein also held that "the form of marriage is one thing, its content quite another. . . . A wife is a God-given helpmeet, flesh of her husband's flesh. But the form of Jewish marriage is more concrete. It represents a transaction, a conveyance of rights. If the marriage is romance in content, it is purchase in form."[39]

However, even when this allowance for actual social conditions is made, several serious obstacles to the simple equation of mōhar with "purchase price" can be advanced. They are well covered by Burrows[40] and include: the comparative independence of the Israelite wives, the above-mentioned distinction between the wife and the concubine who was bought for money, the wife's continued connection with her father's family, the return of part or all of the mōhar to the bride as a dowry, and the sociological fact that the institution of marriage is older than that of sale and purchase.[41] An objection not mentioned by Burrows, but significant, is the fact that although trading in human property was perfectly legal at a certain

37. P. 508.
38. "Le 'Mohar' Israelite," *Comptes Rendus de l'Academie des Inscriptions et Belles-Lettres*, 1935, p. 151.
39. *The Jewish Marriage Contract* (New York: Jewish Theological Seminary, 1927), p. 59.
40. Ch. IV.
41. Cf. also Driver and Miles, *The Assyrian Laws*, p. 144.

level (cf. Exod. 21:21; Lev. 25:45-46), a man could not sell his
wife—even one captured in war (Deut. 21:14)—nor resell a
woman whom he had "selected for himself," if he found no pleasure
in her (Exod. 21:8, NIV). All of this raises doubts about the
suitability of the term "purchase" to describe Israelite marriage.

These doubts are strengthened by the consideration that there
is no unambiguous example in the Old Testament of a marriage
being described in terms of buying and selling. *Laban's daughters*
complain of being sold (*mkr,* Gen. 31:14-16); but this "does not
prove the existence of marriage by purchase among the Israelites,
since there would have been no point in complaining if it had been
customary for fathers to sell their daughters."[42] It appears rather that
Laban was violating some accepted custom in turning their
marriage into a mere sale of property and consuming for himself
what should have come to them. The action of *Boaz,* described in
Ruth 4:10, is often cited as evidence of a wife being bought. But
the verb used is *qnh,* which is a verb of general acquisition and does
not necessarily imply purchase. The passage was closely studied by
David H. Weiss, who concludes:

> The root *qnh* is ill-suited for normal use in connection with regular
> marriage because of its predominant connotation of purchase. . . .
> However, when marriage (or betrothal) is discussed in conjunction
> with salable objects (like the belongings of Elimelech, etc., or the
> field of Naomi), biblical Hebrew, just as Mishnaic, uses a term
> which will embrace the latter as well; hence the term *qnyty* in Ruth
> 4:10. This usage is merely stylistic and devoid of any institutional
> significance.[43]

It is also salutary to remember, considering the amount that has
been written about the *mōhar,* that the root *mhr* occurs only three
times in the Old Testament (Gen. 34:12, for Dinah; Exod. 22:16-17,

42. Millar Burrows, "The Complaint of Laban's Daughters," *JAOS* 57 (1937):
265.

43. "The Use of חנה in Connection with Marriage," *Harvard Theological
Review* 57 (1964): 248. See also Donald A. Leggett, *The Levirate and Goel Institutions in the Old Testament,* pp. 225-29, for a detailed and documented survey of
the interpretation of this text.

for a violated maiden; 1 Sam. 18:25, David's valor for Michal).
None of these can be regarded as normal or typical. Understanding
of the term has therefore had to rely heavily on comparative
materials from Arabia, Mesopotamia, and Ugarit, which can have
no final deciding weight for the precise social significance of the
term in the Old Testament and are in any case themselves subject
to disputed interpretations.[44]

It is very interesting, in conclusion, to note that the more recent
work of field anthropologists generally rejects the view that ex-
changes of money and gifts at marriage among primitive peoples
constitute simple purchase of the bride. Research in different societies where such customs still prevail has confirmed rather the idea
of "compensation gift."[45] Emphasis has been laid on the special
place of these gifts in cementing the relationships between the two
families and in promoting or recognizing the stability of the
marriage.[46] Recent work of this nature is surveyed by J. F. Thiel.[47]
This modern anthropological perspective is brought to bear on the
study of Mesopotamian (and indirectly on Old Testament) marriage
laws and customs by Johannes Renger.[48]

b. The Terms ba'al and be'ûlâ

As was seen in the survey of literature, the designation of the
husband as *ba'al* is frequently used as evidence not only of his
lordship over his wife but also of his ownership of her person. This

44. Cf. Driver and Miles, *The Assyrian Laws,* pp. 142ff.

45. Cf., e.g., E. E. Evans-Pritchard, *Kinship and Marriage among the Nuer*
(Oxford: Oxford University Press, 1951), pp. 58ff., and 89ff.

46. Thus, e.g., Anita Jacobson's thorough study of marriage in Congo-Gabon
describes the bridegift as one of several means of giving expression to "a strongly
positive attitude towards the value of marriage stability as such" (*Marriage and
Money.* Studia Ethnographica Uppsalensia 28 [Lund: Berlingska Boktryckeriet,
1967], p. 165).

47. "The Institution of Marriage: An Anthropological Perspective," *Concilium*
6/5 (1970): 13-24.

48. "Who Are all Those People?" pp. 259-273 in *Approaches to the Study of
the Ancient Near East.* Festschrift Ignace Jay Gelb, ed. Giorgio Buccellati. *Orientalia* 42 (1973).

too goes back to the authority of Robertson Smith, who in fact
coined the phrase "*ba'al* marriage" and explained it: "the husband
in this kind of marriage is called . . . the woman's 'lord' or
'owner.' "[49] Since then, however, scholars have disputed the meaning of the term within the context of marriage. Johannes Pedersen
argued that *ba'al* was a term used within the context of a relationship and did not denote one-sided sovereignty (for which *'āḏôn* was
used).[50] Millar Burrows' careful distinction between ownership and
authority has also already been mentioned. Neufeld, however,
criticizes both Pedersen and Burrows, maintaining that the concept
of ownership, as well as subordination, *was* an essential part of the
meaning of the word, though only in a strictly legal sense.[51]

In a later work, Robertson Smith qualified his "*ba'al* marriage"
concept in an interesting way.

> How *baal* [sic] comes to mean husband is not perfectly clear; the
> name is certainly associated with monandry and the appropriation
> of the wife to her husband, but it does not imply a servile relation,
> for the slave-girl does not call her master ba'l [sic]. Probably the key
> is to be found in the notion that the wife is her husband's tillage.[52]

This idea is supported by the use of the term *be'ûlâ* to describe the
land in its recovered fertility in Isa. 62:4, particularly in view of the
immediately following comparison with marriage in v. 5. It is
possible, therefore, that the significance of the husband being called
ba'al lies more in his "fertilizing" and procreative capacity, and that
be'ûlâ, rather than "owned one," means "one made fruitful." This
fits in very well with the view noted above (p. 188) that what a
husband owned was not his wife's person but her sexuality.

The analogy with the land is interesting since, as we have seen,
an Israelite did not strictly own the land itself, but its fruitfulness.
Property rights in land were really rights of usufruct; the land itself
belonged to Yahweh. Similarly then, in marriage a man did not

49. *Kinship and Marriage in Early Arabia*, p. 75.
50. *Israel* 1:62-63, 69.
51. *Ancient Hebrew Marriage Laws*, p. 232.
52. *Lectures on the Religion of the Semites* (rev. ed. 1894), p. 108, n. 1.

exercise unconditional ownership over his wife as a piece of property; but as her *ba'al* he did have exclusive rights to her sexuality and fertility, and certainly his children, the result of her fruitfulness, were regarded legitimately as his property.

Thus, while the use of *ba'al* and *be'ûlâ* in the context of marriage undoubtedly signified the *authority* of the husband, there are good grounds for doubting that it also signified his *ownership of her person.* Rather, it denoted the exclusiveness of the marriage bond in respect of the husband's sole claim to his wife's sexuality and fertility.

c. The Tenth Commandment

The Tenth Commandment could be called a "stock argument," in that it is usually just referred to without further comment in support of the view that a wife was numbered among her husband's goods.[53] Even Burrows affords it little comment, simply including it in "Other Indications of Ownership," though he wonders if Deut. 5:21, which places the wife first, is perhaps a "sign of social progress."[54] This is an echo of Elizabeth M. MacDonald's note that "the Deuteronomic writers were interested in raising woman's status,"[55] a fact which we have seen carried to something of an extreme by Anthony Phillips (see above, pp. 90-92). However, William L. Moran has strongly argued against using the Tenth Commandment, in either form, as indicative of woman's social status, or the change of order as indicative of social change.

> . . . From a comparison of the two recensions nothing can be concluded about the social status of women. For if Dt 5,21b is a typical list of common possessions subject to sale, exchange or inheritance, then there is no place in it for a man's wife, for no more in Israel than at Ugarit was she from a legal viewpoint a property in the same sense as other possessions; she was not, for example, subject to sale. And consequently there is nothing more

---

53. E.g., "The wife is considered as the property of her husband (Exod. 20:17)" (Neufeld, *Ancient Hebrew Marriage Laws*, p. 231). Cf. above, n. 27.

54. *The Basis of Israelite Marriage*, p. 27.

55. *The Position of Women*, p. 56.

archaic about the list in Ex 20,17, which cannot be understood in the sense that a man's wife was just a common chattel; at the most it implies that she was a possession in some sense. . . .[56]

Proper perspective is gained when it is seen that what the items have in common is not that they are pieces of property, but that they are typical of what may be the object of a neighbor's coveting. There are obviously various motives for covetous desire; oxen and asses represent property which is coveted for its economic value, but it can scarcely ever have been the case that a man coveted his neighbor's wife merely with a view to adding her to his possessions. It is surely her sexuality which is his desire and which was in the legislator's mind when he included her in the list appended to the commandment. So while the commandment forbids the coveting of anything or anyone belonging to a neighbor, the nature of the belonging and the coveting is clearly not uniform. The commandment is concerned with a man's relationship with his neighbor and tells us nothing about the nature of the neighbor's relationship with his own wife. It is thus a misleading and somewhat absurd simplification to use this passage as a "proof" of the chattel status of the wife.

d. Everyday Life

When one writer describes the wife's position in everyday life as no better than the cattle in her husband's herd[57] and another, using the same evidence, speaks of her as something more like a queen in her own world,[58] one suspects that either the evidence is somewhat ambiguous or that writers' opinions are determined by other presuppositions or other evidence to which they attach greater weight. Bearing this in mind by way of caution, we shall nevertheless briefly survey the relevant material and assess its implications. Domestic, social, and cultic life may be mentioned.

(1) What glimpses we get in the Old Testament of wives *in the*

56. "The Conclusion of the Decalogue (Ex 20,17 = Dt 5,21)," *CBQ* 29 (1967): 552.
57. Engert, p. 59.
58. Mace, p. 263.

home fail to bear out the first, lowly opinion of the wife's status mentioned above. There are no instances of exceptionally harsh treatment of a wife,[59] though there is plenty to show that the husband had full authority over her. Yet equally there are examples, especially in the patriarchal stories, of wives exercising considerable influence over husbands.[60] Not only influence, but initiative within the family circle was also exercised by some wives,[61] and the intimacy of marriage is referred to sufficiently often to render Engert's view unlikely.[62] Furthermore, there is the high position of respect accorded to the mother which was entirely equal to the father's in point of law,[63] and is amply illustrated in the narrative, prophetic, and poetic texts.[64] It would seem hard to reconcile within the family unit this attitude of honor and respect for the mother with the alleged inferiority and oppression of the wife. Could children have been expected to render deference equal to that rendered to their father to one whom he regarded as a chattel and treated like a sheep? One is much rather inclined to agree with Raphael Loewe, who feels that the highly exalted position of womanhood within the family in Judaism must have had its roots in the Old Testament.[65]

(2) As regards *social and national life,* the Old Testament is rich in examples of women taking an active part, mixing freely with their menfolk and frequently showing greater initiative and resourcefulness. On occasions indeed, Israel's national security or the survival of a leader depended on the actions of women,[66] and there are instances of the initiative and social freedom of lesser women.[67]

59. The treatment of daughters or concubines is not under consideration here, though as has been noted it is sometimes loosely used with reference to the alleged property status of wives.

60. E.g., Gen. 16, 20, 27.

61. E.g., Josh. 15:18-19; 1 Sam. 25.

62. E.g., Gen. 24:67; 29:18; 1 Sam. 1:8; 2 Sam. 3:16.

63. E.g., Exod. 20:12; 21:15, 17; Lev. 19:3; 20:9; Deut. 5:16; 21:18-19.

64. E.g., Gen. 24:55; 28:7; Judg. 14:2ff.; 17:2ff.; Ezek. 22:7; Prov. 10:1; 20:20; 23:22, etc. Cf. also the mother's part in certain judicial proceedings; see below, p. 219.

65. *The Position of Women in Judaism* (London: SPCK and Hillel, 1966).

66. E.g., Judg. 4:4ff., 17ff.; 1 Sam. 19:11-17; 2 Sam. 17:17-20.

67. E.g., Judg. 9:53; Ruth; 1 Sam. 25; 2 Sam. 14:1-20; 20:16-22; 1 Kgs. 1:15-22; 2:13-22; 2 Kgs. 4:18ff.

Some writers who maintain the chattel status of women concede
these examples as exceptions due to wealth or character, but some
of them were quite ordinary, anonymous, unexceptional folk, so that
is hardly valid. MacDonald notes: "Under subjugation, her initiative would have disappeared, but it is difficult to find an Old
Testament reference where a wife was at a loss, while indications
of her resourcefulness and instances where she had the upper hand
are numerous. A cowed, slave-like race of women would have
afforded none of these."[68]

(3) The position of women in the *religious life* of ancient Israel
has already been discussed in Chapter 3, where it was seen clearly
that the wife was undoubtedly included within the religious community by belonging within a household. As regards the actual cult,
there is evidence that—with the exception of the priesthood—every
aspect was open to women during the Old Testament period. As long
ago as 1898, Ismar J. Peritz made a comprehensive survey of all this
evidence, as well as of such comparative Semitic material as was
then available, and his conclusion was unambiguous:

> The conclusion to which the facts thus treated have led me . . . is
> that the Semites in general, and the Hebrews in particular, and the
> latter especially in the earlier periods of their history, exhibit no
> tendency to discriminate between man and woman so far as
> regards participation in religious practices, but that woman partic-
> ipates in all the essentials of the cult, both as worshiper and as
> official [presumably referring to prophetesses]; and that only in
> later time, with the progress in development of the cult itself, a
> tendency appears, not so much, however, to exclude woman from
> the cult, as rather to make man prominent in it.[69]

From the foregoing it can be seen that there is little to support
the contention of Engert and like-minded more recent views, and
much that makes them highly improbable. On the evidence of her
position within the family, her relative social freedom, and her

68. P. 57.
69. "Woman in the Ancient Hebrew Cult," *JBL* 17 (1898): 114. Cf. also
Clarence J. Vos, *Women in Old Testament Worship* (Delft: Judels & Brinkman,
1967).

participation in religious life, it can be asserted with confidence that in everyday life the Israelite wife did not behave—and was not regarded—as the mere chattel property of her husband.

This survey of literature and arguments has raised, however, one particular issue which needs to be examined more closely. We have seen that some scholars, including quite recent ones, who accept that the social conditions of wives in actual life were not unduly harsh nevertheless maintain that the wife's *legal* status was still that of property belonging to her husband. In the next section, therefore, we undertake a study of the laws involving women, to see if this contention is tenable.

B. THE LEGAL STATUS OF WIVES

Simply for organizational purposes, we shall discuss the laws relevant to our inquiry in the following order: first, laws involving the death penalty; second, laws of a civil nature; and third, family laws.

1. Capital Laws

a. Adultery

> You shall not commit adultery. (Exod. 20:14)

> If a man is found lying with the wife of another man, both of them shall die, the man who lay with the woman, and the woman; so shall you purge the evil from Israel. (Deut. 22:22)

> You shall not lie carnally with your neighbor's wife, and defile yourself with her. (Lev. 18:20)

> If a man commits adultery with the wife of his neighbor, both the adulterer and the adulteress shall be put to death. (Lev. 20:10)

In the light of the foregoing survey it is no surprise that those scholars who hold that a wife was her husband's property also describe adultery as a form of property offense. Statements like the following could be multiplied:

> The general point of view is that adultery with a married woman is an offense against a neighbor's property.[70]

> If a man had relationship with a woman whom he had not regularly purchased, he was interfering with the property rights of some other man.... Under Hebrew law not only adultery, but also other sex offenses are in the nature of damage to the rights of private property.[71]

There is, of course, an obvious logic in these views. Granted the premise that marriage was in fact a property relationship in Israel, adultery (or its equivalent, the violation of a betrothed girl) must have been a property offense. But it is important to be clear that to classify adultery in this way *is only an inference* from a presupposition about the character of Israelite marriage, and not something which can be deduced from the legal texts concerning adultery themselves. It follows therefore, that if that presupposition is called into question, then the inference concerning adultery is rendered equally dubious. In other words, the claim that adultery was a property offense cannot be used *in support of* the alleged legal property status of wives, since it is a derivative of that allegation— an allegation which we have seen to be increasingly abandoned.

There is, however, a much more formidable objection to the theory which is either not recognized by those who advocate the theory or is inadequately met. It is the severity of the penalty for adultery, which was death for both parties.[72] At the very least it may be asked why, if it were simply a violation of property rights, the "property" should have been destroyed (in the execution of the woman) as well as the offending man. But more important is the

---

70. Cyrill W. Emmett, "Marriage," p. 586 in *A Dictionary of the Bible,* ed. Hastings (1909).

71. Louis Wallis, *The Bible is Human,* p. 273; the quotation is preceded by the assertion, "The woman, in fact, was in the category of property" (p. 272).

72. See above, p. 91, against Phillips' view that the execution of the woman was a Deuteronomic innovation, replacing divorce as the penalty.

difficulty of explaining this penalty in the light of the rest of Israel's property legislation. Indeed, it is characteristic of this legislation that the death penalty was not applied to offenses involving property.[73] This principle included offenses where the property involved *was a person* and the offense was *sexual:* the rape of an unbetrothed virgin (Exod. 22:16) or of a betrothed, but unredeemed, slave girl (Lev. 19:20-21). Hence, it cannot be said that the reason for the severity of the punishment in the case of adultery lies in the fact that the "property" was a person, nor in some special heinousness attaching to illicit sexual intercourse.

Wherein then does it lie? David R. Mace finds it in the importance of legitimate paternity and family continuance.

> The Hebrew horror of adultery, and the ruthlessness of the law in dealing with it, rested squarely upon the immensely important principle that a man must be sure that his children were his own. The whole conception of the family continuity was adamant in allowing no deviation from that principle.[74]

Anthony Phillips agrees:

> ... Through her [the wife] ... his name continued. The purpose of the legislation prohibiting adultery was therefore to protect the

73. I use the term "characteristic" rather than "axiomatic" or some such term, in view of Bernard S. Jackson's criticisms of rigid assertions about the religious values that allegedly governed Israelite law ("Reflections on Biblical Criminal Law"). But see above, pp. 162ff., for some countercriticisms where I feel that Jackson may have gone too far in excluding such "religious values." His article (pp. 34ff.) is concerned with adultery. Jackson disputes the view that monetary composition for adultery was always excluded in Israel by the statutory death penalty. He cites as "the most important text" in his favor Prov. 6:35, which says of the aggrieved husband:

> He will accept no compensation,
> nor be appeased though you multiply gifts.

But this text need not necessarily be taken to mean that the offering of money to the jealous husband was *legally* accepted or prescribed. As in the modern offense of "compounding a felony," the money may well have been offered (illegally) in the hope of preventing the matter's being taken to public jurisdiction, with possibly fatal consequences for the offender.

74. P. 242.

husband's name by assuring him that his children would be his
own. . . . There is no thought of sexual ethics as such, but of
paternity.[75]

But is this an adequate reason by itself for the death penalty? Is it,
indeed, strictly true? Legitimate paternity does not seem to have
been exclusively confined to biological parentage, as is shown by
the fact that the offspring of the levirate "fiction" was reckoned as
the heir and son of the nonbiological father. Possible confusion of
offspring is never explicitly mentioned as a justification of the
penalty in any of the laws prohibiting adultery. And in any case,
pregnancy is not an inevitable result of an act of adultery. There can
be no doubt that family continuity was a matter of utmost importance (as we have emphasized above, pp. 151-59), but it is by no
means certain that it was thought to be so threatened by an act of
adultery that both parties should deserve death only or mainly on
that account. A far greater and more immediate threat to a family's
continuity was posed by the refusal of the brother of a man who had
died childless to perform his levirate duty for the widow. Yet he
could be neither compelled to do so nor judicially punished (beyond
a public disgrace)—let alone executed.

The inadequacy of this explanation is further revealed by
examination of Lev. 19:20.

If a man lies with a woman and she is a slave girl betrothed to a
man but not yet ransomed nor given her freedom, compensation
shall be paid.[76] They shall not be put to death because she had not
yet been freed.

---

75. *Ancient Israel's Criminal Law,* p. 117. See further on adultery Henry
McKeating, "Sanctions against Adultery in Ancient Israelite Society, with some
reflections on Methodology in the study of Old Testament Ethics," *JSOT* 11 (1979):
57-72; and Anthony Phillips, "Another Look at Adultery," *JSOT* 20 (1981): 3-25.

76. I have adopted here E. A. Speiser's explanation of the phrase *biqqōreṯ*
tihyeh in terms of compensation, as preferable to the uncharacteristically vague "an
inquiry shall be held" (cf. RSV and NEB). What was special about this case that
needed an investigation to be thus specified? Cf. Speiser, "Leviticus and the Critics,"
pp. 33-36 in *Yehezkel Kaufmann Jubilee Volume.* This interpretation is also adopted
by Martin Noth, *Leviticus,* p. 143.

Mace argues that in this case of violation of a girl "of the concubine class ... adultery is by comparison venial [because] ... the function of the woman is not that of raising legitimate heirs to her owner."[77] But, in fact, in three Old Testament cases where men took concubines the purpose explicitly was to raise legitimate children and heirs (Gen. 16; 30:3, 9). And in common life (excluding royal harems) it is likely that men took concubines for the purpose of gaining or increasing their offspring. In any case, it is not clear from the passage that the girl concerned was in fact being bought in order to become a concubine. The references to freedom may mean that she was destined to become a full wife, once the price for her freedom was paid. So it need not have been her lower prospective marital status that reduced the penalty. If, on the other hand, Mace means by "owner" the girl's *present* master, to whom she is simply a slave in no kind of marital relationship, then it is not a case of adultery at all, and it makes no sense to speak of it as "venial" or otherwise.

Edward Neufeld, too, is inconsistent in his use of this passage, for although he first says it is not strictly a case of "adultery proper," he later claims it as an illustration of property rights "in Biblical law in general *and in the law of adultery in particular.*"[78] But, on the contrary, it is rather an illustration of property rights in persons where the law of adultery did *not* apply. The wording of the law itself makes this clear, in the last phrase of Lev. 19:20: "they are not to be put to death, *because she was not free* (NIV 'had not been freed')." When the offense took place the girl was still legally the *property* of her master, and the offense was therefore one of property damages for which compensation was payable,[79] *not* the capital offense of adultery.[80] The principle is the same as the compensation paid to the father of the violated virgin daughter (Exod. 22:16-17; Deut. 22:28ff.). On the other hand, had the girl been *free* (i.e., no

77. P. 243.

78. *Ancient Hebrew Marriage Laws*, pp. 165-66 (my italics).

79. The compensation would be payable to the slave girl's owner, of course, unless the prospective husband had made some kind of deposit.

80. Cf. further on this point Phillips, *Ancient Israel's Criminal Law*, p. 114.

longer property) as well as betrothed, then the laws of Deut. 22:23-27 would have been relevant; it would have been adultery proper and no longer merely a property offense.

Lev. 19:20 was introduced to show the inadequacy of Mace's explanation of why the death penalty was not imposed. But it has now led us to see that there was a clear legal distinction between adultery with a wife or a betrothed free woman, on the one hand, and sexual assault on women who were the property of another man, such as unbetrothed daughters or betrothed but unredeemed slave girls, on the other hand. The former was a capital offense; the latter was remedied by compensation, like other property offenses. It is therefore quite mistaken to describe adultery as a violation of property rights, for it stands in a quite distinct category of law. This conclusion having been reached, the immediate purpose of this section has been realized, inasmuch as it has been shown that in cases of adultery a wife was *not* treated as having the legal status of property. But for the wider purpose of our argument, more may be said concerning the capital nature of the crime.

Mace offers two further reasons for the severity of the punishment for adultery in Israel: that it was a crime against society as a whole,[81] and that in some way it was also a crime against Yahweh.[82] But he does not clearly explain *why* adultery should have been so regarded. Phillips goes further still. Notwithstanding the view he expresses elsewhere that wives were legally their husbands' property, he argues that

> it is too simple a view of the law of adultery to regard the wife as merely part of her husband's property, for, in distinction from a daughter, by virtue of her marriage, she became an extension of the husband himself (Gen. 2:24). . . .[83]

81. "Whatever attitude be taken towards the adulterous wife, the fact remains that her partner in guilt has perpetrated an outrage against the stability of the whole social structure of Israel" (p. 244).

82. Mace cites Gen. 20:2-7; 39:7-9; 2 Sam. 12:13-14. He still insists, however, that "in law adultery is treated as an offence against the husband's property" (p. 244), as "robbery" (p. 245).

83. P. 117.

This is a view which is necessary, of course, to Phillips' interpretation of the Decalog as Israel's criminal (= capital) law. The Seventh Commandment cannot be merely a property offense, for if it were it would be neither capital nor, *ex hypothesi*, part of the Decalog. Thus he continues:

> The act of adultery was a crime which involved the person of a fellow member of the covenant community, and not a tort on his property. . . . But as adultery was a crime, it was regarded as a repudiation of Yahweh . . . and, therefore, like other crimes threatened the covenant relationship.

Neither Mace nor Phillips, however, seem to me to have recovered the fundamental basis of the severity of the Old Testament attitude toward adultery. Indeed, there is a suspicion of circularity about Phillips' argument as quoted above, for he appears to be saying that adultery was a sin against (or repudiation of) Yahweh because it was a "crime," whereas the burden of his thesis is to show that certain acts were "crimes" because they constituted repudiations of Yahweh. That is, he seems to be using as part of his argument a definition which he is seeking to prove. This is not to say that Phillips is not *right* to describe adultery as a "crime" in his defined sense, but simply to say that I do not think he has established it on firm grounds. As regards Mace, it is insufficient to say that adultery was condemned because it was an offense against society *and* against God, when in fact there is a causal connection between these two respects which lies behind them both. It is a connection which rests upon what has been emphasized frequently hitherto, namely, the socio-theological importance of the family.

Adultery was a crime against God inasmuch as it was a crime against the relationship between God and his people, Israel; and it was a crime against that relationship inasmuch as it was an attack upon the social basis on which it rested. We have seen repeatedly that any attack on the stability of the household unit was a potential threat to the nation's relationship with God. This applied internally, if there was disruption of the *domestic authority* within the family—hence the importance of the Fifth Commandment and related injunctions (see above, pp. 151-59). It applied externally as well, if the *economic viability* of the household was threatened by theft, debt, eviction, and so forth, hence the significance of the Eighth and Tenth Commandments and related prophetic protests (see above, pp. 131-140). It can now be seen that the Seventh Commandment also comes into this category and is based on the same principle, since adultery strikes at the very heart of the stability of the household by shattering the *sexual integrity* of the marriage.

From the general perspective of biblical sexual ethics, adultery is an act of immorality condemned on the basis of the biblical concept of marriage. But from the particular, historical perspective of Israel's relationship with Yahweh and the central importance of the household to it, adultery acquired an additional dimension of gravity which transcended private sexual morality[84] (as well as, of course, civil property law), and raised it to the level of national concern. This explains why it is so frequently singled out by the prophets for condemnation[85] and why it is included in the Decalog—because both were concerned above all to preserve the relationship between Israel and Yahweh, which they saw to be threatened at its familial roots by the crime of adultery. So then, while Mace and Phillips and others of like mind are quite right in asserting that adultery was an offense against society, against God, and against the "covenant relationship," I believe it is this sociotheological dimension of the importance of the household that reveals more clearly and rationally *why* they are right.

It is also significant that these legal and theological aspects of adultery as a capital offense, far from standing in any discrepancy with the more practical and economic viewpoint of Proverbs, as we

---

84. It did not, however, "neutralize" the moral aspect. When Phillips says that "the law of adultery is restricted to sexual intercourse with a married woman, but does not seek to impose sexual fidelity on the husband" (p. 117), he is right in strictly legal terms. But when he continues: "There is no thought of sexual ethics as such . . . ," he seems to ignore that even in the case of nonadulterous sexual assault (Lev. 19:20ff.) the offender was required to offer sacrifice as well as to make restitution— presumably for the moral guilt of his action. Likewise, Hos. 4:14 militates against the common view that *only women* could be guilty of marital infidelity. Morally, if not legally, *male* promiscuity is condemned.

85. E.g., Hos. 4:2; Jer. 7:9; 23:10; Ezek. 18:6, 11, 15; 22:11; 33:26; Mal. 3:5. These do not include the figurative use of adultery for apostasy.

sought to elucidate it above (pp. 92-97), actually tie in very closely with it. Indeed, our interpretation here is reinforced by the Wisdom approach, for it is in those passages in Proverbs that we saw most clearly portrayed the disastrous effects of adultery precisely on an Israelite's household.

b. Intercourse With a Father's Wife

Do not have sexual relations with your father's wife; that would dishonor your father. (Lev. 18:8, NIV)

If a man sleeps with his father's wife, he has dishonored his father. Both the man and the woman must be put to death; their blood will be on their own heads. (Lev. 20:11, NIV)

A man is not to marry his father's wife; he must not dishonor his father's bed. (Deut. 22:30, NIV)

Cursed is the man who sleeps with his father's wife, for he dishonors his father's bed. (Deut. 27:20, NIV)

It is not altogether clear from these texts what the position of the woman in question was. She may have been (1) a stepmother, married after the death of the son's uterine mother (and quite possibly younger than the son), or (2) another of the father's wives in a polygamous situation.[86] We examine both possibilities.

(1) It has been suggested that the purpose of the law is to prevent a man's wife or wives passing, on his death, to his heir along with the rest of his estate,[87] a practice known outside Israel.[88] A son would thus have "acquired" his stepmother by inheritance. Neither

---

86. The majority of commentators prefer the view that she was a stepmother. Karl Elliger, however, believes it was a polygamous wife (*Leviticus*, p. 240).

87. Cf. S. R. Driver, *Deuteronomy*, p. 258; Phillips, *Ancient Israel's Criminal Law*, p. 122.

88. Cf. Driver, *Deuteronomy*, p. 258; and Robertson Smith, *Kinship and Marriage in Early Arabia*, pp. 86ff.

the law itself in any of its forms nor the prophetic condemnation of the practice (Ezek. 22:10, which uses the legal terminology) actually mentions the death of the father. Nevertheless, this interpretation is supported by the fact that in the only historical reference to a man marrying his father's *wife*[89] the woman was his stepmother, who had been married by the father in old age (sixty years old) and was then married by the son after his father's death (1 Chr. 2:21, 24). If this was in fact the purpose of the prohibition, then it shows that the wife was not to be treated as part of her husband's property, to be inherited along with the rest of his estate on his death.[90] In this case, therefore, a wife's legal status was decidedly *not* equivalent to property.

(2) If, on the other hand, the law did not relate to inheritance but merely to intercourse with a father's polygamous wives, it is still not possible to regard the act as an offense against the father's property. The epexegetical clauses of the law show that it was rather considered as a crime against the *person* of the father himself (cf. the references to "his *father's* nakedness" [RSV] and "his *father's* skirt"[91] [KJV]). There is therefore a similarity in this respect between this offense and adultery, which was also seen to be an offense against the *person* of the husband, not against his property.

J. Roy Porter, in his study of Lev. 18 and 20,[92] sets the familial

---

89. Other "examples" are given by some scholars, but in fact only 1 Chr. 2:21, 24 refers to a father's *wife*. Gen. 35:22 (to which Gen. 49:4 and 1 Chr. 5:1 are references) describes Reuben's intercourse with Bilhah, his father's *concubine*. Likewise, 2 Sam. 16:22 describes Absalom's public intercourse with David's concubines, and in 2 Sam. 3:7 and 12:8, which are also sometimes cited in connection with this law, the concubines do not even belong to a father! Abishag, whom Bathsheba requests to be given to Adonijah, had been David's nurse, explicitly without sexual relations (1 Kgs. 1:4; 2:22), not his wife. In any case, these latter cases have to do more with claims to monarchical succession and legitimacy than with normal family relationships.

90. Schaeffer is therefore mistaken in saying: "As part of their husband's estate wives would naturally fall to the heir along with the rest of the property" (*Social Legislation*, p. 39). The texts he quotes as "evidence" are those mentioned above, n. 89, which do not in fact support him.

91. Anthony Phillips, "Uncovering the Father's Skirt," *VT* 30 (1980): 38-43.

92. *The Extended Family in the Old Testament.* Occasional Papers in Social and Economic Administration 6 (London: Edutext, 1967).

aspect of the offense in the context of the desired harmony of the
whole household group. On this specific case he comments: "The
ground of the prohibition here is that intercourse with such a wife
would be an invasion of the rights of the father and thus an obvious
cause of dissension within the kin-group" (p. 14). Thus again, as
Porter's study demonstrates in other respects too, it was the interests
of the stability of the household which dictated the policy and
severity of the law in this and related cases—not simply concern
for sexual propriety. This entirely accords with our remarks at the
end of the section on adultery.

2. Civil Laws

It is in the realm of civil law that disputes over property are normally
found, so it is in this category that laws involving wives must be
carefully scrutinized to see whether they do present or presuppose
the legal property status of wives. Phillips asserts that "the Book of
the Covenant provides ample evidence that a woman had no independent legal status but was treated as the personal property first of
her father, *and then of her husband.*"[93] But does lack of *independent*
legal status necessarily imply a *property* legal status? Exod. 22:16
may show this to be true for a daughter, but the evidence is far from
"ample" in the case of a wife. Phillips rests his case at this point on
his interpretation of Exod. 21:22ff., to which we now turn.

a. Premature Birth or Miscarriage Caused by Injury (Exod. 21:22-25)

22 *If men who are fighting hit a pregnant woman and she gives
     birth prematurely but there is no serious injury, the offender
     must be fined whatever the woman's husband demands and the
     court allows.*
23 *But if there is serious injury, you are to take life for life,*
24 *eye for eye, tooth for tooth, hand for hand, foot for foot,*
25 *burn for burn, wound for wound, bruise for bruise. (NIV)*

93. "Family Law," p. 351 (my italics).

Compensation is clearly involved in the proceedings, but Phillips'
summary of the issue is somewhat misleading: "As a wife was
deemed her husband's property, he naturally received the damages";[94] "when a man injured another's wife, he would have to
compensate her husband."[95] For this is not just a general case of
compensation for injury to a man's wife in any circumstances with
unspecified results,[96] but a special case of injury to a *pregnant* wife
which *actually* results in the premature birth or loss of the fetus.
The compensation, therefore, is payable primarily in respect of the
fetus and not for physical injury to the wife. It is the *child* who has
been put in danger, maimed, or lost altogether, and it is for the child,
considered as the father's property, that compensation is to be paid.
If, according to the common interpretation of the law in its present
form,[97] the "harm" (*'āsôn*) of Exod. 21:22-23 refers to further injury
to the wife beyond the miscarriage or premature birth, then the
punishment is *not* compensation to the husband but talionic retribution (vv. 24-25) or, if the woman dies, death (v. 23b).

It is widely recognized, however, that Exod. 21:22-25 does not
represent the original form of the law. Scholars have suggested
various interpolations and theories of its development, but no
definitive exegesis has emerged. However, Bernard S. Jackson, in
a lengthy article, has attempted "to explain how and why it came to
assume its present form."[98] He enumerates all the internal and
external difficulties of the law and provides extensive bibliographical information on attempts to solve them, from rabbinic to
modern commentators. His own proposals may be summarized as
follows.

(1) The original law consisted only of vv. 22-23 and referred

---

94. *Ancient Israel's Criminal Law,* p. 90.

95. "Family Law," p. 351.

96. Even if it had been, would it have proved that the wife was thereby deemed
her husband's property? Compensation could have been related to the loss of her
services through injury, as a working member of the household, not to "devaluation"
as a piece of chattel property.

97. E.g., Shalom M. Paul, *Studies in the Book of the Covenant,* pp. 72ff.;
J. Philip Hyatt, *Exodus,* p. 233.

98. "The Problem of Exod. XXI 22-25 (*Ius Talionis*)," *VT* 23 (1973): 273-304,
repr. pp. 75-107 in *Essays.*

GOD'S PEOPLE IN GOD'S LAND

exclusively to the consequences of the injury for the *fetus*. If it was prematurely born ("her child goes forth"), there was to be monetary compensation. According to Jackson, "The fact that the lives of the foetus and the woman were endangered may be a sufficient reason for liability" (p. 296). If the fetus was miscarried or stillborn (*'āsôn*, "calamity," in the original law—referring to the fetus, not to the mother), then the offender was to substitute a child of his own for the one lost—taking the phrase, "life for life" in v. 23, not as a formula for the death sentence, but as requiring the substitution of an equivalent, as it does in Lev. 24:18.[99]

(2) Subsequently, a radical change was effected in the law by the interpolation of Exod. 21:24-25. Since some of the injuries in the interpolated talionic series could not apply to a fetus (e.g., the loss of a tooth), the "harm" now had to be taken as referring to the mother. Thus the phrase "life for life" in v. 23, since it no longer stood at the conclusion of the law but now at the head of the list of talionic punishments, took on the meaning of capital punishment for the offender if the mother died.[100] The first part of v. 22 could then only refer to miscarriage, for which compensation, and no longer substitution, became the remedy. Premature birth, to which the original law had referred, was no longer considered to need remedial compensation.

This is a comprehensive and broadly convincing attempt to solve the problems of the law. If it is correct, what bearing does it have on the legal status of wives? Nothing can be inferred on this question from the original form of the law as Jackson isolates it, for as we have seen it was framed to remedy the consequences to a fetus of an accidental blow to the mother by compensating the father. Injury to the *wife* herself formed no part, or at most an incidental part, of the compensation. On the other hand, the modifications introduced by the talionic interpolation show that when the possible further injury to the woman *was* taken into consideration, the

99. Assyrian law also provides for the substitution of a child in the case of a miscarriage caused by a blow; see MAL A 50.

100. Thus was introduced one of the external difficulties of the law, namely, the inconsistency between the death penalty here, for a homicide which was hardly deliberate, and the provisions of the law on unpremeditated homicide in v. 13.

penalty was *not* restricted to compensating the husband, as though for damage to his property, but was retributive, talionic punishment. Compensation was still reserved for the loss of the fetus.[101] The conclusion to be drawn therefore is that, concerning the legal status of the wife, the original form of the law gives us no information because it was solely concerned with the child, and the later development tells us that she was not treated simply as her husband's property, but as a person, injury to whom merited talionic punishment.

b. Absence of Virginity in a Bride (Deut. 22:13-21)

13 *If a man takes a wife and, after lying with her, dislikes her*

14 *and slanders her and gives her a bad name, saying, "I married this woman, but when I approached her, I did not find proof of her virginity,"*

15 *then the girl's father and mother shall bring proof that she was a virgin to the town elders at the gate.*

16 *The girl's father will say to the elders, "I gave my daughter in marriage to this man, but he dislikes her.*

17 *Now he has slandered her and said, 'I did not find your daughter to be a virgin.' But here is the proof of my daughter's virginity." Then her parents shall display the cloth before the elders of the town,*

18 *and the elders shall take the man and punish him.*

19 *They shall fine him a hundred shekels of silver and give them to the girl's father, because this man has given an Israelite virgin a bad name. She shall continue to be his wife; he must not divorce her as long as he lives.*

20 *If, however, the charge is true and no proof of the girl's virginity can be found,*

21 *she shall be brought to the door of her father's house and there the men of her town shall stone her to death. She has done a*

---

101. In Assyrian law also the issues of the fate of the fetus and of the wife are kept clearly separate. For the lost fetus substitution was required, but for injury to the mother a blow was to be stuck at the wife of the offender—a kind of vicarious talionic punishment which is not found in Old Testament law.

*disgraceful thing in Israel by being promiscuous while still in
her father's house. You must purge the evil from among you.
(NIV)*

In this case, a man has made some charge against his wife (soon
after the wedding, as v. 13 implies) which constitutes both a moral
affront to and a judicial accusation against her parents. The issue is
thus a civil dispute between the husband and the father in which the
wife has no independent legal status except as the "object" of the
dispute. The nature and circumstances of the charge, however, are
somewhat obscure, owing to the difficulty of ascertaining the
meaning of $b^e t\hat{u}l\hat{\imath}m$. In vv. 14 and 20 it appears to refer to some
physical fact about the girl, but in vv. 15 and 17 it is apparently some
garment *(śimlâ)* in the parents' possession.

The common understanding of the word as "proof" (NEB),
"evidence" (JB), or "tokens" (RSV) of *virginity* has recently been
disputed by Gordon J. Wenham.[102] Wenham argues that the singular
$b^e t\hat{u}l\hat{a}$ does not denote a *virgo intacta,* but an adolescent girl of
marriageable age (pp. 331ff.). He points out with respect to this law
that the wife is described as a $b^e t\hat{u}l\hat{a}$ in v. 19, even though the
circumstances described in v. 13 almost certainly mean that she was
no longer physically a virgin. Thus $b^e t\hat{u}l\hat{\imath}m$, as an abstract noun
similar in form to $n^{e\prime}\hat{u}r\hat{\imath}m$ ("youth") and $z^e q\hat{u}n\hat{\imath}m$ ("old age"), means
female adolescence and, in the context of this law, the evidence of
adolescence, that is, regular menstruation. What the parents produce in v. 15 is one of the girl's garments, worn before the wedding,
with menstrual bloodstains. However, in view of the fact that the
girl was to be executed if the husband's charge proved true, it cannot
simply have been that he was complaining that the father had given
him a wife who was not yet nubile and menstruating. Rather, her
failure to menstruate in the early months of marriage was, he
suspected, because she was already pregnant by someone else. The
parents' production of the garment was then taken as evidence that
she had not been pregnant prior to the wedding. If the parents could
produce no such garment, then v. 20 would refer to some kind of

102. "$B^e t\hat{u}l\bar{a}h$ 'A Girl of Marriageable Age,'" *VT* 22 (1972): 326-348.

pregnancy test which might eventually prove the husband right—
for example, if the girl bore a child well before nine months had
elapsed after the wedding.

The punishment of the husband if his charge proved false
reflects the gravity of his accusation: whipping, a one-hundred
shekel compensation to the father,[103] and loss of the right of subsequent divorce. There is clearly a deterrent element in these severe
measures—but deterrent from what? What motive could induce a
man to bring such a charge falsely against a bride? He cannot have
been merely seeking a divorce. First, it was not necessary for a
husband to allege and prove legal grounds for divorcing his wife;
rather, it was a matter of his private discretion under family law.
Second, the effect of his charge, if it stood, would be the death and
not the divorce of his wife. One can only conclude that the man was
aware of and intended this legal consequence, in the hope that the
girl's parents would not be able to refute his charge.[104] The law
therefore represents a strong protective measure for the wife, in
view of her lack of legal standing and vulnerability in such a case.
Not only was it designed to protect her good name (vv. 14, 19), but
also to provide for her future security. After such an incident the
man might have been inclined to divorce the woman he "spurned"
and marry another. The law prevented such a divorce, taking the

103. Wenham explains the one hundred shekels in terms of the laws of theft
(Exod. 22:7) and of false witness (Deut. 19:19). The husband making the false
charge was in effect accusing the father of theft of the *mōhar* on false pretences and
was claiming double restitution of the figure set as fifty shekels in Deut. 22:29.
When his charge proved false he was required by the principle of Deut. 19:19 to
pay to the man he had falsely accused the sum he had been trying to get from him—
namely, one hundred shekels (p. 332).

104. Nevertheless, the fact that he intended his wife's death by means of a
false charge was not regarded as a crime deserving the death penalty, as one might
have expected on the basis of Ðeut. 19:19. This shows that a wife did not have the
necessary legal standing as a victim of false witness for that law to apply in her
case. Wenham suggests that it may be evidence that it was possible in Israel to
commute the death sentence for adultery to a monetary settlement: "The penalty
here of 100 shekels suggests composition was possible in the case of adultery"
(p. 333). But this is misleading. The penalty of one hundred shekels was in respect
of the false accusation of fraud against the *father,* not the accusation of adultery or
premarital unchastity against his wife.

view that the security and provision of a household—even the
household of such a man—was preferable to the insecurity and
likely fate of a divorcée.

As regards her legal status, the law does indeed show that a
wife did not have independent legal status over against her husband.
If she were to be defended, it must be by her father. But in this
particular case the woman in fact has a dual status, since the litigants
are her father and her husband, and her legal relationship to each of
them was not identical. The concept of property only legitimately
applies to her position as *daughter* before her marriage, when she
was her father's property and responsibility. Hence, if the charge
was false the compensation was to be paid to the father, and, if it
proved true, the execution of the girl was to take place outside his
house. In other words, the only sense in which the woman in this
case could be described as property would be that she was property
as daughter and not property as wife.

3. Family Law

a. Subordination

The extent of the domestic judicial authority of the head of the
household was examined in Chapter 3, particularly as it affected
children. The wife or wives were also, of course, subject to his
authority, though we have seen that a distinction must be made
between authority and ownership, and that subordination for the
wife did not entail chattel status. This general authority of the
husband is illustrated by two examples of family law: divorce and
vows.

(1) *Deut. 24:1-4* is the only legal passage concerned with
divorce, and two points arise from it relevant to our inquiry.[105] First,
it shows that divorce itself was a matter of internal family law and
not a matter of public jurisdiction. Strictly speaking, it is not a

105. It is not necessary to our purpose to give a detailed account of what is
known of divorce in Old Testament times. Cf. Roland de Vaux, *Ancient Israel,* pp.
34ff.; Reuven Yaron, "On Divorce in Old Testament Times," *RIDA,* 3rd ser.
4 (1957): 117-128; Phillips, "Family Law."

measure providing for divorce itself, but regulating and protecting
the position of the woman after a divorce has taken place and a third
party has become involved.[106] Second, the passage puts no *legal*[107]
obstacle to divorce before the husband (except in cases where Deut.
22:19 or 29 applied). His legal right to divorce his wife (to which
she had apparently no reciprocal right) was a matter of his domestic
jurisdiction, free from external control. The most vehement prophetic denunciation of divorce in the Old Testament, Mal. 2:13-16,
is based on moral and theological grounds, and makes no appeal to
the requirements of any law.

(2) *Num. 30:2-15* concerns liability for *vows,* and places responsibility firmly in the hands of the head of the household for any
vows or oaths sworn by female members of the house. He may
tacitly ratify them or he may nullify them, provided he does so on
the day he hears of them. A "rash promise" (vv. 6, 8) might well
recoil on other members of the house besides the woman; hence
final responsibility, in the interests of the whole family, must rest
with the head of the household. This reflects, of course, the gravity
with which the consequences of vows and oaths were regarded, but
it is also a perfect illustration of the solidarity of the "father's house"
and the paternal responsibility of the head for its welfare. Verse 3
reveals that this is the critical factor by specifying the circumstance,
"within her father's house." By contrast, a widow or divorcée, not
being a subject member of any household, was responsible for her
own vows, unless they had been nullified by her husband while she
had been in his house. It is also repeated that if the vow of a wife
or daughter is nullified by husband or father, "the LORD will forgive
[NIV 'release'] her" (vv. 5, 8, 12). Otherwise she would have been
held accountable for her "rash promise" and liable to its consequences, which could have been to her own hurt (v. 13). There is,
therefore, even in this subordination an element of protection for
the wife, along with the rest of the house.

106. The bill of divorce was a necessary protection for the woman, enabling
her to have proof of the dissolution of her marriage. Otherwise she could be open
to the charge of adultery if she married again, and so could her second husband.
    107. There may, of course, have been moral and social pressures against
divorce. Mal. 2:13-16 shows the depth of feeling at one particular period.

b. Protection

Both of the above laws, while clearly illustrative of the general domestic authority of the husband, contain elements of protection for the wife. There are other illustrations of this protective spirit which show that the husband's power over his wife was far from absolute.

(1) One may presume that a wife can hardly have enjoyed lesser benefits than a concubine, for whom there existed a law, *Exod. 21:7-11*,[108] with three protective stipulations:

(a) The concubine might not be sold outside the community.
(b) Sexually, she was to belong to one man only.[109]
(c) She was to receive undiminished maintenance if another concubine was acquired.

The fact that these provisions were necessary for concubines suggests that there was indeed a tendency for them to be treated in accordance with their legal status as purchased property. But conversely, the *absence of any similar law for wives* shows that they were generally treated consistently with their higher status in customary and family law. No need was therefore felt to frame legislation defining or protecting their legal rights.

(2) There was one case, however, where a law *was* required, not to define the status of a wife but, in presupposing it, to ensure that it was properly acknowledged in a situation where the position of the woman in question was rather ambiguous. This was the case of the female captive of war, *Deut. 21:10-14*. The woman had been acquired by capture and might therefore be legitimately regarded as the man's property. But if he takes the step of formalizing her position by making her his legal wife,[110] then her status is raised

108. It is important to note clearly that this law concerns a concubine (*'āmâ*) and not a wife. The RSV's translation of *'āmâ* by "wife" in v. 10 is misleading.

109. This must be the implication of v. 9. If he designated her for his son then he must treat her as a daughter, i.e., have no sexual relations with her himself. Disregard of this law may well be what Amos was denouncing in Amos 2:7.

110. The Hebrew makes it unmistakeably clear that the woman was being taken as a wife, not a concubine (cf. *wᵉlāqaḥtā lᵉ kā lᵉ'iššâ* [v. 11], *ûbᵉ'altāh* and

accordingly and she may not subsequently be treated like property, for example, as a concubine or slave. She could only be divorced, not sold nor treated harshly. The fact that she was not an Israelite and that she had been acquired by capture and without payment of a *mōhar* was not to justify any diminution of her legal rights as a wife. If this measure of protection, particularly the prohibition on sale, was extended to a foreign wife acquired by capture, the implications for an Israelite wife acquired by normal means are clear.[111]

c. Co-authority

The dignity of the mother in the Israelite family has already been noted. She was not, however, confined to the passive role of "being respected," for there is evidence that it was possible for her to take an active part alongside her husband in legal proceedings which concerned the family. In the case of the wife accused of unchastity by her husband (Deut. 22:15ff.), her father *and mother* appear before the elders to display the *bᵉtûlîm* as evidence of her innocence. Likewise, in the case of the rebellious son who resists all correction (Deut. 21:18ff.), *both* parents are required to bring him before the elders and the charge is made jointly.[112]

Thus, husband *and* wife are seen taking joint legal action in defense or prosecution of a member of the household. In both cases the reason for the required joint action was probably the criminal

---

wᵉhayᵉtâ lᵉkā lᵉ'iššâ [v. 13]). For this reason S. R. Driver is mistaken, it seems, in regarding the prohibition on selling the woman as "in virtual agreement with the provision laid down in Exod. 21:8 for the case of a man who has taken his female bondservant to wife, and afterwards desires to part with her" (*Deuteronomy*, p. 245). In the Exodus law, as pointed out above, the woman is *not* a wife and the restriction is only that she shall not be sold outside her own community. In this law the woman is explicitly made a wife, and the prohibition on selling her is absolute. Her position is clearly and intentionally distinguished from that of a slave or concubine.

111. Cf. J. Gaudemet, "Familie I (Familienrecht), IV, Israel," in *Reallexikon für Antike und Christentum*, ed. Theodor Klauser (Stuttgart: Anton Kiersemann, 1969) 7:299.

112. The role of the mother in these laws was also emphasized by Louis-Germain Lévy, *La Famille dans l'Antiquité Israëlite*, p. 237.

and capital nature of the charges which had to be either rebutted or substantiated. This does not mean, of course, that the wife had equal or independent legal status. It simply shows that in matters of a certain gravity where the integrity or authority of the household was directly threatened, she *shared* her husband's authority and status and could stand alongside him in taking legal action.

CONCLUSION

From this study of the laws involving women, excluding cultic and ritual regulations, it emerges that the assertion that a wife was legally the property of her husband is certainly too simple and almost certainly mistaken. It is too simple because the legal position of the wife was not a constant and definable thing, but varied according to the circumstances of the case and the position of her husband in it. In *civil* law she was sometimes, in the nature of the case, little more than the object of the dispute, though not as a piece of property. In *family* law her position varied considerably. Normally in a position of complete subordination to her husband's domestic authority, she could nevertheless assume a position of co-authority and joint legal activity with him in matters involving the honor or stability of the family. In *criminal* cases she could be thought of as part of her husband's person, so that an offense against her was an offense against him. The assertion is almost certainly also mistaken because, as examination of the laws shows, while it was not possible in every case to define what the wife's precise legal position was, in *no* case was it necessary to postulate that she was legally her husband's property in order to explain the law; indeed, in *some* cases the law very clearly showed that her status was *not* equivalent to property. On the basis of the laws available to us, therefore, we are led to the conclusion that wives did *not* have the legal status of personal property belonging to their husbands.

Is it possible, finally, to say anything more positive? Wives were not their husbands' property, but neither did they have independent legal status. How then are they to be regarded? The suggestion of Phillips in his discussion of adultery, that the wife was regarded as "an extension of the husband himself,"[113] has much to commend it. She was part of her husband's person, so that husband and wife constituted a single legal unit. This is supported by the fact that some criminal offenses of sexual nature (e.g., intercourse with a father's wife and adultery) were regarded as offenses against the husand's person, not against his property. It is also confirmed by Malachi's denunciation of divorce as an attack on one's own "life," as well as being against God.[114] Furthermore, it is arguable that the fact that the sabbath commandment mentions the whole household with the sole exception of the wife—far from indicating that the Decalog was not originally binding on women (cf. above, pp. 90-91)—is rather evidence that she was automatically included along with her husband and did not need separate mention.[115] It is likewise notable that Achan's wife is not included in the catalogue of his household and possessions in Josh. 7:24, though it is fairly certain that she shared his fate. All of this may serve to indicate that the wife's legal status was essentially complementary to her husband's, thus constituting a legal counterpart to the theological concept of "one flesh" (Gen. 2:24).[116] At any rate, the results of this study place beyond doubt, to my mind, that a wife was decidedly not regarded by Israelite law as merely part of her husband's personal goods and chattels.

113. *Ancient Israel's Criminal Law*, p. 117.

114. For this interpretation of the phrase in Mal. 2:15b *(w^{e}nišmartem b^{e}rûḥ^{a}kem)*, see the balanced and helpful exegesis of this very difficult verse by Albin van Hoonacker, *Les douze petits prophètes*, pp. 726-27.

115. This is the view expressed by B. Jacob, "The Jewish Woman," p. 9 in *The Jewish Library*, vol. 3: *Women*, ed. Leo Jung (London and New York: Macmillan, 1970).

116. The legal significance of the unity of "male and female" in the creation narratives was argued by August Dillman, *Die Genesis*, 4th ed. Kurzgefasstes exegetisches Handbuch zum Alten Testament (Leipzig: S. Hirzel, 1882), p. 32; and Hermann Gunkel, *Genesis*, 3rd ed. Handkommentar zum Alten Testament (Göttingen: Vandenhoeck & Ruprecht, 1910), p. 100.

7 *Children*

The role played by children in the religious and cultic life of the family and their theological significance in the continuance of Israel's relationship with Yahweh through successive generations was discussed in Chapter 3. There too it was seen that children shared the "glory" of inclusion within the community of Yahweh's people as long as they belonged within an Israelite household. Our concern in this chapter is to examine the practical effects of children's *legal* status. It is widely agreed, on the basis of evidence which we shall briefly outline at the outset, that this status was that of property belonging to the father. We must then carefully assess a particular view of some scholars that children could be deemed the property of their parents in judicial proceedings in such a way that parents could be punished through the loss or suffering of their children. Finally, we shall discuss legislation of a protective nature in view of the divergent scholarly opinions as to the actual social treatment of children in Israel.

A. CHILDREN'S STATUS AS PROPERTY

The fact that a man's children were regarded in law as part of his total possessions and had a more or less calculable economic value can be demonstrated from several laws. In common with other ancient Near Eastern laws,[1] the Old Testament protected the child before its birth and regarded it even then as the property of the father. Exod. 21:22 prescribes that a man who injures or destroys its prenatal life should pay compensation to the father (see above, pp. 210-13). The economic value of a daughter was bound up with her prospective marriage and the *mōhar* to be received at that time. If she was violated while still unbetrothed, then the offender must compensate the father for the presumed loss or reduction of any future *mōhar* by paying him its equivalent.[2] The Deuteronomic form of this law (Deut. 22:28-29) comes in a series of sexual offenses, but in its original legal context in the Book of the Covenant (Exod. 22:16-17) it concludes a section dealing wholly with property offenses. The basic purpose of the law, therefore, was to make good the economic loss sustained by the father for the damage to his "property." Deuteronomy modified the law slightly, probably in the interests of the victim, by making marriage obligatory and removing the offender's right of divorce. The father's financial interest in his daughter's chastity is further illustrated in the law concerning false charges made by the husband (Deut. 22:13-19; see above, pp. 213-16). Finally there is the fact that a man might sell his daughter as an *ʾāmâ* (Exod. 21:7ff.), probably, in view of the whole contents of that law, for the purpose of concubinage, though Neh. 5:5 implies the giving of children as pledges for loans also.

Thus, children in the Old Testament did have an economic value which became relevant (1) if they were harmed or "devalued" and (2) if financial extremities forced a man to realize even such personal "assets." The legality of using children as salable property in certain circumstances was open to abuse, however, and such abuse was denounced. Amos 2:6-7 may well refer to the forced sale of children for trifling debts. The prophetic protest is all the more pointed if what was happening was technically legal. Likewise, there was apparently nothing *illegal* in the attempt of the creditor to enslave a widow's sons for their father's debts (2 Kgs. 4:1-7). In

1. Cf. MAL A 21, 50-52; CH 209-214; HL 17-18.
2. On the phrase *mōhar habbᵉtûlōt* (Exod. 22:16), cf. Millar Burrows, *The Basis of Israelite Marriage*, pp. 55-63.

the story, Elisha does not condemn the man but simply provides the widow with the means to pay the debt and live in freedom. In the situation recorded in Neh. 5:1-13, only the taking of interest was illegal; the release of the pledged children and mortgaged property was only achieved by Nehemiah's appeal to the creditors' consciences and the spirit of brotherhood.

B. CHILDREN IN JUDICIAL PROCEEDINGS

A number of incidents in the Old Testament record instances where a whole family, or particularly the children, suffer because of the sin or crime of one member of the family, usually the father. These have been explained in the past by theories of communal responsibility and corporate personality, as expounded by H. Wheeler Robinson, Johannes Pedersen, and Aubrey R. Johnson.[3] However, a number of important criticisms of these terms and theories have since been advanced. George E. Mendenhall raises questions about the presuppositions lying behind them as regards the socio-political life of the nation.[4] J. Roy Porter rejects their validity in the legal sphere.[5] John W. Rogerson probes their anthropological basis and exposes its weaknesses.[6] One of the earliest criticisms, and the one

3. H. Wheeler Robinson (esp.), "The Hebrew Conception of Corporate Personality," pp. 49-62 in *Werden und Wesen des Alten Testaments*. BZAW 66 (1936); Johannes Pedersen, *Israel: Its Life and Culture,* 1/2, *passim;* Aubrey R. Johnson, *The One and the Many in the Israelite Conception of God,* 2nd ed. (Cardiff: University of Wales, 1961).

4. "The Relation of the Individual to Political Society in Ancient Israel."

5. "The Legal Aspects of the Concept of 'Corporate Personality' in the Old Testament," *VT* 15 (1965): 361-380.

6. "The Hebrew Conception of Corporate Personality: A Re-examination," *JTS* N.S. 21 (1970): 1-16. This study has the most serious implications for the theory since it exposes the very weak foundations on which it rests—namely, the theories of "primitive mentality" which are now widely rejected by modern anthropologists. Rogerson claims that "in the interests of clarity it would therefore be best to drop the term corporate personality completely, and at the same time to abandon any attempt to explain Old Testament phenomena in terms of primitive mentality" (p. 14). Cf. also the earlier work of Jean de Fraine, "Individu et société dans la religion de l'Ancien Testament (II)," *Bibl* 33 (1952): 461ff.

which we wish to take up here, was made by David Daube,[7] who offered an original suggestion as an alternative explanation of this kind of event, a concept which he termed "ruler punishment."

Daube begins by examining three incidents in the life of David: the rape of his harem in punishment for his adultery with Bathsheba (2 Sam. 12:11; 16:22), the death of Bathsheba's son by David (2 Sam. 12:14), and the plague which followed his census of the people (2 Sam. 24). In all of these episodes someone other than David suffers for David's sins. Daube, however, denies that these events are explicable in terms of corporate personality or communal responsibility, and proposes as a more appropriate concept the term "ruler punishment." In his own words, this means

> . . . a type of punishment which, though free persons other than the real offender were affected, had nothing to do with communal responsibility; but must be accounted for by the fact that a sinner might be punished by being deprived of human "property" (his men if he was a king, his son if he was a father, his wife if he was a husband) just as well as being deprived of any other goods. (p. 165)

Now, as regards the incidents referred to in the life of David, Daube's concept may be accorded some validity. But as he himself says, these examples "are all from the domain of theology: in all of them it is a matter of God exacting retribution from a sinner" (p. 166). Not one of them illustrates normal judicial procedure in any way at all. When, in fact, we do turn to judicial procedure, not only is the concept of ruler punishment not found as a legal principle in any law, but it is explicitly excluded in at least one case and tacitly in several others. This is contrary to what Daube leads us to expect:

> What we may expect [in the province of ordinary law] is cases of a father being deprived of his son (as David was of the child borne by Bathsheba) . . . .What we may expect, for example, is to find a husband being deprived of his wife because he has deprived another man of his wife (as David's harem was appropriated by Absalom because he had appropriated the wife of Uriah). (p. 166)

7. "Communal Responsibility," pp. 154-189 in *Studies in Biblical Law.*

But in fact we find neither of these, either in law or in narrative illustrating legal practices (which the above examples are not). On the contrary, we find such forms of punishment being avoided or excluded.

1. Laws

a. In the case of the goring ox (Exod. 21:28-32), if the ox gores a child, the owner is to be dealt with according to the same legal rules as if it had gored a man or woman. Nothing is to be done to the owner's child. This contrasts with CH 230, in which a builder's son was to be executed if faulty building on his father's part caused the death of the resident's son. Daube points out that the very form of this passage in Exodus gives it the appearance of an amendment deliberately intended to replace an original ruling which was probably closer to that in CH, with the purpose of excluding the sort of punishment there prescribed.[8]

b. Something similar is found in the case of injury to a pregnant woman which causes a miscarriage (Exod. 21:22-23). Other Mesopotamian laws prescribe substitution by the offender of one of his own children for the lost child (see above, p. 212, n. 99). This may have been the earliest form of the Old Testament law too, if Bernard S. Jackson's account of its history is correct; but the point is that it has been changed in such a way as to remove the requirement of substitution and prescribe monetary compensation as the only penalty if the child alone is hurt or killed. Thus here too the idea of "ruler punishment"—punishing a man through his child regarded as his property—is certainly absent and possibly excluded deliberately. In normal judicial procedure, therefore, we have no examples of children being treated as a man's property for the purpose of punishing him. On the contrary, the idea is rejected.[9]

---

8. Bernard S. Jackson, however, regards this clause as a "scholastic addition," not an intentional exclusion of vicarious punishment ("The Goring Ox Again," pp. 90ff.).

9. Deut. 24:16, which is also relevant to this point, is discussed below, pp. 235-37.

2. Narratives

Three incidents are often cited where children (or whole families) suffer for the sins of a parent: the rebellion of *Korah, Dathan, and Abiram* (Num. 16; the complex literary-critical problem of this chapter is not germane to this discussion), the crime and execution of *Achan* (Josh. 7), and the vengeance of the *Gibeonites on the sons of Saul* (2 Sam. 21:1-9). First of all it must be repeated that none of these is a typical or normal example of judicial procedures, any more than are the events cited from the life of David. Porter has shown that they can all be accounted for on grounds other than the idea of a man's family being treated as his property—though Porter allows this as a *possibility* in some cases; his main purpose is to show that they do not support the theory of corporate personality.

In the first two cases it is certainly the nature and gravity of the offenses which produce the collective punishment. Dathan and Abiram have rebelled and committed apostasy; Achan has violated the most sacred obligation of the ḥerem ("ban," or "devotion to destruction"). One aspect of their deeds is that they have "broken" the all-important holiness of the nation, thus bringing upon themselves and those most closely associated with them, their immediate families, the "contagion" of violated holiness. This is clearly brought out in the story of Korah and his company by the way in which the rest of the people are told to keep away from them and all their possessions, as though from an infectious and fatal disease. Of Josh. 7 Porter says: "what is holy contagiously infects everything that has had contact with it, in this case Achan's household and possessions, and therefore they must be treated as suffering from the disease also."[10] But more important, both acts are fundamentally violations of the national relationship with Yahweh, by which the offenders have placed themselves outside the privileges and protection of that relationship. The fact that their families are included in their punishment is simply a further illustration of the principle we have reiterated hitherto, that the family was the basic unit of the relationship with Yahweh and that the standing of the head of the household

10. " 'Corporate Personality,' " p. 372.

within or outside it determined that of his household also. What is
involved here, therefore, is the solidarity of kin within the religious
structure of the nation, the concept of the household as a unit which
"stands or falls" together. But family solidarity need not imply
corporate personality or ruler punishment. Indeed, the latter is surely
quite simply excluded by the fact that in both cases the offenders are
themselves destroyed *along with* their families. They are not being
punished through the *loss* of their "property in persons."

In the third case, that of the Gibeonites and the sons of Saul,
the main operative factor, according to the interpretation in the text,
is the ancient concept of bloodguilt and its ability to "cling" to
successive generations. So Saul's sons are put to death rather as an
expiation of his bloodguilt and its consequences on the land than as
a means of punishing Saul through the loss of his "property." If the
dead Saul can be said to be suffering punishment at all, it is surely
not by being deprived of "property" in the loss of his sons, but by
the loss of posterity upon whom his personal "name" and "survival"
depended.[11] In any case, not only is this incident not typical of
judicial practice, it is not even typical of Israelite practice, since the
Gibeonites were Canaanites.[12]

3. The Second Commandment

Finally, the phrase in the Second Commandment about God "visiting the iniquity of the fathers upon the children to the third and

11. On this aspect of the incident, cf. Herbert C. Brichto, "Kin, Cult, Land and
Afterlife," p. 37.

12. This is a point emphasized by P. J. Verdam, " 'On ne fera point mourir les
enfants pour les pères' en droit biblique," *RIDA*, 1st ser. 3 (1949): 402. The close
parallels with known Canaanite sacrificial rituals are listed by Roland de Vaux,
Studies in Old Testament Sacrifice (Cardiff: University of Wales, 1964 and Mystic,
Conn.: Verry, 1966), pp. 61-62. Other aspects of this strange event (e.g., its links
with fertility cults and dynastic struggles) are discussed by Arvid S. Kapelrud,
"King and Fertility: A Discussion of II Sam. 21:1-14," pp. 113-122 in *Interpretationes ad Vetus Testamentum Pertinentes*. Festschrift Sigmund Mowinckel, ed.
Nils A. Dahl and Kapelrud. Norsk teologisk Tidsskrift 56 (Oslo: 1955); and
Henri S. Cazelles, "David's Monarchy and the Gibeonite Claim (II Sam XXI,1-
14)," *PEQ* 87 (1955): 165-175. All of this makes it a very unstable foundation on
which to build any theory of *Israelite* judicial (or other) concepts.

fourth generation" (Exod. 20:5) has been raised in this context. Porter leaves open the possibility that this does reflect actual legal concepts, in which case it would describe something like Daube's ruler punishment—namely, punishing the fathers by visiting their sins upon their descendants.[13] But it is extremely unlikely that any actual legal concept or human judicial practice is being set forth in this phrase (1) because the Decalog, as we have seen (above, pp. 135-36), is not concerned to specify penalties for human jurisdiction; (2) because God himself is clearly the active subject throughout this part of the commandment; and (3) because of the immediately following reference to blessing on thousands of generations—which it would be absurd to imagine as a legal concept or practice.[14] The whole double-edged sanction of this commandment is theological, not juridical, and the reference to the third and fourth generation is best understood as the effects of an Israelite's sin on the whole of his household group, which could include up to four living generations. Again, it is the solidarity of the family group which is the operative principle, not the idea of the family as a person's property.

In conclusion, therefore, it can be said that there is no evidence that in judicial proceedings a man's children were regarded or treated as his property in such a way that he could be punished through their suffering or death. Though stated negatively, this is a conclusion of considerable positive significance, for it shows that the "property value" of children was confined to those civil cases in which compensation was to be paid (the circumstances being

13. Porter, " 'Corporate Personality,' " p. 377.

14. The view of Édouard Cuq, which contrasts this "law" unfavorably with Babylonian law, is therefore to be rejected. "The right of executing the son or daughter of a man who caused the death of someone else's son or daughter is limited (in the Code of Hammurabi) to the first generation and is only allowed in three cases (CH 116, 210, 230). Among the Hebrews, the crimes of the father could be punished as far as the third and fourth generation, according to divine law, if not by the courts" (*Études sur le droit babylonien, les lois assyriennes et les lois hittites* [Paris: P. Geunthner, 1929], pp. 35ff.). But the "if not" of the last sentence is the crucial point which renders the comparison totally invalid. The Babylonian form of "vicarious" punishment was prohibited in Israelite judicial assemblies. Cf. Verdam, p. 415; and the discussion of Deut. 24:16 below, pp. 235-37.

clearly defined) and to the enforced selling or pledging of children for debt. It was not to be extended to include using children as pieces of property for the purpose of "punishing" their parents. There did exist, therefore, defined practical limits to the *legitimate* realization of the property status of children.

C. PROTECTIVE LEGISLATION

Scholars have diverged almost as widely over the social position, rights, and treatment of children in Israel as they have concerning women. Some have held that the Israelite father exercised a virtually unlimited *patria potestas* ("paternal power") over his children, which extended—at least in Israel's early history—to the right of life and death.[15] Others oppose this view, contending that in general patriarchy in Israel was benevolent throughout the people's history and that children were harshly treated only in extreme circumstances, such as irredeemable bankruptcy or as a result of an apostate and perverted religious zeal which is everywhere condemned.[16]

1. Judicial Limitation of Paternal Power

In this context Deut. 21:18-21, concerning the rebellious son, has been seen as setting a legal limit on the exercise of paternal power by placing the power of execution of a son in the hands of a court of elders and no longer in the hands of the father—that is, bringing into the realm of civil jurisdiction what may have originally been

15. E.g., Thaddaeus Engert, *Ehe und Familienrecht der Hebräer*, pp. 52ff.; Edward Neufeld, *Ancient Hebrew Marriage Laws*, pp. 253-54. Alfred Bertholet, *A History of Hebrew Civilization*, pp. 138, 152.

16. E.g., Henry Schaeffer, who dislikes the connotations of the phrase *patria potestas:* "*Patria potestas* of the Roman type cannot be fully applied to Hebrew society of historical times. Relics of what appears to be an original *jus necisque [sic]* may possibly be found in the ancient practice of sacrificing children to the deity. But the full exercise of *patria potestas*, if it ever did exist, was soon checked by public opinion, later incorporated in the book of Deuteronomy" (*The Social Legislation of the Primitive Semites*, pp. 9-10).

exclusively a matter of family law.[17] It is probable that this was not a revolutionary innovation, but legally encapsulated what was already common practice. It may have been that in the earliest period Israelite fathers had the right of execution over their children, but the evidence is not as strong as some scholarly footnotes imply. Gen. 19:8 and Judg. 19:24, cited by Edward Neufeld, concern a father's willingness to sacrifice his daughter's virginity and honor, *not* his power of life and death over them. Gen. 38:24 is better, in that it is a judicial case where the death sentence is passed by the head of the household, though the accused is a daughter-in-law. There are, however, no examples of such judicial prerogatives being exercised by heads of households in the postpatriarchal narratives. The part played by the mother in the particular case in Deut. 21:18-21 has already been remarked upon. It represented an added element of protection for the son, in that the consent of both parents was required to make the charge actionable.

2. Prohibition of Child Sacrifice

Sometimes child sacrifice is cited as an example of the extent of paternal power.[18] But although this phenomenon and the laws concerning it must now be considered, it ought to be clearly distinguished from the legal right of life and death. The latter is the *judicial* right of a father to execute a child legally when he or she is guilty of an offense. But the sacrifice of a (legally) innocent child, being a *religious* or propitiatory rite with no judicial justification, is clearly something different. This important distinction is not made in some earlier works on Hebrew family customs.

The sacrifice of children in ancient Israel is something about which there is a good deal of confusion and obscurity. Older views that it was once a legitimate part of Yahwism are now usually discounted.[19] On the other hand, the legal terminology (Lev. 18:21;

17. Cf. Bertholet, *A History of Hebrew Civilization,* p. 152.
18. E.g., Neufeld, *Ancient Hebrew Marriage Laws,* p. 253.
19. Cf. Arthur M. Brown, "The Concept of Inheritance in the Old Testament," p. 297. Further, on the issue of the consecration and redemption of the firstborn and

20:2; Deut. 18:10) speaks literally of "dedicating" *(ntn)* and "passing over (hiphil *'br)* one's offspring to Molech.[20] It is not explicitly clear that actual sacrifice is intended. The contexts in these three cases suggest a possible connection between this Molech cult and either sexual perversions[21] or various magical, divinatory rites, or both. On the other hand, Deut. 12:31 specifies child *sacrifice* (using the verb *śārap*) as the nadir of those Canaanite abominations which Israel was to eschew. Morton Cogan deduces from these two facts that in the legal literature the cult of Molech was a divinatory fire cult which did not involve child sacrifice, as distinct from another Canaanite practice of actual immolation of children.[22] Such a distinction, however, is not maintained in the prophetic literature,[23] and it is doubtful if this is due only to a literary fusing or lack of interest in specific points of ritual, as Cogan believes.[24] It probably rather

---

the problem of Ezek. 20:25-26, see de Vaux, *Studies in Old Testament Sacrifice*, pp. 70-73. Although, as de Vaux says, it is absurd to think that the law of the firstborn ever seriously intended the sacrifice of every firstborn son, it is possible that when child sacrifices were perpetrated in Israel this law was used as an excuse or justification, thus necessitating the addition of the clauses requiring that the firstborn be redeemed. The suggestion of this possibility was made to me by Ronald E. Clements.

20. The identity of "Molech" is the most puzzling aspect of the complex range of texts about child sacrifice. On the basis of Carthaginian evidence, Otto Eissfeldt showed that the word was descriptive of a kind of sacrifice, not the name of a particular deity (*Molk als Opferbegriff im Punischen und Hebräischen und das Ende des Gottes Moloch.* Beiträge zur Religionsgeschichte des Altertums 3 [Halle: M. Niemeyer, 1935]). Ugaritic texts witness to similar rites in Phoenicia, whence undoubtedly the Israelites absorbed the practice. Some of the biblical texts, however, can only be understood on the assumption that they are referring to an actual divinity called Molech or Melek, probably owing to confusion as the syncretism developed. Jer. 19:5 illustrates this confusion in accusing the Judaeans of sacrificing children to *Ba'al.* For a thorough survey of the evidence and literature on the problem, cf. de Vaux, *Studies in Old Testament Sacrifice*, pp. 73-90.

21. Norman H. Snaith, "The Cult of Molech," *VT* 16 (1966): 123-24, connects it with ritual prostitution. Following this, Anthony Phillips suggested that the children offered may have been, or may have particularly included, the children of ritual prostitution (*Ancient Israel's Criminal Law*, pp. 128ff.).

22. *Imperialism and Religion: Assyria, Judah and Israel in the Eighth and Seventh Centuries B.C.E.* SBL Monograph 19 (Missoula: Scholars Press, 1974), p. 77.

23. The vocabulary becomes much less precise. Cf. Jer. 3:24; 7:31; 19:5; 32:35; Ezek. 16:20-21; 20:31; 23:37-39; and possibly Zeph. 1:5.

24. Cogan, pp. 78-79.

reflects an actual situation which was more complex and conflated than Cogan's neat distinction allows for. Although such a distinction may well have existed in Canaanite cultic practice, it need not necessarily have been accurately preserved by Israelite syncretism, particularly in the later period of the Monarchy.

Historical attestation of child sacrifice in Israel (apart from the exceptional case of Jephthah's daughter) is limited both in time and location.[25] It is mainly concentrated in the reigns of Ahaz (2 Kgs. 16:3) and Manasseh (2 Kgs. 21:6), whose apostasy and pagan practices were notorious. 2 Kgs. 17:17 records, though without historical detail, that it had happened in the northern kingdom of Israel as well; and v. 31 indicates that the practice was continued, after the destruction of Samaria, by the Sepharvites. This restricts the recorded incidence of child sacrifice to the late seventh and early sixth centuries, during the period of Assyrian domination. Recent studies, however, have convincingly disputed the view that child sacrifice was a religious imposition of Assyrian imperialism—an act of political necessity, later construed as pagan idolatry by the Deuteronomists.[26] Rather, it was a feature of a widespread reversion to a variety of pagan practices, with the evidence pointing much more positively to the perennial Canaanite influence than to Assyrian compulsion. John W. McKay notes:

> . . . The cultic innovations of Ahaz and Manasseh, heretofore interpreted in terms of the overlord's imposition of religious sanctions, do not appear to have been acts of Assyrianization, but rather reflect many different forms of digression from traditional Yahwism and apostasy to a wide variety of indigenous and foreign practices.[27]

25. Cf. the conclusion of de Vaux's chapter on human sacrifice: ". . . It is evident that this custom, brought in from outside, limited to the region of Jerusalem, restricted in time and condemned by all who stood for Yahwism, cannot prove that human sacrifices were ever lawful in Israel" (*Studies in Old Testament Sacrifice*, p. 90).

26. Cogan; and John W. McKay, *Religion in Judah under the Assyrians, 732–609 B.C.* SBT, 2nd ser. 26 (1973).

27. McKay, p. 67.

If not performed under compulsion, then, the child sacrifices of this
period were indeed part of this "voluntary" apostasy, and the
Deuteronomistic condemnations cannot be set aside as theological
misconstruction. Cogan observes:

> The Deuteronomistic historian viewed the age of Manasseh as
> unprecedented both in the nature and scope of its "apostasy." Our
> literary and archaeological study has confirmed this evaluation.
> ... The feeling that such enormities as described in 2 Kgs. 21:1-16
> could only be expiated through destruction and exile need not be
> late exilic rationalization ... [nor] ... ascribed to schematized
> historiography.[28]

The laws against child sacrifice were introduced in this section
as a further illustration of the concern to protect children from abuse
of their property status. But it may be objected that, in the light of
the foregoing paragraphs, the legal prohibition and prophetic protest against the rite were in fact based on its pagan and idolatrous
nature, rather than on the use of children in it. The laws therefore,
it might be said, represent concern for the purity of Yahweh's cult
and not, at least not primarily, for the lives of the children. However,
among all the relevant texts there are some whose language betrays
more than cultic purity as the grounds of their vehemence against
child sacrifice.

(1) Deut. 12:31 comes as the climax of a passage prohibiting
Israel from following the abominations of Canaan. The special
disgust felt at the sacrifice of one's own children is expressively
compressed into the Hebrew particle *gam* ("even") and the emphatic position of the object before the main verb: "Even their sons
and their daughters they sacrifice in the fire" (author's translation).

(2) Jer. 19:4 describes the child sacrifices which took place in
the valley of Hinnom as shedding the *"blood of innocents."*

(3) Ps. 106:37-38 uses similar language. The sacrifice of children was a shedding of "innocent blood" which "polluted" the land
with blood. Both expressions are used frequently elsewhere of the

crimes of murder and violence (e.g., Deut. 21:8-9; 27:25; 1 Sam. 19:5; 2 Kgs. 21:16; 24:4 [of Manasseh, probably including his child sacrifices]; Prov. 6:17; Num. 35:33).

(4) Ezek. 23:37 also associates child sacrifice with "blood upon [the] hands" of both Judah and Israel.

This language strongly supports the view that the universal condemnation of child sacrifice went well beyond the polemic against idolatry and regarded it as an act of murder also, and that this aspect of it was as much a factor in the severity of the law (Lev. 20:2 prescribes death by stoning) as the idolatrous nature of the rite. We are justified, therefore, in including this material on the prohibition of child sacrifice among evidence of the protection of children in Israel. The legal property status of children did not entail that their lives were simply at the disposal of the head of the household. They may have had an economic value in some circumstances, but they retained basic human rights as persons.

3. Exclusion of Collective Judicial Punishments

This protection of the child's life is further illustrated by the law of *Deut. 24:16,* forbidding the linking together of generations in judicial punishment: "The fathers shall not be put to death for the children, nor shall the children put to death for the fathers; [each] shall be put to death for his own sin." In discussing this law, David Daube asks (but does not answer): "Against which idea is the famous injunction 'The fathers shall not be put to death for the children . . .' directed, communal responsibility, or ruler punishment? Or against both?"[29] The answer must be that it is certainly not directed against the second. The concept of ruler punishment is excluded by the form of the first phrase of the law, for how could the death of a father be regarded in any sense as the punishment of the son through his "personal property"?[30]

29. "Communal Responsibility," p. 184.
30. Further criticisms of Daube's general argument are made by Verdam, p. 406.

Linguistically, the verse could be taken to refer to vicarious punishment, since Hebrew *al is as versatile as English "for."[31] But the best, and generally accepted, sense is obtained by taking the verse to mean collective punishment, in which several members of a family suffer along with the actual criminal. The verse should then be rendered: "The fathers shall not be put to death *together with* the children. . . ." This interpretation is supported by the interesting reference to the law in 2 Kgs. 14:5-6, where Amaziah, in accordance with this law, refrains from executing the children of the regicides in addition to the regicides themselves. Whatever view one takes of the literary relationship between the law in Deuteronomy and its citation in 2 Kgs. 14, the fact remains that it was understood collectively by the historian.

It is no longer held, however, that the Deuteronomic regulation was a revolutionary innovation, demanding individual responsibility as opposed to a then general rule of communal liability and collective punishment. The older view of a development in Israelite society and law from primitive collectivism to individualism is being generally abandoned. Particularly in the legal documents the principle of individual liability is recognized and applied from the earliest period.[32] The existence of this law, however, shows that there was felt to be a danger of collective punishments being administered, and the Amaziah incident shows the kind of circumstances in which it might have occurred.[33]

31. BDB, *al II.1.f.(b) (p. 754), quotes this text as an example of *al meaning "on account of," which could presumably be taken to include the sense "instead of," though it is somewhat ambiguous.

32. "The whole Book of the Covenant knows nothing of such corporate liability within the family. Therefore we must reckon with the possibility that our Deuteronomic regulation is after all much earlier than was formerly assumed" (Gerhard von Rad, *Deuteronomy*, p. 152). The same point is stressed by Porter: "As far as the whole Hebrew legal system is concerned, there seems little reason to depart from the picture suggested by the Book of the Covenant that the law operated on the basis of the individual rather than the group and was concerned to fix individual guilt and inflict individual punishment" (" 'Corporate Personality,' " p. 379). Further criticisms and a survey of literature on the subject of the "collective to individual" theory was made by de Fraine.

33. Regarding the historicity of the event, J. M. Salmon comments: "Rejection of its validity on the grounds that such ethical ideas in Israel—specifically that of

In this law, then, we have a measure which is strongly protective of the person and life of the child, designed to prevent his being included in any judicial punishment of his father under the normal processes of law. Inevitably, of course, the judicial punishment of a man cannot but have an effect upon his children—especially if his offense were capital. But this is surely precisely the point of the reference in the Second Commandment to the "third and fourth generation." The commandment describes the natural effects of sin and its punishment on the family; Deut. 24:16 prescribes only for the realm of the human administration of justice. The distinction is most clearly drawn by S. R. Driver:

> There [in the Second Commandment] the reference is to the providence of God, operating naturally through the normal constitution of society: children are linked to their parents by ties, physical and social, from which they cannot free themselves; and they suffer, not because they are *guilty* of their fathers' sins, but because by the self-acting operation of natural laws their fathers' sins entail disgrace or misfortune upon them. Here [in Deut. 24:16] a law is prescribed for *human action*, and a principle is laid down for the administration of justice by the State: the family of the criminal is not to be punished judicially with him. The two cases are thus altogether different: it is one thing that, in virtue of the physical and social conditions in which they live, children should suffer for their fathers' sins; it is another that, by the deliberate intervention of human authority they should be punished for criminal acts which they have not committed.[34]

CONCLUSION

The result of our survey in this chapter, then, shows that, while children were entirely subject to the authority of the head of the

individual responsibility—had not yet developed to this point is not only arbitrary, but . . . based on a demonstrably incorrect interpretation of judicial development in Israel" ("Judicial Authority in Early Israel," p. 107).

34. *Deuteronomy*, pp. 277-78.

household and counted legally as his property, the practical effects
of children's status as property were quite restricted. There were, in
fact, only two legitimate grounds for a father to "realize" the
economic value of his children: (1) if they sustained "damage" or
"devaluation" (as in the cases of premature birth or miscarriage and
the violation of a virgin daughter), and (2) if financial extremity
forced him to sell their services as slaves or as pledges. He did not
have arbitrary power over their lives, either in the judicial case of
incorrigible disobedience or in the cultic rite of sacrifice. Children
could not be used judicially as a means of punishing their father,
nor could they be made to suffer judicially along with him for
offenses of which he alone was guilty. Taking into consideration the
extent of the father's duties as outlined in Chapter 3, it is apparent
that there was a much greater concern in the Old Testament with
the *responsibility* of the father for his children than with his *rights*
over them.

8 | Slaves

> Man is the shadow of a god, a slave is the
> shadow of a man . . .

Akkadian proverb[1]

In contrast to the proverb quoted here, the height of Old Testament thinking on slavery is reached in the words of Job 31:15:

> Did not he who made me in the womb make him?
> And did not one fashion us in the womb?

Although this is the clearest expression of the slave's fellow-humanity,[2] it is not the only evidence for such an awareness in ancient Israel. There is very wide agreement among scholars that the Israelites' attitude toward slavery, particularly as it becomes apparent in some of their laws, was undoubtedly unique in the ancient Near Eastern

---

1. "Akkadian Proverbs and Counsels," V.(3), trans. Robert H. Pfeiffer, p. 426 in *Ancient Near Eastern Texts*, 3rd ed., ed. James B. Pritchard (Princeton: Princeton University Press, 1969).

2. This verse is also a most explicit example of the presupposition of the doctrine of creation as a source of moral value and obligation. This is a theme which is expounded in detail from Job 31 in S. Y. Tang's dissertation, "The Ethical Content of Job 31." See esp. pp. 161-67 and ch. 6, pp. 206ff.

world.[3] While it is obvious that Israel regarded slaves as the property of their masters, in common with what J. P. M. van der Ploeg calls the *ius gentium* ("law of the nations," i.e., common legal conventions) of the time,[4] there was also a sense that slavery was inherently unnatural and abhorrent—indeed, the result of a curse in the case of the Canaanites, who probably made up the bulk of slaves in early Israel (Gen. 9:25; Josh. 9:23). This feeling produced a trait of humanity even in laws where the property status of slaves is at its starkest. Mayer Sulzberger notes: "Among the Hebrews the slave was not obliged to struggle for recognition as a human being."[5] Furthermore, this attitude was not something that arose by social or ethical evolution. It seems on the contrary to have been present in Israelite legal traditions from the earliest period and to be bound up with Israel's belief that their own history as a nation had begun in slavery. Indeed, it is precisely in this area—namely, Israel's attitude toward slaves and other classes of oppressed and vulnerable people—that their foundational tradition of national delivery from slavery through the Exodus had its most profound ethical impact.

A. GENERAL LAWS

1. A Fatal Beating (Exod. 21:20-21)

20 If a man beats his male or female slave with a rod and the slave dies under his hand, he must surely be avenged.

21 But if the slave dies after a day or two, he is not to be punished, for the slave is his money. (author's translation)

No law illustrates so well as this the ambivalence of the Old Testament's slavery laws. The second part of the law is an unqual-

---

3. Even as extreme a writer as Thaddaeus Engert, whose severe views on women and children have been noted, concedes to the Israelites "a humane slave law," which he compares favorably with that of surrounding nations (*Ehe und Familienrecht der Hebräer*, p. 76).

4. "Slavery in the Old Testament," *VTS* 22 (1972): 72-87.

5. "The Status of Labor in Ancient Israel," p. 251.

ified acceptance of the general view that a slave was his master's financial property, so much so that it could be assumed that an Israelite would not intentionally deprive himself of his own property. So if the slave died several days after a beating, homicidal guilt could be discounted: the man's loss of property was sufficient punishment. On the other hand, the first clause of the law is entirely unparalleled in ancient Near Eastern law codes in making a person's treatment of *his own* slave a matter of public judicial action. This unique aspect of the law is true, whatever construction is put upon the phrase *nāqōm yinnāqēm*, "he shall surely be avenged."

The phrase is problematic. The common use of *nqm* elsewhere would support the view that it here means the taking of vengeance for blood—that is, the death of the murderous master.[6] Against this it is argued (for example, by Brevard S. Childs) first, that this law is in the section concerning compensation for bodily injury and not in the previous section on homicide, and second, that a master would not have been executed for killing his own slave. But the "categories" of the Book of the Covenant are not so beyond dispute (homicide occurs again in 21:29) as to predetermine the meaning of this law. Moreover, the second point is an *a priori* argument that lacks external support inasmuch as this text is the only evidence we actually have regarding the legal attitude toward the murder of a slave in Israel. Stronger arguments are needed to justify departing from the natural sense of the words even though they cause difficulty, as has been recognized since the earliest interpreters.[7] Van der Ploeg remarks: "Translating has first to be in accordance with the laws of philology. Therefore *nāqōm yinnāqēm* means 'he shall be

6. Brevard S. Childs lists those who take it thus, though he disagrees himself (*The Book of Exodus*, p. 471). In addition to those mentioned by Childs, cf. Frank Michaeli: "Without doubt, it is the death penalty, in accordance with the general concept that bloodshed demands the death of the guilty person" (*Le Livre de l'Exode*. Commentaire de l'Ancien Testament 2 [Neuchâtel: Delachaux & Niestle, 1974], p. 200). Cf. also Martin Noth: "The word used for 'punishment' however means blood-vengeance and thus the death of the killer" (*Exodus*. OTL [1962], p. 181).

7. The Samaritan Pentateuch interpreted it as a death penalty, by reading *môt yûmāt;* but this, as van der Ploeg observes, "is rather an old interpretation than a variant" ("Slavery in the Old Testament," p. 79).

avenged,' which implies the shedding of the blood of the master of the slave. But one must admit that this leaves us perplexed."[8]

If the death penalty is excluded, one is left with the problem of what the phrase could then refer to. "Apparently," suggests Childs, "the determination of the required penalty was left to the discretion of the judge."[9] But would such an indeterminate punishment not have been expressed by a more general verb, such as *pqd*, rather than a specific verb for vengeance? J. M. Salmon argues that the law was to ensure that a slave, whose family would not have been in a position to avenge his murder, should nevertheless "enjoy" the right of vengeance exercised on his behalf by the civil authorities. He also argues that the penalty was death.[10] Martin Noth makes the same conjecture:

> It is not said who is to carry out this blood-vengeance in the case of a slave, vengeance which is the duty of the clan of the man who has been killed. Perhaps blood-vengeance, which begins automatically and is therefore not demanded by law, is here required because it is to be executed for the slave by the legal assembly.[11]

This accords with what has been seen of the limitations on the powers of the head of the household. He did not have an arbitrary right of life and death over his wife or children—even though the latter were undoubtedly his property. It is reasonable therefore to expect that he did not have such power over the lives of his slaves either, and that to beat a slave to death would have been treated as criminal homicide.

8. "Slavery in the Old Testament," p. 80.

9. P. 471.

10. ". . . If the deed were an offense at all, it was wilful homicide, or murder, and must be punished by death. Nor was it necessary to specify by whom the punishment should be administered; it can only be by the community, that is by the city authorities. The point was that the murderer must indeed be punished, and it is this requirement to which the law gives expression: *nāqōm yinnāqēm*" ("Judicial Authority in Early Israel," p. 175).

11. *Exodus*, p. 181.

2. Freedom for Injury (Exod. 21:26-27)

26 *When a man strikes the eye of his slave, male or female, and destroys it, he shall let the slave go free for the eye's sake.*
27 *If he knocks out the tooth of his slave, male or female, he shall let the slave go free for the tooth's sake.*

This law is equally unparalleled in protecting the male or female slave from arbitrary assault by the master. The granting of freedom, as Noth points out, is a kind of reparation since it represents a forfeiture of the purchase price of the slave. The inclusion of the "tooth" indicates that the law does not intend only grievous bodily harm, but any unwarranted assault. The basic humanity of the slave is given precedence over his property status. According to Childs, "A slave is not freed because of property damage, but because he is an oppressed human being. For this reason the loss of a tooth represents an act of abuse as well as the loss of an eye"[12]—that is, even though loss of a tooth could not detrimentally affect his usefulness as working "property."

a. Slaves' Judicial Rights?

One very significant implication of the law appears to have been overlooked hitherto by commentators. This is not an injunction to charitable concern for the oppressed, such as is common in Israelite law. It does not fall into one of the sections of humanitarian exhortation included in the Book of the Covenant in its present form, which command or prohibit certain behavior without specifying punishment. On the contrary, it is one of a series of civil laws concerning disputes over assault, injury, compensation, and so forth in which plaintiffs, defendants, and judicial decisions are involved and remedies specified. Does this then indicate that a civil case could arise in which a slave was the plaintiff against his own master? It is hard to see what else the content and position of the law could imply, or how else the law could have been seriously intended to be observed. Slaveowners could hardly have been relied on spontaneously to grant freedom on the spot to slaves they had injured.

12. P. 473.

To repeat, this is not "Deuteronomic" exhortation but civil law. Presumably therefore the judicial authorities must have been able to enforce the law by compelling the offender to free the slave. But on whose suit and on what evidence? Only the slave could show the physical evidence and produce whatever witnesses he could to the assault. The conclusion seems unavoidable that a slave could initiate a legal dispute with his master.

Anthony Phillips cites this law and the preceding one on the murder of a slave as exceptional examples of the courts' curtailing the independence of the head of the household under family law: "The slave's freedom would have been enforced by the courts . . . [who would] *intervene*."[13] But how, and on whose initiative, did this intervention occur if, according to Phillips, "a slave could normally not have brought an action for damages for assault against his master"? The law, if it were to have any meaningful legal (as distinct from merely charitable) force, must presuppose that there were *some* circumstances in which a slave could appeal to judicial authority against his own master, that in *some* situations a slave could have definite legal status as a person, notwithstanding his normal status as purchased property.

Unfortunately there is no historical evidence of such a case, but it seems to me that this view can be supported by consideration of the context of the quotation from Job cited at the beginning of this chapter, namely, Job 31:13-15.

b. Job 31:13-14

13 *If I have denied justice to my male and female slaves*
    when they had a case against me,
14 *What will I do when God confronts me?*
    What will I answer when he calls me to account? (author's
    translation)

Commentators on these verses in general admire the exalted ethical nature of the sentiment and then contrast it with the gloomy picture

13. "Some Aspects of Family Law in Pre-exilic Israel," p. 358 (my italics).

of slaves' alleged *lack* of rights in actual life. Exod. 21:1-11 is often cited, but not the law protecting the slave from assault by his master (vv. 26-27) nor that on vengeance for a slave's murder (vv. 20-21). Job is taken to be speaking only metaphorically or hypothetically, not referring to any actual legal dispute.

> Before the law slaves had some (Exod. 21:1-11), but few rights; but Job, when his slaves had anything to urge against him, even though they might have been *unable to make a case of it at law* against him, did not turn them contemptuously away.[14]

> The rights of slaves were few (Exod. 21.1-11). . . . But Job recognized his slaves as fellow creatures (verse 15), who had rights *even though they were not enforceable at law.*[15]

Édouard P. Dhorme's comment is somewhat ambiguous:

> The rights of slaves were reduced to a minimum in Hebrew Law (Exod. 21:1-11). *Job admits* that the slave has the right to argue with or press a claim against his master.[16]

Presumably this means a *moral* right which Job "admits," in the absence of any actual legal right. A similar ambiguity attaches to Francis I. Andersen's comment, though he comes nearest to the understanding of the passage that I wish to advance here.

> But in [Job's] *valuation* a slave is not a chattel, but a human person with rights at law. . . . Verse 13 shows that *Job believed* that a slave had the right to initiate a suit against his master.[17]

Again, it is implied that this is Job's personal view of what the slave's rights in law should have been, in point of ethics, not necessarily what they actually were in point of fact. Job's assertion,

---

14. (S. R. Driver and) George Buchanan Gray, *A Critical and Exegetical Commentary on the Book of Job.* ICC (1921), p. 266 (my italics).

15. H. H. Rowley, *The Book of Job.* NCBC (1980), pp. 200-201 (my italics).

16. *A Commentary on the Book of Job* (London and Nashville:Thomas Nelson, 1967; repr. 1984), pp. 455-56 (my italics).

17. *Job.* Tyndale Old Testament Commentary (Leicester and Downers Grove: InterVarsity, 1976), p. 242 (my italics).

in other words, concerns his *personal* attitude toward and treatment of his own slaves, irrespective of their *actual* legal status or facilities. Georg Fohrer puts it more forcefully still:

> Here he has gone far beyond the mere legal point of view. . . . The equality of having been created by the same God demands equality before the law, which has its origin in the divine will, and this has ethical and legal consequences. This is a revolutionary idea in a period when slaves, like cattle, were regarded as part of the property.[18]

Now, it is beyond doubt that the ethical appeal of Job 31:15 is something new and that it transcends legal categories. But this need not imply that what is envisaged in v. 13 is "revolutionary" or, from a judicial point of view, purely hypothetical. In view of the existence of such laws as Exod. 21:20-21 and 21:26-27, we must surely reckon with at least the possibility that the *mišpaṭ* ("justice") and *rîb* ("cause") of Job 31:13 refer to actual judicial proceedings between Job and one of his slaves. Several points may be made in defense of this possibility.

1. The words themselves, though they do have metaphorical uses, are such as are frequently used of actual judicial cases and disputes,[19] and there is no *a priori* reason why they may not have a literal sense in this verse. Furthermore, the syntax indicates that the slaves "on their part began the dispute (for, as the Talmud correctly points out, it is not בְּרִיבִי עִמָּם, but בְּרִיבָם עִמָּדִי)"[20] (i.e., not "my dispute with them" but "their dispute with me").

2. There is significance in the logical sequence of thought between v. 13 and v. 14. In v. 14 Job refers again to his oft-expressed desire for a proper lawsuit with God (cf. Job 13:3, 18; 23:3-7; 31:35)—a lawsuit he confidently expected to win. It makes sense, therefore, to see a reference to a lawsuit in 31:13 and expand the

---

18. "The Righteous Man in Job 31," p. 15 in *Essays in Old Testament Ethics: J. Philip Hyatt, In Memoriam,* ed. James L. Crenshaw and John T. Willis (New York: Ktav, 1974).

19. Cf. particularly the use of *rîb* concerning the poor man's legal suit in Exod. 23:3.

20. Franz Delitzsch in Carl F. Keil and Delitzsch, *Commentary on the Old Testament,* IV: *Job* II, p. 181.

meaning thus: if when one of his own slaves brought a suit against him Job had been in the habit of treating it with contempt,[21] how then could he, God's servant (1:8; 2:3), expect a fair hearing in his own controversy with God?

3. This chapter forms the climax to Job's last speech, which also incorporates chs. 29 and 30. A prominent feature of those chapters is Job's complaint that whereas he had once played a leading and respected role in the judicial affairs of his community, his loss of family, estate, and health had deprived him of all that and made him an object of scorn (cf. above, pp. 80-81). However, not only does the context thus include reference to legal proceedings, but Job has particularly and at length recounted his successful championing of the legal rights of the poor and unprivileged (29:12-17). It is not unnatural, therefore, to take 31:13 as a reference to his consistency in such matters, even where the plaintiff was his own slave and he himself the defendant. As the kind of person who would thoroughly examine the suit of a stranger (29:16),[22] Job would not dismiss with contempt the suit of his own slave (31:13); *rîḇ* is used in both texts.

4. Form-critical investigations of Job 31 have yielded interesting results which bear on our proposal. In 1953 Gerhard von Rad included Job 31 with other examples of protestations of righteousness in the Old Testament, as variants of a form which he found in some of the Testaments of the Patriarchs and, at a still later stage, in Paul's "hymn to love" in 1 Corinthians 13:4-7.[23] He regarded the form as basically cultic in origin and usage but, in view of 1 Sam. 12:3, reckoned with the possibility of a legal use also. Fohrer, however, regards legal usage as the primary background to the *form* of the chapter, which he sees as modelled on the "oath of purity" and self-imprecations.[24] But the *content* of the chapter Fohrer attributes rather to the influence of Wisdom teaching.

21. This paraphrase is justified by the use of the imperfect *'em'as* rather than a perfect form.

22. "What is extraordinary is the fact of taking an interest in the cause of a stranger" (Dhorme, p. 425, commenting on 29:16).

23. "The Early History of the Form-Category of *I Corinthians* XIII.4-7," pp. 301-317 in *The Problem of the Hexateuch*.

24. "The Righteous Man in Job 31," pp. 10-13.

> Thus, although the Joban poet has used the form of the judicial
> oath of purity of the accused which originated in the legal realm,
> . . . the transgressions which are mentioned . . . are neither actual
> and public crimes nor legal variable acts in general. Rather, Job is
> concerned about attitudes in man which cannot be controlled
> legally, attitudes which can only lead to sinful acts, or about secret
> sins among the suspected crimes which had not been exposed.
> This concern is based on the Wisdom teaching, and not on the Law.
> (p. 13)

But the contents can hardly be classified into a single uniform
category.[25] It would be truer to say that *some* of the strophes of the
chapter *are* concerned with "actual crimes" and "legal acts" while
others are not. The legal background can only be assessed, therefore, at the level of particular strophes. The fact that the ethos of the
whole chapter does indeed utterly transcend a narrow legalism does
not detract from Job's claim to have obeyed the law, where a
particular law can be discerned as the basis of any of his self-
imprecations. Indeed, the use of curse formulae would seem to
make a greater impact if there were a strong legal basis to the ethical
claims of his protestation—however much it may be agreed that
the influence of Wisdom teaching has molded the language and
"atmosphere."

If, therefore, pursuing these considerations, we ask whether
any law lies behind the particular profession of innocence in Job
31:13, it can be plausibly suggested that a protective law like Exod.
21:26-27 is in mind. Job is denying having ever sought to obstruct
or prevent the judicial hearing of a suit against himself by one of
his own slaves. Thus it may be argued that the protective legislation
of the Book of the Covenant and this passage in Job's *apologia* are
mutually illuminatory and present to us a picture of the slave in
Israel as being far from a creature of no rights, but rather as one

25. Andersen's comments on the composition of Job's protestation are apt:
"The list of crimes in Job's negative confession is neither systematic nor complete.
It was not drawn up by an articled clerk. It is a poem, recited by a miserable outcast
on the city rubbish dump, not by a prisoner in the dock. It is Job's last passionate
outburst, and the author has given it an earnestness and a torrential quality" (*Job*,
p. 239).

who, though legally of property status, was nevertheless accorded basic human and legal rights—rights which in some circumstances could be exercised over against his own master.

3. Other Laws

The rest of the general laws concerning slaves in the Old Testament may be more briefly summarized. As in other societies, one who injured a slave was required to compensate the owner. Exod. 21:32 illustrates this as regards the goring of a slave and Lev. 19:20-22 as regards the violation of a betrothed slave girl. The law concerning the acceptance of permanent slavery by a Hebrew slave (Exod. 21:6) is really a question of private family law.[26] It illustrates yet again the magnetic force of the household and the priority of security within a household as preferable to a parlous freedom. Finally, there existed several customary laws of a charitable sort. Apart from the inclusion of slaves in the "rest" of the sabbath day (Exod. 20:10), there was the Deuteronomic exhortation to generosity on release of the Hebrew slave after his six years of service (Deut. 15:12-18) and the unique and somewhat astonishing law of asylum (Deut. 23:15-16). It is astonishing in that it is quite the reverse of the common law of the ancient Near East, in which severe penalties were imposed (both in domestic law and international treaties) for harboring runaway slaves.[27]

B. SLAVE RELEASE LAWS

In Chapter 5, when we were considering the institutions connected with the seventh year, it was proposed to keep the land aspects

26. I find quite convincing Phillips' presentation of this ceremony as a household affair, taking place before the household *'elōhîm* and therefore as a facet of family law. See *Ancient Israel's Criminal Law*, pp. 60ff., 136-37 (and literature there cited); and "Family Law," p. 357. Cf. also Shalom M. Paul, *Studies in the Book of the Covenant*, p. 50.

27. See Isaac Mendelsohn, *Slavery in the Ancient Near East* (Oxford: Oxford University Press, 1949), pp. 58-64; and van der Ploeg, "Slavery in the Old Testament," pp. 83-84.

separate from the question of slave release (see above, p. 147). In turning now to the latter question we find it as complicated as the other. The major problem, to which this final section attempts to suggest a solution, is the relationship between the legislation of Exod. 21:1-6 and Deut. 15:12-18, on the one hand, with their six-year release, and the provisions of Lev. 25:39-43, on the other, which provides for a release in the Jubilee or fiftieth year.

The most common approach to these texts has been to assume that there is a straightforward discrepancy between the laws and to account for it in terms of the different periods from which they come, on the grounds that the later legislator was modifying or repealing the earlier law. Thus, for example, S. R. Driver comments: "Experience had shown that . . . the limit of service fixed by Exodus and Deuteronomy could not be enforced."[28] The extension to fifty years was mitigated by the exhortation to kindness. Roland de Vaux notes: "These laws [Exod. 21 and Deut. 15] were not obeyed. . . . It is because of this difficulty that the ideal law of Lv 25 allows for an extension which may amount to fifty years, but puts the master under the obligation of treating his slave like a wage-earner or a guest."[29] It is thus regarded as a compromising reform.

But this view is open to major objections. It seems inconceivable that *any* amelioration of treatment or conditions should have been regarded as adequate compensation for changing a comparatively brief period of servitude into what in most cases would be slavery for life. And if it had proved impossible to enforce the original six-year limit, how could the rather vague injunctions to leniency be enforced if a creditor chose to ignore them? The only beneficiaries of such a "reform" would be the wealthy creditors. Indeed, E. Ginzberg regards it as having been designed with precisely their interests in view. The legislator "hoped that a fifty year period might be sufficiently long to safeguard the private property of the rich and still retain the institution of manumission."[30] It was, in short, a "com-

28. *Deuteronomy,* p. 185.

29. *Ancient Israel,* p. 83. Cf. also Ze'ev W. Falk, *Hebrew Law in Biblical Times* (Jerusalem, 1949), p. 91; Phillips, *Ancient Israel's Criminal Law,* p. 78; Henry Schaeffer, *Social Legislation,* p. 92.

30. "Economics," p. 349.

promising" law, to "placate the rich and obtain their support for the measure as a whole" (p. 389). But it is impossible to see how such an attitude, allegedly obtaining in the exilic period, can be reconciled with the weight of the prophetic indictment of the rich and their economic oppression—an indictment which was believed to have been vindicated by the judgment of the Exile. Jer. 34:17 directly links the doom of the Captivity with disobedience of the law of slave release. If one objects that this is a Deuteronomistic viewpoint, whereas Lev. 25 represents Priestly sources, one need only point to the essentially similar conception of the reason for the Exile offered by the same Priestly sources in Lev. 26:34ff. (see above, pp. 149-151). In other respects the effect of the Exile appears to have been to induce almost fanatical efforts to keep the law (e.g., the increased zeal for sabbath observance), in the belief that judgment had fallen on the nation for disobedience. It would be quite extraordinary if on this issue a legislator had taken the contradictory view that, because people had failed to obey this law in the past, it should be abandoned in practice and replaced by a law which, by allowing lifetime slavery, was the antithesis of what the original law had tried to achieve. For these reasons, then, the "modification," "reform," or "replacement" theories must be rejected.

The problem is tackled with literary-critical methods by Martin Noth[31] and recently also by Niels P. Lemche.[32] Noth reckons that Lev. 25:40b and 41, which "looks out of place," may be an addition to the original paragraph in the "*mûk* series" (see above, p. 121), inserted when that series was combined with the Jubilee provisions. Originally the paragraph vv. 39ff. (minus vv. 40b and 41) had tacitly assumed the seventh year release laws of Exodus and Deuteronomy. But later, and "rather mechanically," a reference to the Jubilee has been inserted "which appears to ignore the older slave laws" and is, in fact, in "considerable tension" with them. Lemche also reckons with (un-identified) secondary passages in vv. 39-54, and proposes to under-stand the "Jobel" manumission as originally a *seven*-yearly matter, in accordance with Exodus and Deuteronomy. Later, the redactor of Lev.

31. *Leviticus*, p. 192.
32. "The Manumission of Slaves," pp. 49-51.

25 turned the "Jobel" into a *seventh* sabbatical year, perhaps owing to "practical and economic motives" (p. 51), and thus the discrepancy arose. Both these theories, however, "cut the knot" rather than "unravelling" it, and neither is very convincing. The likelihood of finding a solution along these lines is rejected by Karl Elliger.[33]

Other scholars have suggested harmonizing the texts, applying the theory that freedom was to be granted after the sixth year of a slave's service unless the Jubilee came first, in which case the slave was lucky enough to be released earlier. This is favored by a number of conservative scholars[34] and is also Elliger's explanation of how the texts would have been understood in the context of the completed Pentateuch.[35] But one would have expected such a relationship to be expressed more clearly—at least in the Leviticus text. Such a view makes the texts incomprehensible without the others. But it is a dubious exegesis that requires us, as Henry L. Ellison puts it, in rejecting this view, "to treat the Bible as a kind of jig-saw puzzle."[36]

A discrepancy, however, only exists if it be assumed (as it usually is) that Exodus, Deuteronomy, and Leviticus are all concerned with the same thing—a straightforward release of slaves—and that the only major difference is the matter of the length of enslavement. The discrepancy disappears if in fact the two sets of provisions (treating Exod. 21:1-6 and Deut. 15:12-18 as basically the same law) deal with *two distinct sets of circumstances.*

Isaac Mendelsohn proposed that the laws dealt with different phenomena, but the distinction he draws is rather odd.[37] The slave

---

33. *Leviticus*, p. 360.

34. E.g., Keil and Delitzsch, *The Pentateuch* 2:464-65; Oswald T. Allis, "Leviticus," p. 165 in *The Eerdmans Bible Commentary*, 3rd ed., ed. Donald Guthrie, *et al.* (Grand Rapids: Wm. B. Eerdmans, 1970), published in Great Britain as *The New Bible Commentary: Revised* (London: Inter-Varsity, 1970); Robert A. Cole, *Exodus*. Tyndale Old Testament Commentaries (London and Downers Grove: InterVarsity, 1973), p. 165.

35. "In the context of the completed Pentateuch the discrepancy would have been resolved thus: in normal circumstances a man's slavery would come to an end after six years; but if he was lucky, he would go free sooner, if a Jubilee happened to fall within his six year period" (Elliger, p. 360).

36. "The Hebrew Slave: A Study in Early Israelite Society," *Evangelical Quarterly* 45 (1973): 30. Cf. also S. R. Driver, *Deuteronomy*, p. 185.

37. P. 89.

of Exodus and Deuteronomy was the *defaulting* debtor who had actually been seized by his creditor. But the "subject of the Levitical law is the poor Hebrew who sold himself into perpetual slavery either to a fellow-Hebrew or to a stranger" (p. 89). The distinction rested on whether the slavery had been entered by compulsion or voluntarily (though in both cases because of insolvency). But this has the surely impossible implication that an Israelite who voluntarily deprived himself of freedom in order to pay his debts—or just to survive—could have his whole family enslaved for a generation or more, whereas a person who had to be seized by his creditor (e.g., for [deliberate?] failure to repay a debt) served a mere six years. Mendelsohn's theory is improbable and ignores other differences between the laws.

A more fruitful approach is to take the word *"Hebrew"* in Exodus and Deuteronomy as the key to the distinction.[38] Thus, the original law in the Book of the Covenant had to do with the "Hebrew" in the *social,* not ethnic, sense,[39] that is, with the *landless* person, who survived by selling his services to an Israelite household. Lev. 25:39ff., by contrast, deals with the one who is an *Israelite landholder* but who has been forced by poverty to mortgage it and then to sell his family and himself into the service of a fellow Israelite. The first is "Hebrew" class slavery; the second is Israelite debt slavery. This essential difference between the two sets of provisions becomes clear when a close scrutiny of the three texts reveals the following distinctions.

1. In the Jubilee text of Lev. 25 the word "Hebrew" *nowhere* appears. The importance of this is obscured by the common habit

---

38. This is the approach adopted by Ellison, which I believe can be amplified and substantiated by the arguments set out below.

39. It is now widely agreed that *'ibrî* is related to the various forms of *'apiru*, and that the latter term described a "relatively unified entity with much in common linguistically, sociologically and culturally, but an 'international' class of men, a social stratum . . ." (Manfred Weippert, *The Settlement of the Israelite Tribes in Palestine.* SBT, 2nd ser. 21 [1971], p. 65). Weippert provides a comprehensive account of the Hebrew/*'apiru* question (pp. 63-102). Cf. also Norman K. Gottwald, *The Tribes of Yahweh*; and Marvin L. Chaney, "Ancient Palestinian Peasant Movements and the Formation of Pre-monarchic Israel," pp. 52-57, 72-83. A very thorough survey of the whole question is Nadav Na'aman, "Ḥabiru and Hebrews: The Transfer of a Social Term to the Literary Sphere," *JNES* 45 (1986): 271-288.

of scholars and commentators of speaking of *Hebrews* being released in the Jubilee.[40] It is also commonly assumed that "Hebrew" in at least the Deuteronomic passage[41] and, according to some, also in the Book of the Covenant[42] has become synonymous with "Israelite." But is this necessarily so? Lemche argues strongly for maintaining the sociological interpretation of "Hebrew" in Exod. 21:2 (following Albrecht Alt),[43] on the grounds that the laws of the first part of the Book of the Covenant are pre-Israelite and that, even when brought into an Israelite context, the "Hebrew slave" law was still understood to refer to the social class of that name and not simply to ethnic Israelites.[44] The situation need not be different in Deut. 15:12. Manfred Weippert argues that "here the 'Hebrew' is described as the 'brother' of the person addressed in the legal text and is, therefore, defined as an Israelite."[45] But the word *'āḥîḵā* ("your brother") is of very wide meaning,[46] and the phrasing of Deut. 15:12a shows rather that it is the "brother" who is being defined (i.e., limited and qualified) as a "Hebrew," not vice versa. That is, the phrase "Hebrew" (designating male or female) is a specific qualification of the broader term *"your brother" for the purpose of indicating clearly the social* status, not the *nationality*, of the person referred to—namely, a "Hebrew." If it were merely ethnic in sense, the phrase would surely be tautologous. Precisely the same can be said of the defining use of *'iḇrî* in Jer. 34:9, 14; the slaves are Jews and brothers, but their social status and condition is described by the term "Hebrew" (cf. also below, p. 259).

In Lev. 25:39, however, the term "your brother" is not qualified by any further noun or adjective. It is simply stated that he has "sunk into poverty" (*yāmûḵ*; cf. NEB). That is, the fact that he

---

40. E.g., S. R. Driver, *Deuteronomy*, p. 185; Falk, p. 91.

41. Gerhard von Rad, *Deuteronomy*, p. 107; de Vaux, *Ancient Israel*, p. 83.

42. Childs, p. 468; J. Philip Hyatt, *Exodus*, p. 228.

43. "The Origins of Israelite Law," pp. 93-95.

44. "The 'Hebrew Slave': Comments on the Slave Law Ex. xxi 2-11," *VT* 25 (1975): 129-144.

45. P. 87.

46. Thus, BDB points out that it could be extended to include the sojourner (p. 26a).

has *become* poor is given as the *explanation* of why he should be
selling himself into the service of a fellow Israelite, whereas in
Exodus and Deuteronomy no explanation is advanced. It was
sufficiently understood in those texts that a person described as a
"Hebrew" belonged to a landless class of people who sold themselves or were acquired[47] as their way of life or means of livelihood—not as the result of a sudden reversal of fortune such as is
implied by the *mûk* paragraphs.

2. In Exodus and Deuteronomy the Hebrew's service as a slave
is unqualified. He serves (*'āḇaḏ*) for six years. By contrast, the
impoverished brother is emphatically *not* to be made to serve as a
slave (literally, "you shall not enslave upon him the slavery of a
slave," Lev. 25:39b), nor may he be sold as a slave (cf. the similar
form of words in v. 42b: literally, "they must not be sold according
to the selling of slaves"). Rather, he is to dwell like a hired worker
or resident laborer under the employment[48] of his creditor. That it
is in fact a creditor-debtor relationship is fairly clear from vv. 35-37.
Such a relationship, however, is not at all specified or presupposed
in the "Hebrew" law.

3. Neither Exodus nor Deuteronomy speaks of any right of
redemption for the "Hebrew" slave—understandably, since the
redemption of land or persons was a family or clan affair and the
"Hebrew," as defined above, would hardly have had wealthy family
connections. In Lev. 25, however, the debt servitude of the Israelite
is brought into close contact with the redemption regulations. They
are specified in vv. 47ff., where the creditor was an alien, and it is
very probable that similar procedure was applicable where the
creditor was an Israelite.

4. Another difference which concerned the family was that a
"Hebrew" might forfeit his wife and children on release, if he had
gained them during his six years. She and they remained the
property of his master. In the Jubilee release, however, the phrase

---

47. Alt prefers the *yimmāḵēr* of Deut. 15:12 as the original text of the law, and
gives the niphal a reflexive sense ("The Origins of Israelite Law," pp. 93-94). The
view advanced here is supported by Na'aman.

48. Cf. above, Chapter 3, n. 59, for this meaning of *'im*.

"... and his children with him" occurs twice (Lev. 25:41, 54). The man has land to which he can return and thus is able to maintain the integrity of his family.[49] As was noted above (pp. 124-25), the main purpose of the Jubilee was to restore the family ownership of land and to limit the effects of debt and poverty to roughly a single generation. But such ambitions were irrelevant to legislation for the "Hebrews" since they had no stake in the kinship-land structure of the nation.

5. The *occasion* of release is markedly different in the two provisions. It was simply a domestic affair in the "Hebrew's" case, taking place in the seventh year of an individual's service. But, as presented in Lev. 25, the Jubilee release was a festival of national scope and importance in a fixed year.

6. The *effects* of the release in the two cases represent a yet more significant difference. The "Hebrew," on release, becomes a *hopšî*, "freedman" (Exod. 21:2b; Deut. 15:12b). The term is un- doubtedly related to the class of *hupšu* found in Canaanite and Assyrian texts, though the precise sociological meaning of the latter term is still a matter of debate.[50] It seems to have involved a kind of freedom, but within a low and dependent social class. Mendel- sohn describes the *hopšîm* as "legally free, but *without land* or any other means of existence" and therefore obliged to "hire themselves out as day-laborers or settle on a rich man's land as tenant- farmers."[51] Lemche sees two possibilities from the comparative evidence: that the *hopšî* "entered into a private clientage to his former master, or . . . passed into a sort of collective depen- dency. . . . A חפשי should be socially ranged somewhere between

---

49. The possession of land was a basic factor in being able to retain control over one's family. The Israelite of Lev. 25:35ff. had not *lost* his land technically, and so "he is only a semi-slave, for he retains control over his family, something denied to the slave" (Ellison, pp. 33-34). Neh. 5:5b, however, shows the powerless- ness of being in such a situation: "it is not in our power to help it [the pledging of children], for other men have our fields and our vineyards." Cf. Mic. 2:9 and above, pp.97-99, for the link between dispossession and the breakup of families.

50. Cf. Weippert, p. 72, n. 63, for a survey of the debate. See also Oswald Loretz, *Habiru-Hebraër*. BZAW 160 (1984): 252-263.

51. Isaac Mendelsohn, "The Canaanite Term for 'Free Proletarian,' " *BASOR* 83 (1941): 38 (my italics).

a slave and a freedsman."[52] For the "Hebrew," therefore, release after six years' service probably entailed a change of residence and employment rather than any great rise in social status or privilege.

Significantly, the word is totally absent from the Jubilee provision in Lev. 25. There the keyword is "return" *(šûb)*. The debtor "goes forth" and "returns" to his "kin group" and to his ancestral property (25:10). The subject of the Jubilee law, therefore, was a member of an Israelite clan who had a legal title to his family land and could "return" to full possession of it—a very different case from the landless, dependent "Hebrew," for whom the idea of a "return" was irrelevant. The term *šûb* is accordingly quite absent from the Exodus and Deuteronomy texts—as absent as *hopšî* is from Leviticus.

Thus, the primary concern of the "Hebrew" legislation was to prevent the indefinite exploitation of a member of that social class by any one owner, whereas that of the Jubilee was to preserve or restore the integrity, independence, and property of Israelite households—on theological grounds that we have already examined.

7. Even the *theological* motive, which is present in both laws, is differently expressed. Deut. 15:15 gives as a motive for "Hebrew" release the memory of Israel's own experience of slavery in Egypt.[53] Just over half of the occurrences of the word '*ibrî* are in the Egyptian context.[54] The argument thus is: "Because *you* were once a slave ('Hebrew') in Egypt, but are now free because Yahweh redeemed you, you must show like generosity to those who are now slaves ('Hebrews') among you." Lev. 25:42, however, reads: "For *they* [the Israelite debtors] are *my* servants, whom I brought out of the land of Egypt. . . ." The legislator puts creditor and debtor on the same social and theological footing before God. All Israelites are God's purchased slaves (cf. v. 55) and are therefore forbidden to enslave one another.

---

52. "The 'Hebrew Slave,' " p. 142.

53. Many scholars believe that the same motive is implicitly present in Exodus, in that the "Hebrew" release law has been placed at the beginning of the Book of the Covenant. Its humaneness is thus emphasized as an ethical obligation arising out of the redemption from Egypt.

54. Seventeen out of thirty-three occurrences. For the details, see Weippert, p. 84.

CONCLUSION

All these differences between the laws confirm the view that they are concerned with essentially different phenomena: one with the "class slavery" of the "Hebrews," a landless and rootless substratum of society who lived by selling their services to Israelite households; the other, with Israelites who entered the service of another out of an increasing burden of poverty and debt but who in theory retain the legal ownership of their land and can "return" to it.

This latter fact about the Jubilee is an added point in favor of its early origin, for it envisages a situation where every family did have a patrimony to which, if temporary alienation had been forced upon them, they could "return" in the Jubilee. Such could have been the general situation in the early period of tribal settlements and land allotment, but the economic history of the Monarchy period reveals a process of increasing dispossession and the growth of large, nonpatrimonial estates.[55] The concept of a "return" must soon have become meaningless for large numbers of the newly dispossessed and *landless* poor and their descendants. By the same token this explains the absence of historical reference to a Jubilee being practiced.

It also explains why Jer. 34 does not invoke the Jubilee provisions but instead refers to the "Hebrew" legislation in its Deuteronomic form. This does not imply that the Jubilee law was entirely nonexistent at the time (as Roland de Vaux believes[56]), but rather that the economic conditions it presupposes no longer obtained. The slaves released by Zedekiah were not mortgaged debtors with estates to return to, but dispossessed people working like serfs on land no longer theirs. Freedom for them would mean joining the ranks of the *hopšîm* (Jer. 34:9-10, 16). Their status in fact corre-

55. Cf. the literature on this cited above, pp.105-6, particularly Edward Neufeld, "The Emergence of a Royal-Urban Society in Ancient Israel." Neufeld thinks that attempts may well have been made to revive the Jubilee (along with the *šᵉmiṭṭâ*) during periods such as the revolution of Jehu and the reforms of Hezekiah and Josiah, though there is no clear evidence. Cf. Neufeld, "Socio-economic Background of *Yōbēl* and *Šᵉmiṭṭâ*," pp. 117ff.

56. *Ancient Israel*, p. 176.

sponded with that of the "Hebrews" of the early laws, and so
Jeremiah invokes that legislation as relevant to their situation. They
were Judaean by nationality, but "Hebrew" in social condition.

It is significant that in Jer. 34 the word $š^e miṭṭâ$ is *not* used, even
though the dependence upon Deut. 15 is extensive. Indeed, Jer.
34:14 begins with identical wording to Deut. 15:1 ("At the end of
seven years . . .") *but* then skips over the $š^e miṭṭâ$ law to the "Hebrew" release law beginning at Deut. 15:12. This makes sense only
in the light of the understanding of the $š^e miṭṭâ$ that we developed
above (pp. 142ff. and 167ff.), that it involved release of pledged
land to its true owner in the Sabbatical Year. Jer. 34, however, is not
concerned with release of *land* or the suspension of debts for a year,
and probably was not actually related to a regular Sabbatical Year.[57]
Rather, it was concerned with the permanent release of *persons*
from slavery. The fact that it omits reference to the $š^e miṭṭâ$ confirms,
therefore, our view that the $š^e miṭṭâ$ was primarily concerned with
property pledges and should be kept distinct from straightforward
slave release.

On the other hand, Jer. 34 uses the word $d^e rôr$ ("release") for
the release of persons—a word *not found at all* in Deut. 15, but a
technical expression from the Jubilee milieu (cf. Lev. 25:10; Ezek.
46:17).[58] The other Jubilee concepts (return, redemption) could
clearly not be used because they were no longer applicable and thus
irrelevant, but $d^e rôr$ could be used for the manumission of the
slaves' *persons*. Their economic conditions, however, particularly
their landlessness, made the "Hebrew" legislation of Deut. 15 the
appropriate law to invoke.

57. As against Nahum M. Sarna, "Zedekiah's Emancipation of Slaves and the
Sabbatical Year." See above, p. 149.
58. The absence of $š^e miṭṭâ$ and the use of $d^e rôr$ in Jer. 34 is noted by Martin
Kessler, "The Law of Manumission in Jer 34," *Biblische Zeitschrift* N.S. 15 (1971):
106, but without further explanation.

Conclusion to Part Three

In the Introduction to this third part of our study it was said that we must beware of simplistic statements about the property status of dependent persons in Israel. Our analysis in each of the last three chapters has borne this out. In each case we have seen that the persons concerned cannot be called "property"—legally or socially—without important qualifications and limitations. This does not mean, of course, that we can go to the other extreme and adopt a sentimental view which ignores the facts. Wives were not chattel property; but they did not have the kind of free independent equality so sought after in the modern world. Children did have an economic "value," and undoubtedly this could lead to suffering and harsh treatment in times of poverty and acute need. Slaves were slaves, and the basic procedures of purchase and sale—at least as regards foreign slaves—was not changed in Old Testament Israel, though there were certainly protective measures to mitigate the system, as we have seen.

Nevertheless, our survey of the available evidence in each case has shown that there was a strong element of humaneness in Old Testament society, expressed in both social custom and attitudes, and also given concrete form in practical legislation. Theodore H. Robinson considered this to be ". . . the central truth which was fundamental to their earlier thought, the supreme value of people as against things."[1] This has become something of a truism in Christian ethical language: "People matter more than things." But the evidence examined in the preceding chapters gives us solid proof that in the case of Old Testament Israel this was not merely a matter of sentiment or wishful piety, but of actual sociological fact.

At the end of Parts One and Two we tried briefly to see ways in which the material in those sections could be applied ethically. We saw a typological link between the testaments in the way that Old Testament land theology provides a socio-economic background to the New Testament concept and practice of *koinonia* fellowship. We also saw how Old Testament laws concerning property, with its varied rights and responsibilities, can be handled paradigmatically—seeking to apply the moral principles and social objectives in different but comparable modern contexts. In some ways the material concerning persons may seem easier to apply— at least in general terms—since the ethical value of persons is already high on the agenda of Christian ethics.

Dependent persons in particular—the same three groups, in fact, as have been discussed in the last three chapters—feature significantly in the New Testament. Jesus' positive attitude and caring actions towards women and children are well known and commented on. Paul and Peter specifically address wives, children, and slaves as an integral part of the Christian household communities to which they belonged, both in terms of how they should behave and how they should be treated. It seems that both Jesus and the apostles were recovering an authentically Old Testament (i.e., for them, scriptural) perspective on the status, value, and rights of such people, in contrast both to contemporary Jewish society (which had slipped a long way from the Old Testament in its treatment of women in particular) and also to the wider Graeco-Roman world.[2]

When it comes to more specific application of particular texts,

1. "The Old Testament and the Modern World," in *The Old Testament and Modern Study*, ed. H. H. Rowley (Oxford: Oxford University Press, 1951), p. 369.
2. I have discussed the role of the family and these groups as recorded in the New Testament more fully in *An Eye for an Eye/Living as the People of God*, pp. 190-96.

then the paradigmatic approach again becomes necessary. We instinctively adopt it already in our handling of certain aspects of New Testament ethical teaching. For example, we take Paul's instructions to slaves and their masters and apply it to the whole realm of working relationships between employers and employees, because we can see that similar principles are involved, similar dangers, and similar ethical demands of the gospel, though in a changed economic context. But then, Paul himself recognized the paradigmatic principle in his use of Old Testament laws. He perceives the essential principle within the law concerning threshing oxen, for example, and applies it to Christian laborers, for God is concerned for both (1 Cor. 9:8-12). Similarly, when examining any Old Testament law concerning persons, we need to ask: What is the primary objective of this law? Is it designed to protect someone who is vulnerable? Is it designed to limit or remove circumstances of potential danger or oppression? How is it related to (1) the family and (2) the wider civil structure? Then, having grasped these dimensions of the law in Israel's own context, we need to inquire what practical means would embody the same concern for people in comparable conditions today.

"Comparable conditions today" is, of course, a very wide phrase, if one thinks on a worldwide scale. The ease or difficulty of applying Old Testament law paradigmatically depends to some extent on the degree of "distance" from the social conditions of ancient Israel. To people unaccustomed to anything else but the highly urbanized, technological, and sophisticated Western culture, many Old Testament laws must appear at first sight quaint, primitive, and quite unrelated to anything in their environment. But first sight is deceptive. The larger the culture gap, the more carefully we need to look at our own society to discover those groups of people who do in fact stand in a highly comparable position to the major groups of dependent persons in Israel. We may have technically abolished slavery, but there are those whose almost total dependence on others, on "the market," or on one particular institution or employer reduces them to a kind of inescapable bondage. Then there are unemployed youth, one-parent families, the homeless, the immigrant communities—some might want to add the unborn child, symbol of total dependency. What are the social objectives, policies, and actions which conform to the Old Testament models for justice for such groups?

However, the great majority of the world's population does not in fact live in the kind of Western society referred to above. For many millions, the life and society of ancient Israel would be perfectly recognizable as comparable to their own, including even many features of agricultural practice and some family customs. Furthermore, very similar social and economic problems afflict the same groups of dependent persons in many countries of the Two Thirds World as are the target of the Old Testament prophets' protest—vastly unequal land distribution, exploitation of farmers, oppression of the landless, injustice and corruption in the courts and political authority, vulnerability of women and children, poverty of casual laborers.

At a personal level, while I was teaching in India I was acutely impressed with the almost direct relevance of Old Testament laws in some cases. It was, for example, a most interesting exercise to ask a class of seminary students to reflect on the impact it would make on Indian society if many of the laws in Lev. 19, and some others in Deuteronomy, were to be applied more or less directly as written. The paradigmatic "distance" was very short indeed; the point of the laws was usually easy to grasp and apply without very much "cultural translation." In fact, their very closeness to social reality there made them all the more uncomfortable to reflect upon. The discussion generated much more heat, disagreement, and argument than any comparable discussion in the West, because the authority and cutting edge of the text were felt much more keenly.

A still more personal example may underline the point. In the West, any discussion or reflection I ever engaged in regarding the laws of employment in the Old Testament—whether concerning slaves or hired laborers—had always been one step removed from experience for me. I had never employed anybody directly, and was not likely to. The force of these laws always applied to somebody else in my mind. In India, however, we employed a woman as a "servant." She performed some of the tasks for which in the West we would have used (and paid for) machines. Reflecting on her

relationship to us, it struck me how many of the Old Testament laws
and injunctions were directly relevant, and, I believe, ethically
authoritative, for us. As regards her social position, she was comparable to certain features of both the slave and the hired laborer in
the Old Testament (I am, of course, using the words in an objective
sense, without personal or status implications). Being the sole
earner for her family, she was in that respect totally dependent on
our household for her livelihood (as the slave was). Like the hired
laborer, she lived by her labor, and the prompt payment of wages
was of vital importance. She was part of that enormous pool of
"casual" labor in India, sometimes called "the informal sector"—a
euphemism for a vast edifice of vulnerability to exploitation,
without protection from law or social convention. One can see why
there is so much in Old Testament law exhorting Israelite households to treat such people with justice and generosity. Thus, we felt
the paradigmatic force of biblical texts about avoiding any kind of
ill treatment (which may seem obvious, but was not so in this
context, even in Christian households), prompt payment, generosity
out of the abundance of God's blessing on us (Deut. 15:14), justice
in any grievance (Job 31:13), receiving some share in food prepared
for our benefit (Deut. 25:14), and sabbatical rest (she did not come
on Sundays!).

As regards the last point, it is again striking how the Fourth
Commandment is specifically for the benefit of the working population, and that slaves were included. In other words, *they* were not
to be made to work harder so that *we* could enjoy a rest and feel
religious. Not all Christian households in India who employ servants give them Sunday off by any means. So I was led to wonder
if the fact that we felt we ought to do so was simply a hangover
from sabbatarian legalism. I have concluded that it was not. Rather,
the whole point of the paradigmatic application of the ethical force
of the Old Testament laws lies in the assumption of the moral
consistency of God. That is, if this is what God demanded of his
people *then* in their treatment of dependent persons in their households, then surely, in the light of the love of Christ and our higher
motivation "in the LORD," he demands no less of us *now*. The
experience has shown me in a more direct way what is meant by

the principle, "*Love* is the fulfilling of the *law*." It is the *law* which shows me, in a very practical economic and unmistakable way what it means to *love* a servant.

So then, if I feel it is important that we as Christians should work hard at finding appropriate applications of Old Testament law, it is not merely because we ought to obey the law as such. It is rather because obedience to the law was one important ingredient in fulfilling the more fundamental demand which is the basis of biblical ethics in both the Old and New Testaments—to love the LORD your God, and to love your neighbor as yourself. It is when we ask, "What does it mean to love my neighbor?" that the Old Testament answers: "Here is a model and pattern of what it meant for Israel in their context. This is what God—their God and yours—required of them, in every down-to-earth, demanding detail. Take it and compare it with your own context and the issues you face, and in the light of its authority endorsed by Christ, with the help of the Holy Spirit, it should become clear what the LORD requires of you."

Selected Bibliography

Alt, Albrecht. "The Origins of Israelite Law." In *Essays on Old Testament History and Religion*, pp. 101-171. Oxford: Basil Blackwell, 1966 and Garden City: Doubleday, 1968.

Andersen, Francis I. "Israelite Kinship Terminology and Social Structure." *Bible Translator* 20 (1969): 29-39.

————. "The Socio-Juridical Background of the Naboth Incident." *JBL* 85 (1966): 46-57.

Bess, S. Herbert. "Systems of Land Tenure in Ancient Israel." Ph.D. dissertation, University of Michigan, 1963.

de Boer, P. A. H. *Fatherhood and Motherhood in Israelite and Judean Piety.* Leiden: E. J. Brill, 1974.

Brenner, Athalya. *The Israelite Woman: Social Role and Literary Type in Biblical Narrative.* The Biblical Seminar 2. Sheffield: JSOT Press, 1985.

Brichto, Herbert C. "Kin, Cult, Land and Afterlife—a Biblical Complex." *HUCA* 44 (1973): 1-54.

Brown, Arthur Mason. "The Concept of Inheritance in the Old Testament." Ph.D. dissertation, Columbia University, 1965.

Brueggemann, Walter. *The Land.* Overtures to Biblical Theology. Philadelphia: Fortress, 1977.

Burrows, Millar. *The Basis of Israelite Marriage.* American Oriental Series 15. New Haven: American Oriental Society, 1938.

Clark, W. Malcolm. "The Origin and Development of the Land

Promise Theme in the Old Testament." Ph.D. dissertation, Yale University, 1964.

Clements, Ronald E. *God and Temple: The Idea of Divine Presence in Ancient Israel.* Oxford: Basil Blackwell and Philadelphia: Fortress, 1965.

————. "Temple and Land: A Significant Aspect of Israel's Worship." *Transactions of the Glasgow University Oriental Society* 19 (1961–1962): 16-28.

————, ed. *The World of Ancient Israel: Sociological, Anthropological and Political Perspectives.* SOTS Monograph. Cambridge: Cambridge University Press, 1989.

Daube, David. "Communal Responsibility." In *Studies in Biblical Law,* pp. 154-189. 1947; repr. New York: Ktav, 1969.

Davidson, R. "Some Aspects of the Old Testament Contribution to the Pattern of Christian Ethics." *Scottish Journal of Theology* 12 (1959): 373-387.

Davies, Eryl W. "Inheritance Rights and the Hebrew Levirate Marriage." *VT* 31 (1981): 138-144, 257-268.

Davies, W. D. *The Gospel and the Land: Early Christianity and Jewish Territorial Doctrine.* Berkeley: University of California Press, 1974.

Dearman, John Andrew. *Property Rights in the Eighth-Century Prophets.* SBL Dissertation 106. Atlanta: Scholars Press, 1988.

Diamond, Arthur S. "An Eye for an Eye." *Iraq* 19 (1957): 151-55.

Ellison, Henry L. "The Hebrew Slave: A Study in Early Israelite Society." *Evangelical Quarterly* 45 (1973): 30-35.

Engelhard, David H. "The Lord's Motivated Concern for the Underprivileged." *Calvin Theological Journal* 15 (1980): 5-26.

Evans, Mary J. *Woman in the Bible.* Downers Grove: InterVarsity, 1984.

Falk, Ze'ev W. *Hebrew Law in Biblical Times: An Introduction.* Jerusalem, 1964.

Fensham, F. Charles. "Widow, Orphan and the Poor in Ancient Near Eastern Legal and Wisdom Literature." *JNES* 21 (1962): 129-139.

Fohrer, Georg. "The Righteous Man in Job 31." In *Essays in Old*

Testament Ethics: J. Philip Hyatt, In Memoriam, ed. James L. Crenshaw and John T. Willis, pp. 1-22. New York: Ktav, 1974.

de Geus, C. H. J. *The Tribes of Israel.* Studia Semitica Neerlandica 18. Assen: van Gorcum, 1976.

Gnuse, Robert. *You Shall Not Steal: Community and Property in the Biblical Tradition.* Maryknoll, N.Y.: Orbis, 1985.

Gordon, Cyrus H. "Sabbatical Cycle or Seasonal Pattern." *Orientalia* N.S. 22 (1953): 79-81.

Gottwald, Norman K. *The Tribes of Yahweh: A Sociology of the Religion of Liberated Israel, 1350–1050 B.C.E.* Maryknoll, N.Y.: Orbis, 1979.

Greenberg, Moshe. "Some Postulates of Biblical Criminal Law." In *Yehezkel Kaufmann Memorial Volume,* ed. Menahem Haran, pp. 5-28. Jerusalem: Magnes, 1960.

Hammershaimb, Erling. "On the Ethics of the Old Testament Prophets." *VTS* 7 (1960): 75-101.

Hyatt, J. Philip. "Were There an Ancient Historical Credo in Israel and an Independent Sinai Tradition?" In *Translating and Understanding the Old Testament,* ed. Harry Thomas Frank and William L. Reed, pp. 152-170. Nashville: Abingdon, 1970.

Jackson, Bernard S. *Essays on Jewish and Comparative Legal History.* Studies in Judaism in Late Antiquity 10. Leiden: E. J. Brill, 1975.

————. *Theft in Early Jewish Law.* Oxford: Oxford University Press, 1972.

Jacobson, Anita. *Marriage and Money.* Studia Ethnographica Uppsalensia 28. Lund: Berlingska Boktryckeriet, 1967.

Kaiser, Walter C., Jr. *Toward Old Testament Ethics.* Grand Rapids: Zondervan, 1983.

Lang, Bernhard. "The Social Organization of Peasant Poverty in Biblical Israel." *JSOT* 24 (1982): 47-63.

Leggett, Donald A. *The Levirate and Goel Institutions in the Old Testament.* Cherry Hill, N.J.: Mack, 1974.

Lemche, Niels Peter. "The Manumission of Slaves—The Fallow Year—The Sabbatical Year—The Jobel Year." *VT* 26 (1976): 38-59.

Lind, Millard C. "The Concept of Political Power in Ancient Israel." *Annual of the Swedish Theological Institute* 7 (1968/1969): 4-24.

McCarthy, Dennis J. "Notes on the Love of God in Deuteronomy and the Father-Son Relationship between Yahweh and Israel." *CBQ* 27 (1965): 144-47.

MacDonald, Elizabeth M. *The Position of Women as Reflected in Semitic Codes of Law.* University of Toronto Studies. Oriental Series (1931).

Mace, David R. *Hebrew Marriage: A Sociological Study.* London: Epworth and New York: Philosophical Library, 1953.

Martens, Elmer A. *Plot and Purpose in the Old Testament.* Leicester: Inter-Varsity, 1981. Published in the United States as *God's Design: A Focus on Old Testament Theology.* Grand Rapids: Baker, 1981.

Mason, John. "Biblical Teaching and Assisting the Poor," *Transformation* 4/2 (1987): 1-14.

May, Herbert G. "A Sociological Approach to Hebrew Religion." *Journal of Bible and Religion* 12 (1944): 98-106.

Mendelsohn, Isaac. *Slavery in the Ancient Near East.* New York: Oxford University Press, 1949.

Mendenhall, George E. "The Relation of the Individual to Political Society in Ancient Israel." In *Biblical Studies in Memory of H. C. Alleman,* ed. Jacob M. Myers, O. Reimherr, and H. N. Bream, pp. 89-108. Locust Valley, N. Y.: J. J. Augustin, 1960.

Mettinger, T. N. D. *Solomonic State Officials: A Study of the Civil Government Officials of the Israelite Monarchy.* Coniectanea Biblica, Old Testament 5. Lund: Gleerup, 1971.

Miller, Patrick D., Jr. *The Divine Warrior in Early Israel.* HSM 5. Cambridge, Mass.: Harvard University Press, 1973.

————. "The Gift of God: The Deuteronomic Theology of the Land." *Interpretation* 23 (1969): 451-465.

Muilenburg, James. *The Way of Israel: Biblical Faith and Ethics.* New York: Harper & Row, 1961.

Napier, B. Davie. "Community under Law: On Hebrew Law and its Theological Presuppositions," *Interpretation* 7 (1953): 404-417.

Neufeld, Edward. *Ancient Hebrew Marriage Laws, with Special*

References to General Semitic Laws and Customs. London: Longman, Green, 1944.

————. "Socio-economic Background of *Yōbēl* and *Šᵉmiṭṭâ.*" *Rivista degli Studi Orientali* 33 (1958): 53-124.

Nicholson, Ernest W. *Exodus and Sinai in History and Tradition.* Oxford: Basil Blackwell and Richmond: John Knox, 1973.

North, Robert G. "The Biblical Jubilee and Social Reform." *Scripture* 4 (1951): 323-335.

————. *Sociology of the Biblical Jubilee.* Analecta Biblica 4. Rome: Pontifical Biblical Institute, 1954.

Paul, Shalom M. *Studies in the Book of the Covenant in the Light of Cuneiform and Biblical Law.* VTS 18 (1970).

Phillips, Anthony J. *Ancient Israel's Criminal Law: A New Approach to the Decalogue.* Oxford: Basil Blackwell and New York: Schocken, 1970.

————. "Some Aspects of Family Law in Pre-exilic Israel." *VT* 23 (1973): 349-361.

van der Ploeg, J. P. M. "Slavery in the Old Testament." *VTS* 22 (1972): 72-87.

Porter, J. Roy. *The Extended Family in the Old Testament.* Occasional Papers in Social and Economic Administration 6. London: Edutext, 1967.

————. "The Legal Aspects of the Concept of 'Corporate Personality' in the Old Testament." *VT* 15 (1965): 361-380.

von Rad, Gerhard. "The Promised Land and Yahweh's Land in the Hexateuch." In *The Problem of the Hexateuch and Other Essays,* pp. 79-93. 1966; repr. London: SCM and Philadelphia: Fortress, 1984.

Ringe, Sharon H. *Jesus, Liberation, and the Biblical Jubilee.* Overtures to Biblical Theology 17. Philadelphia: Fortress, 1985.

Salmon, J. M. "Judicial Authority in Early Israel: An Historical Investigation of Old Testament Institutions." Ph.D. dissertation, Princeton University, 1968.

Sarna, Nahum M. "Zedekiah's Emancipation of Slaves and the Sabbatical Year." In *Orient and Occident.* Festschrift Cyrus H. Gordon, ed. Harry A. Hoffner, Jr., pp. 143-49. Alter Orient und Altes Testament 22 (Neukirchen-Vluyn: Neukirchener, 1973).

Schaeffer, Henry. *The Social Legislation of the Primitive Semites.*
New Haven: Yale University Press and London: Oxford University Press, 1915.

Seeligmann, Isaac L. "A Psalm from Pre-regal Times." *VT*
14 (1964): 75-92.

van Selms, Adrianus. "The Goring Ox in Babylonian and Biblical
Law." *Analecta Orientalia* 18 (1950): 321-330.

Smith, William Robertson. *Kinship and Marriage in Early Arabia.*
Cambridge: Cambridge University Press, 1885.

Spina, Frank Anthony. "Israelites as *gērîm,* 'Sojourners,' in Social
and Historical Context." In *The Word of the Lord Shall Go
Forth.* Festschrift David Noel Freedman, ed. Carol L. Meyers
and Michael P. O'Connor, pp. 321-335. Philadelphia: American Schools of Oriental Research, 1983.

Stamm, J. J., and Andrews, M. E. *The Ten Commandments in
Recent Research.* SBT, 2nd ser. 2. London: SCM and Naperville: Allenson, 1967.

Stek, John H. "Salvation, Justice and Liberation in the Old Testament." *Calvin Theological Journal* 13 (1978): 133-165.

Swartley, Willard M. *Slavery, Sabbath, War and Women: Case
Issues in Biblical Interpretation.* Scottdale, Pa.: Herald, 1983.

Swidler, Leonard. *Biblical Affirmations of Woman.* Philadelphia:
Westminster, 1979.

Tang, S.Y. "The Ethical Content of Job 31: A Comparative Study."
Ph.D. dissertation, Edinburgh, 1967.

Thiel, J. F. "The Institution of Marriage: An Anthropological Perspective." *Concilium* 6/5 (1970): 12-24.

de Vaux, Roland. *Ancient Israel: Its Life and Institutions.* New
York: McGraw-Hill and London: Darton, Longman & Todd,
1961.

———. *The Early History of Israel.* Philadelphia: Westminster and
London: Darton, Longman & Todd, 1978.

———. *Studies in Old Testament Sacrifice.* Cardiff: University of
Wales, 1964 and Mystic, Conn.: Verry, 1966.

von Waldow, H. Eberhard. "Israel and Her Land: Some Theological
Considerations." In *A Light unto My Path.* Festschrift Jacob M.

Myers, ed. H. N. Bream, R. D. Heim, and Carey A. Moore, pp. 493-508. Philadelphia: Temple University Press, 1974.

———. "Social Responsibility and Social Structure in Early Israel." *CBQ* 32 (1970): 182-204.

Weinfeld, Moshe. "The Covenant of Grant in the Old Testament and in the Ancient Near East." *JAOS* 90 (1970): 184-203.

Weippert, Manfred. *The Settlement of the Israelite Tribes in Palestine: A Critical Survey of Recent Scholarly Debate.* SBT, 2nd ser. 21. London: SCM and Naperville: Allenson, 1971.

Wenham, Gordon J. *"Beṭûlāh* 'A Girl of Marriageable Age." *VT* 22 (1972): 326-348.

Westbrook, Raymond. "Jubilee Laws." *Israel Law Review* 6 (1971): 209-226.

———. "Redemption of Land." *Israel Law Review* 6 (1971): 367-375.

Wright, Christopher J. H. "The Ethical Relevance of Israel as a Society." *Transformation* 1/4 (1984): 11-21.

———. "The Israelite Household and the Decalogue: The Social Background and Significance of Some Commandments." *Tyndale Bulletin* 30 (1979): 101-124.

———. *Living as the People of God.* Leicester: Inter-Varsity, 1983. Published in the United States as *An Eye for an Eye.* Downers Grove: InterVarsity, 1983.

———. *Using the Bible in Social Ethics.* Nottingham: Grove, 1983.

———. "What Happened Every Seven Years in Israel? Old Testament Sabbatical Institutions for Land, Debts and Slaves." *Evangelical Quarterly* 56 (1984): 129-138, 193-201.

Zimmerli, Walther. *The Old Testament and the World.* London: SPCK and Atlanta: John Knox, 1976.

Index of Authors

McKay, John W., 233
McKeating, Henry, 203
McKenzie, Donald A., 80
McKenzie, John L., 78, 80, 81
Malamat, Abraham, 56, 106
Mann, Thomas W., 35
Marmorstein, E., 101
Martens, Elmer A., 8, 180, 269
Martin, James D., 49
Mason, John, 180, 269
May, Herbert G., 45, 107, 108, 269
Mayes, A. D. H., 74
Mays, James Luther, 26
Mendelsohn, Isaac, 249, 252, 256, 257, 269
Mendenhall, George E., 45, 49, 53, 72, 88, 107, 224, 269
Menes, Abram, 100, 172
Mettinger, T. N. D., 45, 52, 55, 59, 62, 63, 73, 106, 269
Meyers, Carole L., 45, 191, 271
Michaeli, Frank, 241
Michaelis, John David, 183
Miles, John C., 162, 188, 191, 192, 194
Miller, Patrick D., Jr., 8, 36, 38, 39, 40, 41, 45, 76, 269
Miscall, Peter D., 103
Moore, Carey A., 272
Moran, William L., 196
Mowinckel, Sigmund, 35
Muilenburg, James, 269
Mussner, F., 80
Myers, Jacob M., 49, 269

Na'aman, Nadav, 253
Nahmani, Hayyim S., xvii
Napier, B. Davie, xvii, 269
Neufeld, Edward, xv, 105, 120, 187, 188, 191, 192, 195, 196, 204, 230, 231, 258, 269, 270
Nicholson, Ernest W., 14, 15, 42, 270
Nielson, Eduard, 131
North, Robert G., xv, 62, 121, 123, 125, 170, 171, 270

Noth, Martin, 6, 22, 24-25, 36, 46, 47, 52, 74, 120, 144, 146, 147, 149, 203, 241, 242, 251
Nougayrol, Jean, 45

O'Connor, Michael P., 45, 271
Otwell, John H., 190
van Oyen, Hendrik, xiv

Patterson, W. P., 184
Paul, Shalom M., 136, 162, 164, 211, 249, 270
Pedersen, Johannes, 49, 120, 186, 188, 195, 224
Peritz, Ismar J., 199
Pfeiffer, Robert H., 239
Phillips, Anthony, 77, 79, 80, 81, 89-92, 100, 132-33, 134, 137, 139, 143, 145, 153, 157, 165, 166, 168, 169, 173, 189, 196, 201, 202, 203, 204, 205-6, 207, 208, 209, 210-11, 216, 220, 232, 244, 249, 250, 270
Pinches, T. G., 56
van der Ploeg, J. P. M., 80, 125, 240, 241, 249, 270
Plöger, Josef Georg, 8
Porter, J. Roy, 209, 224, 227, 229, 236, 270
Preuss, Horst Dietrich, 64, 102
Pritchard, James B., 239

Rabinowitz, J. J., 59, 166
von Rad, Gerhard, 5-6, 9, 10-12, 14-15, 18, 24, 26, 33, 37, 38, 42, 48, 60, 63, 69, 74, 146, 168, 236, 247, 254, 270
Reed, William L., 14, 76, 268
Reimherr, O., 49, 269
Rémy, P., 136
Renger, Johannes, 194
Reuther, Rosemary Radford, 191
Reventlow, Henning Graf, 58
Ringe, Sharon H., 270
Robertson, David A., 11, 16
Robinson, H. Wheeler, 107, 224

Index of Scripture References